Fresh Insight of Environment and International Society

Fresh Insight of Environment and International Society

Dheeraj Razdan

CYBER TECH PUBLICATIONS
4264/3, Ansari Road, Daryaganj, New Delhi-110002 (India)
Ph.: 011-23244078, 011-43559448 Fax: 011-23280028
E-Mail: cyberpublicationsdelhi@yahoo.com
Website: www.cybertechpublications.com

FRESH INSIGHT OF ENVIRONMENT AND INTERNATIONAL SOCIETY

Dheeraj Razdan, .

First Edition 2011

Published by :

G.S. Rawat for **Cyber Tech Publications**
4264/3, Ansari Road, Daryaganj, New Delhi-110002 (India)
Ph.: 011-23244078, 011-43559448 Fax: 011-23280028
E-Mail: cyberpublicationsdelhi@yahoo.com
Website: www.cybertechpublications.com

Printed at: Asian Offset Printers, Delhi-53

Contents

Preface

The international community legislated on international oil pollution in the oceans. By the 1970s, the regional consequences of pollution and the destruction of flora and fauna were obvious, and by the late 1980s global environmental threats were part of the international community's agenda as scientific evidence identified the potential consequences of ozone depletion, climate change and loss of biodiversity. Local issues were recognised to have transboundary, then regional, and ultimately global consequences. In 1996, the International Court of Justice recognised, for the first time, that there existed rules of general international environmental law, and that a 'general obligation of States to ensure that activities within their jurisdiction and control respect the environment of other States or of areas beyond national control is now part of the corpus of international law relating to the environment'. Since then, specific treaty rules have become more complex and technical, environmental issues have been increasingly integrated into other subject areas (including trade, investment, intellectual property, human rights, and armed conflict), and international environmental jurisprudence has become less exceptional as the case law of international courts and tribunals expands. It was not until the late nineteenth century that communities and states began to recognise the transboundary consequences of activities which affected shared rivers or which led to the destruction of wildlife, such as fur seals, in areas beyond national jurisdiction.

—Author

1

Introduction

THE ENVIRORNMENT AND OTHER VALUES

International environmental law is influenced by a range of non-legal factors. The likelihood of achieving an agreement increases with: greater scientific consensus about the cause and seriousness of a problem; increased public concern; a perception on the part of the negotiating states that other partners are doing their 'fair' share to address the problem; an increase in short-term political benefits; and the existence of previous, related multilateral agreements. Factors which lessen the likelihood of reaching agreement include the upward costs of environmental controls and the increases in the number of states negotiating a treaty or other instrument. Other relevant considerations include the existence of appropriate international fora for the negotiation of the agreement and the nature of arrangements for dealing with non-compliance.

Of all these factors, two have been particularly influential: the impact of science, and the economic costs. Since the first edition of this book, greater attention has also been given to other values, representing neither scientific nor economic considerations. Given that the land – and the sea – and the air-spaces of planet Earth are shared, and are not naturally distributed among the states of the world, and given that world transforming activities, especially economic activities, can have effects directly or cumulatively, on large parts of the world environment, how can international law reconcile the inherent and fundamental interdependence of the world environment? How could legal control of activities adversely affecting the world environment be instituted, given that such activities may be fundamental to the economies of particular states?

Science

The strong concern of states to ensure that their economic interests are taken into account in the development and application of international environmental law has been matchedby an equally firm view that environmental regulations should only be adopted where there is compelling scientific evidence that action is required to prevent environmental damage. This has brought diplomats and international lawyers together with the scientific community in ways not often seen in other areas of international law. The ease with which an international lawyer is able to present a cogent case for international legislation will often turn upon the ability to show that the lack of action by the international community is likely to result in significant adverse effects. Within the past decade the task may have been made substantially less onerous by the broad acceptance and application of the precautionary principle, which provides a basis for action to be taken even in the face of significant scientific uncertainty. The 1985 Vienna Convention (and its 1987 Montreal Protocol), the 1992 Climate Change Convention (and its 1997 Kyoto Protocol), the 1995 Straddling Stocks Agreement and the 2000 Cartagena Protocol on Biosafety may be cited as examples of the numerous international environmental treaties establishing obligations in the face of scientific uncertainty and in the absence of an international consensus on the existence of environmental harm. To these may be added a series of international judicial decisions informed by 'prudence and caution'.

Since the first edition of this book was published in 1995, the place of science in international environmental decision-making has been the subject of vigorous debate, largely focusing around competing claims concerning the lawfulness of restrictions on the use of, and international trade in, modified THE ENVIRONMENT AND INTERNATIONAL SOCIETY foodstuffs, including genetically modified organisms. Disputes under various World Trade Organization (WTO) agreements (relating to beef hormonesand asbestos) and the negotiations leading to the adoption of the Cartagena Protocol on Biosafety have provided opportunities for an airing of states' views as to the degree of scientific evidence and certainty that is required to justify restrictions (as well as the economic and other implications of such decisions, and the extent to which non-scientific and non-economic considerations may be applied in decision-making, on which see below). As to science, in large part the issues have been driven by differences of perspective between the United States and the European Union, with the former strongly in favour of decision-making which is based on 'hard science' and strictly limiting the circumstances in which restrictions may be permitted in the face of uncertainty as to consequences. The extent of the difference – and its implications for the legal order more generally – are reflected in views expressed by one official of the US State Department: the increasing efforts from within the EU . . . could weaken the scientific basis for regulatory decisions that affect trade. This trend poses a challenge not only to US interests but also to the rules-based, global trading system that we have spent the past 50 years building.

Thecontrary position–adoptedbytheEuropean Union–wouldallowdecision-makers a greater 'margin of appreciation' in the face of scientific uncertainty, and is reflected in its arguments to the WTO Appellate Body in the *Beef Hormones* case, and in its Communication on the use of the precautionary principle. The tension in the two approaches has not been resolved at the level of international legislation, and will fall to international adjudicators to determine on a case-by-case basis.

The approaches of the International Court of Justice (in the *Gabcikovo-Nagymaros* case), the International Tribunal for the Law of the Sea (in the *Southern Bluefin Tuna* and *MOX* cases), the WTO Appellate Body (in the *Beef Hormones* case) and the European Patent Office (in the *Plant Genetic Systems* case) merit attention and comparison, indicating THE LEGAL AND INSTITUTIONAL FRAMEWORK a reluctance to move away from traditional approaches, but tempered with a growing recognition as to some appropriate role for precautionary measures.Of particular note, in this regard, is the recognition of a greater role for early 'risk assessment', beyond traditional use of environmental impact assessment.

Economics

The progress of international environmental law reflects the close relationship between environmental protection and economic development. Over the short term, laws adopted to protect the environment can impose potentially significant economic costs. Moreover, certain developed countries will be well placed to benefit from the adoption of stringent environmental standards, including the advantages gained from the sale of environmentally sound technology, while others will be concerned about the threat to their economic competitiveness which results from the failure of other countries to adopt similar stringent standards and may, some argue, relax their environmental standards.

Most environmental treaties do not provide for financial resources to be made available to compensate for the additional costs of protective measures, partly because, it must be said, at the time of their negotiation their economic consequences were not fully considered. The Convention on the International Trade in Endangered Species (CITES), for example, did not provide compensation to African states for the loss of revenue resulting from the 1989 ban on international trade in ivory. This may have limited the desire of many developing countries to support similar measures subsequently. There is also concern that the move towards harmonisation might lead to a lowering of environmental standards to ensure that economic costs can be borne, as reflected in efforts to introduce a principle of 'cost-effectiveness' to guide decision-making under some environmental agreements. Accordingly, some treaties, such as the EC Treaty (as amended since 1992), required certain EC secondary legislation to include a safeguard clause which allows member states to adopt provisional measures for 'non-economic environmental reasons'.

It is hardly surprising, therefore, that in recent years environmental concerns have become interconnnected with economic considerations. Aside from the question of the potential use of economic instruments to achieve environmental objectives, two issues have become particularly acute in recent negotiations. Developing countries have sought to make their acceptance of environmental obligations dependent upon the provision of financial assistance, and some developed countries, in order to prevent the competitive economic advantages which might flow from non-compliance, have striven to ensure that environmental treaties establish effective institutions to verify and ensure that the contracting parties comply with their environmental obligations.

These two features have resulted in environmental treaties breaking new ground in the development of international legal techniques. Some environmental treaties, such as the 1987 Montreal Protocol, the 1992 Climate Change Convention, the`1992 Biodiversity Convention and the 2001 POPs Convention, now provide for 'compensatory' finance to be made available to developing countries to enable them to meet certain 'incremental costs' of implementing their obligations, and provide for subsidiary bodies to verify compliance and implementation. This linkage has in turn led to the creation of specialised funding arrangements within existing institutions,in particular theWorld Bank and the regional development banks, such as the Global Environment Facility (GEF).

The integration of environmental protection and economic development could make international environmental law less marginal. On the other hand, the integration of environmental concerns into international economic arrangements may merely serve to subsume environmental considerations and perpetuate an approach to international economic practices and arrangements which may encourage certain environmental problems. This concern refers to the integration of environment and development which has led to the emergence of the concept of sustainable development, now reflected in many international instruments and the decisions of some international courts.

Other social objectives

Science and economics are not the only factors which influence international environmental decision-making, or international adjudication of decisions premised on environmental arguments. Within the past five years, there has been increasing recognition of a place for social and other values as legitimate factors influencing environmental decision-making. This is reflected, initially, in the EC rules which emerged in 1992 to permit (on a temporary basis) exceptional measures based on non-economic considerations (see above), which were relied upon (in Directive 90/220) by some EC member states to justify temporary bans on the placing on the market of genetically modified maize and oil rapeseed products. More recently, however, it has been taken up in other contexts.The 2000 Biosafety Protocol allowsparties, in reaching decisions under the Protocol, to take into account, consistent with their international obligations, socio-economic considerations arising from the impact of living modified organisms on the conservation and sustainable use of biological diversity, especially with regard to the value of biological diversity to indigenous and local communities.

In a similar vein, in its decision in the *Asbestos* case, also in 2000, the WTO Appellate Body confirmed that an importing state was entitled to take into account (among other factors) consumer tastes and habits in respect of a particular product in order to determine whether it was 'like' another product.This recognises, apparently for the first time, that the characteristics of a product go beyond economic and physical (scientific) considerations.

Sustainable development

The concept of sustainable development may be found expressly or implicitly in many environmental treaties and other instruments in the period prior to the publication of the Brundtland Report in 1987. Nevertheless, the Brundtland Report is commonly viewed as the point at which sustainable development became a broad global policy objective and set the international community on the path which led to UNCED and the body of rules referred to as 'international law in the field of sustainable development', but distinguished from international environmental law. Is there any difference between international law in the field of sustainable development and international environmental law?

The Brundtland Report defined sustainable development as 'development that meets the needs of the present without compromising the ability of future generations to meet their own needs'. Two key concepts are contained within this definition: the concept of needs, in particular the essential needs of the present generation, and the idea of limitations imposed by the state of technology and social organisation on the environment's ability to meet present and future needs. The Brundtland Report identified critical objectives for environment and development policies reflected in the concept of sustainable development:

- reviving growth and changing its quality;
- meeting essential needs for jobs, food, energy, water and sanitation;
- ensuring a sustainable level of population;
- conserving and enhancing the resource base;
- reorienting technology and managing risk; and
- merging environment and economics in decision-making.

The forty chapters of Agenda 21 elaborate upon these issues. Taken together they constitute the framework for international law in the field of sustainable development, now confirmed as an international legal term by the ICJ in the *Gabcikovo-Nagymaros* case and as having practical legal consequences by the WTO Appellate Body in the *Shrimp/Turtle* case. Agenda 21 has been confirmed and, to a limited extent, taken a step further by the Plan of Implementation adopted by the World Summit on Sustainable Development, in September 2002.

The Agenda 21 address issues which are primarily 'environmental', and they provide the subject matter of this book. The international law of sustainable development is therefore broader than international environmental law; apart from environmental issues, it includes the social and economic dimension of development, the participatory role of major groups, and financial and other means of implementation. International environmental law is part of the international law of sustainable development, but is narrower in scope. And, as will be seen in subsequent chapters, the integration of environmental considerations with other social objectives has led to the development of a human rights/environment jurisprudence and the integration of environment into matters such as armed conflict and criminal law (reflected, in a limited way, in the Statute of the International Criminal Court).

THE INTERNATIONAL LEGAL ORDER

Environmental issues pose challenges for the traditional international legal order, in at least three ways. They pose challenges, first, for the legislative, administrative and adjudicative functions of international law; secondly, for the manner in which international legal arrangements are currently organised (i.e. along territorial lines); and, thirdly, for the various actors who are considered to be members of the international community and participants in the various processes and practices of the international legal order. The ability of the international legal order to address these three aspects, in the context of environmental issues, will determine whether international law is up to the task of taking on these new global challenges, or whether it will become 'the faithful friend of a family overtaken by time'. It remains to be seen whether a diminishing conception of sovereignty in the face of a more assertive international judiciary, together with a more inclusive, accessible and diverse international legal order, leads to any greater protection of the environment.

The functions of international law

International law and institutions serve as the principal framework for international co-operation and collaboration between members of the international community in their efforts to protect the local, regional and global environment. At each level, the task becomes progressively more complex as new actors and interests are drawn into the legal process: whereas just two states negotiated the nineteenth-century fishery conservation conventions, more than 150 states negotiated the 1992 Climate Change Convention and the 2000 Biosafety Protocol.

In both cases, however, the principles and rules of public international law and international organisations serve similar functions: to provide a framework within which the various members of the international community may cooperate, establish norms of behaviour and resolve their differences. The proper functions of international law are legislative, administrative and adjudicative functions. The legislative function, which is considered in chapter 4, provides for the creation of legal principles and rules which impose binding obligations requiring states and other members of the international community to conform to certain norms of behaviour. These obligations place limits upon the activities which may be conducted or permitted because of their actual or potential impact upon the environment. The impact might be felt within the borders of a state, or across the boundaries of two or more states, or in areas beyond the jurisdiction and control of any state.

The administrative function of international law allocates tasks to various actors to ensure that the standards imposed by the principles and rules of international environmental law are applied. The adjudicative function of international law aims to provide mechanisms or fora to prevent and peacefully settle differences or disputes which arise between members of the international community involving the use of natural resources or the conduct of activities which will impact upon the environment. As will be seen, since the mid-1990s the adjudicative function has assumed increasing importance in interpreting and applying – and even developing – the rules of international law in the field of the environment.

Sovereignty and territory

The international legal orderregulates the activities of an international community comprising states, international organisations and non-state actors. States have the primary role in the international legal order, as both international law-makers and holders of international rights and obligations. Under international law states are sovereign and have equal rights and duties as members of the international community, notwithstanding differences of an economic, social, political or other nature. The doctrine of the sovereignty and equality of states has three principal corollaries, namely, that states have: (1) a jurisdiction, prima facie exclusive, over a territory and a permanent population living there; (2) a duty of non-intervention in the area of exclusive jurisdiction of other states; and (3) the dependence of obligations arising from customary law and treaties on the consent of obligor.

The sovereignty and exclusive jurisdiction of the 200 or so states over their territory means, in principle, that they alone have the competence to develop policies and laws in respect of the natural resources and the environment of their territory, which comprises:

1. the land within its boundaries, including the subsoil;
2. internal waters, such as lakes, rivers and canals;
3. the territorial sea, which is adjacent to the coast, including its seabed, subsoil and the resources thereof; and
4. the airspace above its land, internal waters and territorial sea, up to the point at which the legal regime of outer space begins.

Additionally, states have limited sovereign rights and jurisdiction over other areas, including: a contiguous zone adjacent to the territorial seas; the resources of the continental shelf, its seabed and subsoil; certain fishing zones; and the 'exclusive economic zone'. It follows that certain areas fall outside the territory of any state, and in respect of these no state has exclusive jurisdiction. These areas, which are sometimes referred to as the 'global commons', include the high seas and its seabed and subsoil, outer space, and, according to a majority of states, the Antarctic. The atmosphere is also sometimes considered to be a part of the global commons. This apparently straightforward international legal order worked satisfactorily as an organising structure until technological developments permeated national boundaries. This structure does not, however, co-exist comfortably with an environmental order which consists of a biosphere of interdependent ecosystems which do not respect artificial national territorial boundaries. Many natural resources and their environmental components are ecologically shared. The use by one state of natural resources within its territory will invariably have consequences for the use of natural resources and their environmental components in another state. This is evident where a river runs through two or more countries, or where living resources migrate between two or more sovereign territories. What has only recently become clear is that apparently innocent activities in one country, such as the release of chlorofluorocarbons or (possibly) genetically modified organisms, can have significant effects upon the environment of other states or in areas beyond national jurisdiction. Ecological interdependence poses a fundamental problem for international law, and explains why international co-operation and the development of international environmental standards are increasingly indispensable: the challenge for international law in the world of sovereign states is to reconcile the fundamental independence of each state with the inherent and fundamental interdependence of the environment.

An additional but related question arises as a result of existing territorial arrangements which leave certain areas outside any state's territory: how can international law ensure the protection of areas beyond national jurisdiction? While it is clear that under international law each state may have environmental obligations to its citizens and to other states which may be harmed by its activities, it is less clear whether such an obligation is owed to the international community as a whole.

International actors

A second salient issue concerns the membership of the international community and the participation of actors in the development and application of the principles and rules of international environmental law.

In the environmental field it is clear that international law is gradually moving away from an approach which treats international society as comprising a community of states, and is increasingly encompassing the persons (both legal and natural) within and among those states.

This is reflected in developments both in relation to law-making and law enforcement. This feature is similar to that which applies in the field of international human rights law, where non-state actors and international organisations also have an expanded role. This reality is reflected in many international legal instruments.

The Rio Declaration and Agenda 21 recognise and call for the further development of the role of international organisations and non-state actors in virtually all aspects of the international legal process which relate to environment and development. The 1998 Aarhus Convention provides clear rules on the rights of participation of non-state actors, in relation to access to information and justice, and the right to participate in environmental decision-making. Although the Convention's requirements are intended to apply at the national level, there is no reason why this rationale should not equally apply at the international level, including in the EU context.

ENVIRONMENT CHALLENGES

It is now widely recognised that the planet faces a diverse and growing range of environmental challenges which can only be addressed through international co-operation. Acid rain, ozone depletion, climate change, loss of biodiversity, toxic and hazardous products and wastes, pollution of rivers and depletion of freshwater resources are some of the issues which international law is being called upon to address. Since the mid-1980s, the early international legal developments which addressed aspects of the conservation of natural resources have crystallised into an important and growing part of public international law. The conditions which have contributed to the emergence of international environmental law are easily identified: environmental issues are accompanied by a recognition that ecological interdependence does not respect national boundaries and that issues previously considered to be matters of domestic concern have international implications. The implications, which may be bilateral, sub-regional, regional or global, can frequently only be addressed by international law and regulation.

The growth of international environmental issues is reflected in the large body of principles and rules of international environmental law which apply bilaterally, regionally and globally, and reflects international interdependence in a 'globalising' world. Progress in developing international legal control of activities has been gradual, piecemeal and often reactive to particular incidents or the availability of new scientific evidence. It was not until the late nineteenth century that communities and states began to recognise the transboundary consequences of activities which affected shared rivers or which led to the destruction of wildlife, such as fur seals, in areas beyond national jurisdiction. In the 1930s, the transboundary consequences of air pollution were acknowledged in the litigation leading to the award of the arbitral tribunal in the *Trail Smelter* case.

In the 1950s, the international community legislated on international oil pollution in the oceans. By the 1970s, the regional consequences of pollution and the destruction of flora and fauna were obvious, and by the late 1980s global environmental threats were part of the international community's agenda as scientific evidence identified the potential consequences of ozone depletion, climate change and loss of biodiversity. Local issues were recognised to have transboundary, then regional, and ultimately global consequences. In 1996, the International Court of Justice recognised, for the first time, that there existed rules of general international environmental law, and that a 'general obligation of States to ensure that activities within their jurisdiction and control respect the environment of other States or of areas beyond national control is now part of the corpus of international law relating to the environment'.

Since then, specific treaty rules have become more complex and technical, environmental issues have been increasingly integrated into other subject areas (including trade, investment, intellectual property, human rights, and armed conflict), and international environmental jurisprudence has become less exceptional as the case law of international courts and tribunals expands. The 1992 UN Conference on Environment and Development (UNCED) provided an opportunity for the international community to prioritise environmental issues and consolidate a vast and unwieldy patchwork of international legal commitments.

The treaties and other international acts adopted before, at and since UNCED reflect the growing range of economic activities which are a legitimate concern of the international community and properly subject to international legal regulation. UNCED agreed environmental priorities which were essentially divided into two categories: those relating to the protection of various environmental media, and those relating to the regulation of particular activities or products. The first category identified the following priorities for the protection and conservation of particular environmental media:

- protection of the atmosphere, in particular by combating climate change, ozone depletion and ground-level and transboundary air pollution;
- protection of land resources;
- halting deforestation;
- conservation of biological diversity;
- protection of freshwater resources; and
- protection of oceans and seas (including coastal areas) and marine living resources.

The second category of major issues identified the products and by-products of human technological and industrial innovation which are considered to be particularly harmful to the environment, and which therefore require international regulation. These include:

- biotechnology;
- toxic chemicals, including their international trade;
- agricultural practices;
- hazardous wastes, including their international trade;
- solid wastes and sewage-related issues; and
- radioactive wastes.

For both categories, the international legal issues are complex, and cannot be considered or addressed properly without taking account of political, cultural, economic and scientific concerns. What level of environmental protection should those standards seek to establish?

Should the standards be set on a uni-formbasis or should they be differentiated to take account of political, economic and ecological circumstances? What regulatory and other techniques exist to apply those standards? How are the standards to be enforced domestically and internationally? What happens if a dispute arises over non-compliance?

In addressing these questions, it is clear that the environment represents a complex system of interconnections, that to understand the evolution and character of a particular environment it is necessary to consider a broad range of apparently unrelated factors, and that these factors should be understood as interacting with each other in a number of ways which do not permit them to be treated as discrete.

The interdependence of environmental issues poses legal challenges: how to develop and apply a comprehensive and effective set of legal requirements aimed at preventing environmental damage by addressing the sources without taking measures which will cause harm elsewhere? Current efforts to develop environmentally-sound energy policies reflect the full extent of this challenge, and require international law-making to respond to environmental complexity.

2

History of the Environment

INTRODUCTION

The first period began with bilateral fisheries treaties in the nineteenth century, and concluded with the creation of the new international organisations in 1945. During this period, peoples and nations began to understand that the process of industrialisation and development required limitations on the exploitation of certain natural resources (flora and fauna) and the adoption of appropriate legal instruments. The second period commenced with the creation of the UN and culminated with the UN Conference on the Human Environment, held in Stockholm in June 1972. Over this period, a range of international organisations with competence in environmental matters was created, and legal instruments were adopted, at both the regional and global level, which addressed particular sources of pollution and the conservation of general and particular environmental resources, such as oil pollution, nuclear testing, wetlands, the marine environment and its living resources, the quality of freshwaters, and the dumping of waste at sea. The third period ran from the 1972 Stockholm Conference and concluded with the UN Conference on Environment and Development (UNCED) in June 1992.

During this period, the UN tried to put in place a system for co-ordinating responses to international environmental issues, regional and global conventions were adopted, and for the first time the production, consumption and international trade in certain products was banned at the global level. The fourth period was set in motion by UNCED, and may be characterised as the period of integration: when environmental concerns should, as a matter of international law and policy, be integrated into all activities. This has also been the period in which increased attention has been paid to compliance with international environmental obligations, with the result that there has been a marked increase in international jurisprudence. In tracing the development of the subject, general tendencies and themes may be discerned. First, thedevelopment of principles and rules of international environmental law – through treaties, other international acts and custom – has tended to react to events or incidents or the availability of scientific evidence, rather than anticipate general or particular environmental threats and put in place an anticipatory legal framework.

Secondly, developments in science and technology have played a significant catalytic role: without the availability of scientific evidence, new rules of law are unlikely to be put in place.

Thirdly, as is reflected throughout this book, the principles and rules of international law have developed as a result of a complex interplay between governments, non-state actors and international organisations. The extent to which a particular area is subject to legal rules will depend upon pressure being imposed by non-state actors, the existence of appropriate institutional fora in which rules can be developed, and sufficient will on the part of states to transform scientific evidence and political pressures into legal obligations.

And, fourthly, it is only very recently – within the past decade – that issues of international environmental law have become a regular subject of international adjudication, and that international courts have begun to contribute to the definition and application of the subject. Modern international environmental law can be traced directly to international legal developments which took place in the second half of the nineteenth century. Thus, although the current form and structure of the subject has become recognisable only since the mid-1980s, a proper understanding of modern principles and rules requires a historic sense of earlier scientific, political and legal developments. International environmental law has evolved over at least four distinct periods, reflecting developments in scientific knowledge, the application of new technologies and an understanding of their impacts, changes in political consciousness and the changing structure of the international legal order and institutions.

FROM STOCKHOLM TO RIO: 1972–1992

The Stockholm Conference set the scene for international activities at the regional and global level, and influenced legal and institutional developments up to and beyond UNCED. Developments in this period are of two types: those directly related to Stockholm and follow-up actions; and those indirectly related thereto. The period was marked by: a proliferation of international environmental organisations (including those established by treaty) and greater efforts byexistinginstitutionsto address environmentalissues; thedevelopmentof new sources of international environmental obligations from acts of such organisations; new environmental norms established by treaty; the development of new techniques for implementing environmental standards, including environmental impact assessment and access to information; and the formal integration of environment and development, particularly in relation to international trade and development assistance.

Post-Stockholm: treaties and other international acts

The creation of the United Nations Environment Programme (UNEP) and the adoption of Principle 21 were the most significant achievements of the Stockholm Conference. UNEP has been responsible for the establishment and implementation of the Regional Seas Programme, including some thirty regional treaties, as well as important global treaties addressing ozone depletion, trade in hazardous waste and biodiversity. In the period immediately after

Stockholm, several other treaties of potentially global application were adopted outside UNEP but within the UN system, to address the dumping of waste at sea, pollution from ships, the trade in endangered species and the protec-tionof world culturalheritage. The most important, viewedover time, is likely to be the United Nations Convention on the Law of the Sea (UNCLOS) which established a comprehensive framework for the establishment of global rules on the protection of the marine environment and marine living resources, including detailed and important institutional arrangements and provisions on environmental assessment, technology transfer, liability and dispute settle-ment. Many of the techniques subsequently adopted in other environmental treaties may be traced directly to UNCLOS.

The Stockholm Conference was followed by important regional developments, including the adoption of EC environmental protection rules, and the creation of an Environment Committee at the OECD. Other notable regional developments included: multilateral treaties dedicated to the protection of all migratory species; the protection of habitats; the prevention of transboundary air pollution; the regulation and prohibition of commercial mineral activities in the Antarctic, and rules on environmental co-operation and behaviour in a compact on development assistance between developed and developing countries.

Towards the end of this period, UN economic and financial organisations began to be faced with the practical implications which national and international environmental law might have for their respective activities. In 1971, the General Agreement on Tariffs and Trade (GATT) had established a Group on Environmental Measures and International Trade (which did not meet until 1991), and as an organisation found itself increasingly faced with environmental issues, including the question of the circumstances in which unilateral trade restrictions adopted in the name of environmental protection could be justified under GATT rules. In the face of increasing public and governmental pressure, the World Bank and the regional development banks were called upon to integrate environmental considerations into their loan-making processes. This led to the establishment of an Environment Department in the World Bank and the adoption of limited environmental impact assessment requirements by most multilateral development banks.Amongst the most significant reflection of the changing times was the integration of environmental obligations into the 1990 Articles establishing the European Bank for Reconstruction and Development. In 1991, the

World Bank, UNEP and the United Nations Development Programme established the Global Environmental Facility to provide financial resourcesto support projects which benefited the global commons. At the same time, theGATT decided to re-activateits long-dormant Group onEnvironmental Measures and International Tra d e.

Prior to UNCED, treaties were adopted in areas not previously subject to international regulation. Under the auspices of the UNECE, treaties addressed environmental impact assessment, the transboundary impacts of industrial accidents, and the protection and use of international watercourses. The International Law Commission (ILC) completed a first reading of its draft Articles on the law of non-navigational uses of international watercourses, while the UN Security Council declared that ecological issues could constitute threats to international peace and security. The UN General Assembly adopted a resolution prohibiting the use of driftnets, the first time that body had adopted a normative rule seeking to establish a worldwide standard.

This was also the period in which the impact of acts of international organisations began to be felt. Many organisations had the power to adopt binding or non-binding decisions, resolutions, recommendations or other acts, and these organisations served as fora in which new international environmental legislation could be proposed, adopted and implemented. There are several examples of such acts which are noteworthy for their consequences on industrial and other economic activity, but three in particular reflect the scale of the changes which had occurred.

These were: the moratorium on commercial whaling adopted by resolution of the International Whaling Commission in 1982; the 1983 moratorium on commercial whaling adopted by resolution of the Consultative Meeting of the parties to the 1972 London Convention;and the decision by the 1989 conference of the parties to the 1973 CITES which placed African elephant ivory on Appendix 1 to the Convention and banned the international trade in ivory. Each of these acts followed public pressure and politico-legal strategies adopted at the national and international levels over several years. Despite strong efforts to reverse these acts, they remained effective in 2002, although their economic impact, and their effect on the activities of indigenous peoples, focused attention on the broader economic and social implications of adopting international environmental regulations.

Several non-binding instruments were adopted under the auspices of intergovernmental and non-governmental organisations. Three such instruments haveplayedan influential role:the 1978 UNEP draftPrinciples,the 1981 Montevideo Programme, and the 1982 World Charter for Nature. Non-governmental efforts lay behind two other initiatives whose impact has been substantial: the collaboration between IUCN, UNEP and the Worldwide Fund for Nature (WWF) which led to the 1980 World Conservation Strategy; and the 1991 document entitled 'Caring for the Earth: A Strategy for Sustainable Living'.

1978 UNEP DRAFT PRINCIPLES

One of the first acts to be adopted by UNEP in the field of international law led to the 1978 draft 'Principles of Conduct in the Field of the Environment for the Guidance of States in the Conservation and Harmonious Utilisation of Natural Resources Shared by Two or More States' (the UNEP draft Principles). The draft Principles resulted from the efforts of an Intergovernmental Working Group established by the UNEP Governing Council in 1976, pursuant to a request by the UN General Assembly. The Working Group agreed to limit the effort to the preparation of principles and guidelines which would not be taken as creating legally binding obligations. This is reflected in the Explanatory Note to the Principles, which states that 'the language used throughout does not seek to prejudice whether or to what extent the conduct envisaged in the principles is already prescribed by existing principles of general international law'. The UNEP draft Principles were annexed to the final report of the Working Group which was adopted by the UNEP Governing Council in May 1978 but never submitted to the General Assembly for its consideration.

The UNEP draft Principles comprise fifteen principles to govern the use of 'shared natural resources', a concept which is not defined but which is understood from the Report of the UNEP Executive

Director to mean something other than the 'global commons'. The fifteen Principles include language presciently similar to some of the provisions which were endorsed by the whole of the international community, fourteen years later at UNCED. Principles 1 and 2 recognise the duty of states to co-operate to control, prevent, reduce and eliminate adverse environmental effects, and requires them, to that end, to endeavour to conclude bilateral or multilateral agreements to secure specific regulation of their conduct. Principle 21 of the Stockholm Declaration, broadly followed by Principles 3 and 4, introduces a requirement that states 'make environmental assessments' before engaging in certain activities. Principles 5 and 6 relate to information exchange, consultation and notification, which are elements of the principle of good faith and good neighbourliness elaborated by Principle 7. The draft Principles include principles on scientific studies and assessments (Principle 8), emergency action (Principle 9) and the use of the 'services' of international organisations (Principle 10). The settlement of disputes and responsibility and liability are addressed by Principles 12 and 13, and Principles 13 and 14 elaborate upon the objectives of non-discrimination and the rights of persons in other jurisdictions who may be adversely affected by environmental damage to the equal right of access to administrative and judicial proceedings. Principle 15 provides that the UNEP draft Principles should be interpreted and applied 'to enhance and not to affect adversely development and the interests of all countries, and in particular the developing countries'.

1981 MONTEVIDEO PROGRAMME

Three years later, an *ad hoc* meeting of senior government officials expert in environmental law was held in Montevideo under UNEP auspices, and the Programme for the Development and Periodic Review of Environmental Law (the Montevideo Programme) was prepared. The Programme was adopted by the UNEP Governing Council in May 1982 and influenced UNEP's legal activities in the period 1982–92, resulting in the development of regional and global treaties and 'soft law' instruments. The Montevideo Programme has also been integrated into the UN System-Wide Medium-Term Environment Programmes (1984–9 and 1990–5). In 1993 and again in 2001, the UNEP Governing Council adopted new Programmes.

The original Montevideo Programme was divided into three parts. The first part proposed that guidelines, principles or agreements should be developed to address: marine pollution from land-based sources; protection of the stratospheric ozone layer; and the transport, handling and disposal of toxic and dangerous wastes. The second part proposed that action should be taken to address eight priority subject areas:

- international co-operation in environmental emergencies;
- coastal zone management;
- soil conservation;
- transboundary air pollution;
- international trade in potentially harmful chemicals;
- the protection of rivers and other inland waters against pollution;
- legal and administrative measures for the prevention and redress of pollution damage; and
- environmental impact assessment.

The third programme area proposed work of a general nature to promote the development of environmental law, including research, writing and teaching of theoretical and practical aspects of environmental law and the dissemination of information.

1982 WORLD CHARTER FOR NATURE

Ten years after the Stockholm Conference, the UN General Assembly adopted the World Charter for Nature, which set forth 'principles of conservation by which all human conduct affecting nature is to be guided and judged'. The Charter, which is divided into three sections, is a non-binding instrument drafted in general language. The Charter differs from the Stockholm Declaration and the UNEP draft Principles in substance and form: it is an avowedly ecological instrument. Whereas the earlier instruments were anthropocentric and focused on the protection of nature for the benefit of mankind, the Charter emphasises the protection of nature as an end in itself. The explanation for this lies in part in its origins

- the Twelfth General Assembly of the IUCN held in Zaire in 1975 - and in its subsequent elaboration by IUCN and an international group of independent experts. The Charter was strongly supported by developing countries, marking a change from the general reluctance which many of these countries had expressed at Stockholm ten years earlier for international environmental policy. The Charter is not binding, and has been characterised as 'an important symbolic expression of an intent among nations to achieve a more harmonious and sustainable relationship between humanity and the rest of the biosphere - between mankind and earth'. As a standard of ethical conduct, however, many of its provisions are now reflected in treaties.

Section I, entitled 'General Principles', contains aspirational language calling for the respect of nature and its essential processes: safeguarding habitats and ensuring the survival of all life forms; providing special protection for unique areas, ecosystems and habitats of endangered species; maintaining 'optimum sustainable productivity' of natural resources without endangering other ecosystems or species; and securing nature against degradation from warfare. Section II, entitled 'Functions', is more operational in character. It calls for the integration of nature into the planning and implementation of development activities, taking into account the long-term capacity of natural systems and the physical constraints, biological productivity and diversity and natural beauty of different areas.

The Charter includes 'rules' governing the use of natural resources which pre-date the concept of sustainable development first used in the 1985 ASEAN Agreement and endorsed by the Brundtland Report in 1987. Living resources should not be used in excess of their natural capacity for regeneration; the productivity of soils should be maintained; resources should be reused or recycled, and non-renewable resources should be used with restraint. The Charter includes language on environmental impact assessment and distinguishes between three activities in the light of such assessments: (1) activities which are likely to cause irreversible damage to nature (which should be avoided); (2) activities which are likely to pose a significant risk to nature (which should be preceded by an exhaustive examination); and (3) activities which may disturbnature (which should be preceded by an assessment of their consequences). The approach is now broadly reflected in international practice. The Charter supports an approach which combines the prevention of natural disasters, the avoidance of discharge of pollutants, and the rehabilitation of degraded areas.

Section III, entitled 'Implementation', includes elements of the approaches endorsed and applied by subsequent environmental treaties and instruments. These techniques include: the dissemination of knowledge of nature, particularly by ecological education; the formulation of conservation strategies and environmental assessments; public access to information for consultation and participation; the provision of funds and administrative structures; scientific research; and early detection of degradation. Implementation includes: co-operation among and between the various actors in the international community (states, public authorities, international organisations, individuals, groups and corporations); the establishment of standards for products and manufacturing processes; the implementation of applicable international legal provisions, and measures to ensure that activities do not cause damage to natural systems within other states or in areas beyond the limits of national

jurisdiction. The Charter recognises the place of non-state actors, including their right and duties relating to participation in the formulation of decisions, access to means of redress when their environment suffers damage, and the responsibility to act in accordance with the provisions of the Charter. 1980 World Conservation Strategy/1991 'Caring for the Earth' Strategy

The 1980 World Conservation Strategy was prepared by IUCN, UNEP, WWF, UNESCO and FAO. The Strategy gave currency to the term 'sustainable development', and has led to the preparation of national and sub-national conservation strategies in most states. It has subsequently influenced international legal developments. The 1980 Strategy emphasised three objectives stressing the interdependence of conservation and development:

1. Essential ecological processes and life-support systems must be maintained;
2. Genetic diversity must be preserved; and
3. Any use of species or ecosystems must be sustainable.

It identified six main obstacles to the fulfilment of these objectives:

1. The failure to recognise that living resource conservation is a process that cuts across all sectors;
2. The failure to integrate conservation with development;
3. A development process that is inadequate in environmental planning and management;
4. Lack of capacity to conserve due to inadequate legislation and lack of enforcement;
5. Lack of awareness of the benefit of conservation; and
6. The inability to deliver conservation-based development where it is most needed, including rural areas of developing countries.

In 1991, the 'Caring for the Earth' Strategy restated the thinking about conservation and development with two aims: securing a commitment to sustainable living; and translating its principles into practice.

The text defines Principles and Additional Actions for Sustainable Living, and proposes guidelines to allow adaptation of the Strategy to needs and capabilities and to implement it. The Strategy includes a commitment to national and international law as essential tools for achieving sustainability by the establishment of standards of social behaviour and the establishment of permanent policies. Specific recommendations include:

1. Establishing a constitutional commitment to the principles of a sustainable society;
2. Establishing a comprehensive system for environmental law, and providing for its implementation and enforcement;
3. Reviewing the adequacy of legal and administrative controls and of implementation and enforcement mechanisms;

4. Making information on the environment more accessible; and
5. Subjecting projects, programmes and policies to environmental impact as-sessment.

National legal measures specifically recommended include: the development of standards; the application of the precautionary principle and the use of best available technology; a liability system that provides for compensation not only for economic losses suffered by other users of the environmental resource in question but also for ecological and intangible losses, and the capacity to require the restoration of damaged ecosystems, or punitive damages where restoration is impossible. Also recommended were strict liability for accidents involving hazardous substances; granting citizens' groups standing in judicial and administrative procedures in order to contribute to enforcement of the law and remedies for environmental damage; and making agencies that are responsible for the implementation and enforcement of environmental law accountable for their actions. The Strategy seeks the development of international law by strengthening existing international agreements, concluding new international agreements to achieve global sustainability, and preparing and adopting a Universal Declaration and Covenant on Sustainability. The Brundtland Report and the Report of the Legal Experts Group

The World Commission on Environment and Development (WCED), chaired by Norwegian Prime Minister Gro Harlem Brundtland, was established in 1983 by the UN General Assembly, and its report (the Brundtland Report) was published in 1987. The Commission was established as an independent body, linked to, but outside the control of, governments and the UN system. It had three objectives: to re-examine critical environment and development issues and formulate realistic proposals for dealing with them; to propose new forms of international co-operation on these issues that would influence policies and events in the direction of needed changes; and to raise levels of understanding and commitment to action of individuals, voluntary organisations, businesses, institutions and governments. Drawing on previous work such as the World Conservation Strategy, the Brundtland

Report was a catalyst for UNCED and the five instruments there adopted. The Brundtland Report signalled changes in the way we look at the world. It provided support for expanding the role of sustainable development, proposed a UN programme on sustainable development, and identified the central legal and institutional issues.

Until recently, the planet was a large world in which human activities and their effects were neatly compartmentalised within nations, within sectors (energy, agriculture, trade) and within broad areas of concern (environmental, economic, social). These compartments have begun to dissolve. This applies in particular to the global 'crises' that have seized public concern, particularly over the last decade. These are not separate crises: an environmental crisis, a development crisis, an energy crisis. They are all one.

On policy matters the Commission focused attention on population, food security, the loss of species and genetic resources, energy, industry and human settlements, recognising that these are connected and cannot be treated in isolation from each other. On international co-operation and institutional reform the focus included: the role of the international economy; managing the global commons; the relationship between peace, security, development and the environment; and institutional and legal change. The Report made specific recommendations in respect of each of these matters that identify challenges for the development of international law, including the impact of national sovereignty and the management of the 'global commons'.

The Brundtland Report identified six priority areas for legal and institutional change, and identified the existing legal order as part of the problem. First, governments, regional organisations and international bodies and agencies were called upon to support development which would be economically and ecologically sustainable, to integrate the environment fully into their goals and activities, and to improve co-ordination and co-operation. Secondly, it sought a reinforcement of the roles and capacities of environmental protection and resource management agencies to deal with effects, including a strengthened UNEP as the principal source for environmental data, assessment and reporting and the principal advocate and agent for change and international co-operation. Thirdly, it called for an extension of the capacity of the international community to identify, assess and report on global risks of irreversible environmental damage, including a new international programme for co-operation among nongovernmental organisations, scientific bodies and industry groups. Fourthly, it recognised the need to expand the rights, roles and participation in development planning, decision-making and project implementation of an informed public, non-governmental organisations, the scientific community, and industry.

Fifthly, in recognising that 'international law is being rapidly out-distanced by the accelerating pace and expanding scale of impacts on the ecological basis of development', the Brundtland Report called on governments to fill gaps in national and international law related to the environment in order to find ways to recognise and protect the rights of present and future generations to an environment adequate for their health and well-being, to prepare under UN auspices a universal declaration on environmental protection and sustainable development and a subsequent convention, and to strengthen procedures for avoiding or resolving disputes on environment and resource management issues. Finally, the Report recognised the need to invest in pollution control by providing financial assistance through the World Bank, the IMF and other regional development banks. The Report also called for a UN Programme on Sustainable Development and an international conference to review progress and to promote follow-up arrangements. Each of these proposals received support from governments at UNCED.

An Experts Groupon Environmental Law was established alongside UNCED. It proposed Legal Principles and Recommendations on Environmental Protection and Sustainable Development (1986 WCED Legal Principles), set out in twenty-two Articles, which are intended to reflect the basic obligations of states based on an assessment of treaties, soft law instruments, and some state practice. The WCED Legal Principles fall into three categories, including 'general principles, rights and responsibilities', and 'principles, rights and obligations governing transboundary natural resources and environmental interference'. These are addressed below.

ENVIRONMENTAL PERSPECTIVE TO THE YEAR 2000 AND BEYOND

In 1987 the United Nations General Assembly adopted the 'Environmental Perspective to the Year 2000 and Beyond' as a framework to guide national action and international co-operation in policies and programmes aimed at achieving environmentally sound development.

The Perspective had been prepared by a UNEP intergovernmental preparatory committee pursuant to a request from the General Assembly, and focused on the same six key sectoral issues as the Brundtland Commission: population; food and agriculture; energy; industry; health and human settlements; and international economic relations. The Perspective identified four further issues which it considered to be of global concern: oceans and seas; outer space; biological diversity; and security and the environment. For legislation and environmental law, the Perspective identified issues requiring attention:

- The need to conclude conventions for hazards relating to chemicals, the treatment and international transport of hazardous wastes, industrial accidents, climate change, protection of the ozone layer, protection of the marine environment from pollution from land-based sources, and protection of biological diversity; and
- The establishment of legal regimes at international and national levels to improve the environmental management of rivers, lakes and forests.

The Perspective noted, in opaque language which reflected the lack of consensus over future directions, that the 'progressive emergence of general environmental norms and principles and the codification of existing agreements could lead to a global convention on the protection and enhancement of the environment'.It also noted that the International Court of Justice, the Permanent Court of Arbitration and regional mechanisms should facilitate the peaceful settlement of environmental disputes.

Conclusions

By 1990, preparations for UNCED were under way and significant political and legal changes were in place. There was now a discrete area of law called international environmental law. At the global and regional level this included a large number of substantive rules limiting the rights of states to engage in activities which were harmful to the environment. International environmental law was no longer focused on the protection of wildlife. Standards had been adopted and applied for the protection of the marine environment and freshwater resources, the atmosphere and the ozone layer, and the disposal of hazardous and other wastes. New techniques for the implementation of those standards, such as environmental impact assessment and access to environmental information, were being developed and applied. Environmental protection was being addressed in the context of economic matters, such as trade and development lending. Developing countries had succeeded in establishing the principle that financial resources should be made available to help them meet the incremental costs of implementing their international environmental obligations. Differential standards were accepted in the 1985 SO2 Protocol to the 1979 LRTAP Convention and the 1987 Montreal Protocol. New institutions had been created to address regional and global environmental issues, and existing institutions were beginning to integrate environmental considerations into their activities. Subsidiary bodies were being established to ensure innovative implementation and compliance techniques. Principle 21 was broadly considered to reflect a rule of customary international law, and new principles were emerging, such as the polluter-pays principle and the precautionary principle. Perhaps most significantly, in respect of the standards being adopted, and in respect of monitoring and implementation, new international actors, including non-governmental organisations from developed and developing countries, were participating in the international legal process.

UNCED

Report of the UN Conference on Environment and Development, Rio de Janeiro, 3–14 June 1992, UN Doc. A/CONF.151/26/Rev.1

(vols. I–III); A. Adede, 'International Environmental Law from Stockholm to Rio: an Overview of Past Lessons and Future Challenges', 22 *Environmental Policy and Law* 88 (1992); A. C. Kiss and S. Doumbe-Bille, 'La Conference des Nations Unies sur l'Environnement et le Developpement', AFDI 823 (1992); I. M. Porras, 'The Rio Declaration: A New Basis for International Co-operation', 1 RECIEL 245 (1992); G. Speth, 'A Post Rio Compact', 88 *Foreign Policy* 145 (1992); M. Pallemaerts, 'International Environmental Law from Stockholm to Rio: Back to the Future?' 1 RECIEL 254 (1992); P. Sand, 'UNCED and the Development of International Environmental Law', 3 *Yearbook of International Enviromental Law* 3 (1992); N. Robinson (ed.), *International Protection of the Environment: Agenda 21 and the UNCED Proceedings* (1992); D. Freestone, 'The Road from Rio: International Environmental Law after the Earth Summit', 6 JEL 193 (1994); H. Smets, 'The Polluter-Pays Principle in the Early 1990s', in L. Campiglio *et al.* (eds.), *The Environment After Rio* (1994), 131.

In December 1987, the UN General Assembly noted the Brundtland Report,and the following year called for a UN conference on environment and develop-ment. In December 1989, General Assembly Resolution 44/228 convened a UN Conference on Environment and Development for June 1992 in Brazil. The purpose of the Conference was to 'elaborate strategies and measures to halt and reverse the effects of environmental degradation in the context of strengthened national and international efforts to promote sustainable and environmentally sound development in all countries'.

UNCED was held in Rio de Janeiro, Brazil, on 3–14 June 1992, and was attended by 176 states, more than fifty intergovernmental organisations, and several thousand corporations and non-governmental organisations. UNCED adopted three non-binding instruments: the Rio Declaration on Environment and Development (the Rio Declaration); a Non-Legally Binding Authoritative Statement of Principles for a Global Consensus on the Management, Conservation and Sustainable Development of All Types of Forest (the UNCED Forest Principles); and Agenda 21. Two treaties were also opened for signature: the Convention on Biological Diversity;

and the UN Framework Convention on Climate Change. UNCED was the culmination of three separate but related negotiating processes, one of which was the Preparatory Committee for UNCED (PrepComm) which met four times between August 1990 and May 1992. The other two were the Intergovernmental Negotiating Committee for a Framework Convention on Climate Change (INC/FCCC) which held five sessions between February 1991 and May 1992, and the Intergovernmental Negotiating Committee for a Convention on Biological Diversity (INC/CBD) which held five sessions between June 1991 and May 1992. It was also, however, an opportunity to take stock of developments which had taken place in regional and global organisations, in public and private initiatives, and in bilateral, regional and global treaties. It provided an opportunity for the international community to translate initiatives such as the Brundtland Report and the Strategy for Sustainable Living, as well as the many regional preparatory conferences which had taken place, into a coherent strategy of international environmental policy and law for the twenty-first century.

UNCED's contribution to international law will emerge over time, and is likely to include the Commission on Sustainable Development, the endorsement of a new topic area known as the 'international law of sustainable development' (of which international environmental law forms a significant part), a number of the Rio Declaration principles, and the framework established by Agenda 21. It has been suggested that UNCED's endorsement of sustainable development could undermine 'the autonomy of environmental law as a body of rules and standards designed to restrain and prevent the environmentally destructive effects of certain kinds of economic activity', and there might be some reason to fear that the Rio Conference constituted 'the beginning of the decline of international environmental law as an autonomous branch of international law'. This has not been borne out by subsequent developments.

UNCED was concerned with the balance between environmental protection and economic development. Environmentalconcernshave been marginal inthe broader scheme of international legal and institutional arrangements. For them to affect and influence behaviour in significant ways they must be integrated into economic and development activities, without their being overwhelmed by the more powerful rules of international economic co-operation.

The Rio Declaration

The Rio Declaration represents a series of compromises between developed and developing countries and a balance between the objectives of environmental protection and economic development. Thetext wascompleted at the Fourth PrepComm in April 1992 and was not reopened for negotiation at UNCED, despite threats from a number of countries to do so, and was 'endorsed' by the UN General Assembly in December 1992. It comprises twenty-seven Principles which set out the basis upon which states and people are to co-operate and further develop 'international law in the field of sustainable development' (Principle 27). Although it is non-binding, some provisions reflect rules of customary law, others reflect emerging rules, and yet others provide guidance as to future legal developments. A number of the Principles have been referred to with regularity by national and international courts. The Rio Declaration provides a benchmark to measure future developments, and provides a basis for defining 'sustainable development' and its application. It attempts to achieve an acceptable balance between environment and development. The Rio Declaration lost its original title ('Earth Charter'), mainly at the insistence of developing countries, and it bears little resemblance to the Universal Declaration of Human Rights, or to the Universal Covenant which the Brundtland Report had called for.

Principle 1 of the Rio Declaration reflects a shift towards an anthropocentric approach to environmental and developmental issues, declaring that human beings are 'at the centre of concerns for sustainable development', and that they are 'entitled to a healthy and productive life in harmony with nature'; this falls short of recognising a right to a clean and healthy environment. The Rio Declaration reaffirmed Principle 21 of the Stockholm Declaration with one addition. As amended, Principle 2 provides that:

States have, in accordance with the Charter of the United Nations and the principles of international law, the sovereign right to exploit their own resources pursuant to their own environmental and developmental policies, and the responsibility to ensure that activities within their jurisdiction or control do not cause damage to the environment of other states or of areas beyond the limits of national jurisdiction.

The addition of the words 'and developmental' (which is not reflected in Article 3 of the Biodiversity Convention or Principle 2(a) of the Forest Principles), in the context of a negotiation of a document adopted by consensus by 176 states, arguably reflects an 'instant' change in the rule of customary international law which is widely considered to be set forth in Principle 21. It has been suggested that the addition of these two words reveals a 'skilfully masked step backwards' which by its stronger emphasis on development 'upsets the delicate balance struck in Stockholm between the sovereign use of natural resources and the duty of care for the environment'. In fact, a careful reading suggests that the additional words merely affirm that states are entitled to pursue their own development policies. The introduction of these words may even expand the scope of the responsibility not to cause environmental damage to apply to national development policies as well as national environment policies. In practice, the modest amendment has not been identified as having been relied upon by states.

The heart of the Rio Declaration is found in Principles 3 and 4, which should be read together to understand the political context in which they were negotiated and the trade-off they represent. Both Principles were initially controversial. Principle 3 provides that '[t]he right to development must be fulfilled so as to equitably meet developmental and environmental needs of present and future generations'. It represents something of a victory for developing countries and the Group of 77, being the first time that the 'right to development' has been affirmed in an international instrument adopted by consensus. The nature and extent of that right is left open, as is the question of whether such a right attaches to states, peoples or individuals. In return for Principle 3, the developed countries extracted Principle 4, which provides that '[i]n order to achieve sustainable development, environmental protection shall constitute an integral part of the development process and cannot be considered in isolation from it'. This reflects a commitment to moving environmental considerations and objectives from the periphery of international relations to its economic core. In practical terms, Principle 4 can be read as permitting, or requiring, the attachment of environmental conditionalities to all development lending by states and multilateral development banks, and the integration of environmental considerations into all economic and other development.

The Rio Declaration recognises a principle of 'common but differentiated responsibility'. Principle 7 notes the different contributions of countries to regional and global environmental degradation, and provides that:

> [i]n view of the different contributions to global environmental degradation, States have common but differentiated responsibilities. The developed countries acknowledge the responsibility that they bear in the international pursuit of sustainable development in view of the pressures their societies place on the global environment and of the technologies and financial resources they command.

This principle of 'common but differentiated responsibilities' crystallises the provisions in earlier instruments which encourage universal participation in agreements by providing incentives in the form of differentiated standards and 'grace periods', and the provision of financial incentives to subsidise at least some of the incremental costs incurred in fulfilling treaty obligations. The United States rejected an interpretation 'that would imply a recognition or acceptance by the United States of any international obligations or liabilities, or any diminutions in the responsibilities of developing countries.

Principle 11 of the Rio Declaration commits all states to enact 'effective environmental legislation', although the standards, objectives and priorities 'should reflect the environmental and developmental context to which they apply'. Principle 11 also recognises that standards applied by some countries 'may be inappropriate and of unwarranted economic and social cost to other countries, in particular developing countries'.

The Rio Declaration develops general principles of the international law of sustainable development. The 'precautionary approach' is endorsed by Principle 15, and the polluter-pays principle is implicitly recognised in Principle 16. The Rio Declaration takes several steps beyond the Stockholm Declaration by supporting the development of 'procedural' techniques for implementing international standards (including the provision of, and access to, information relating to environmental matters, and recognising the need for participation of concerned citizens) supporting environmental impact assessments, and calling for notification, information exchange and consultation.

Other matters addressed by the Rio Declaration include: the relationship between environmental protection and free trade obligations; the development of national and international law regarding liability and compensation for the victims of pollution and other environmental damage; the need to eradicate poverty and decrease disparities in standards of living; and the reduction and elimination of 'unsustainable patterns of production and consumption'. It promotes 'appropriate demographic policies', endogenous capacity-building and scientific understanding, as well as the transfer of technologies. The Rio Declaration supports the full participation of women, youth and indigenous people and their communities, recognises that war is 'inherently destructive of sustainable development', that peace, development and environmental protection are 'interdependent and indivisible', and that there is a need for the peaceful resolution of environmental disputes.

As apackage, the RioDeclarationincludesprovisionswhichare more specific than those adopted in the Stockholm Declaration. It provides a framework for the development of environmental law at the national and international level whichwillserve as animportant point of reference to guide decision-making. Its contribution to the development of rules of customary law has become clearer over time, although many of its provisions were already found in treaties and other international acts and reflected in the domestic practice of many states.

Agenda 21

Agenda 21 is a non-binding blueprint and action plan for a global partnership for sustainable development. It was conceived as a plan of action by and for the whole of the international community, designed to integrate environment and development concerns for 'the fulfilment of basic needs, improved living standards for all, better protected and managed ecosystems and a safer, more prosperous future. Agenda 21 comprises forty chapters and hundreds of programme areas, the indicative cost of each having been estimated by the UNCED secretariat. The average annual cost of implementing the activities in Agenda 21 was estimated at US$600 billion in the period 1993–2000.

Agenda 21 was negotiated over two years, and 'reflects a global consensus and political commitment at the highest level' towards the implementation of national strategies, plans, policies and processes to be supported and supplemented by international co-operation. The implementation of Agenda 21 is the responsibility of governments, with key roles to be played by the UN system, other international, regional and sub-regional organisations, and with broad public participation and the active involvement of non-governmental organisations. It constitutes an extensive series of programme areas setting out 'the basis for action, objectives, activities and means of implementation' which will be carried out by the various actors according to the different situations, capacities and priorities of countries and regions in full respect of all the principles contained in the Rio Declaration on Environment and Development. It could evolve over time in the light of changing needs and circumstances. This process marks the beginning of a new global partnership for sustainable development.

What contribution has Agenda 21 made to international law? The tangible developments which flow directly from the text are limited. It recommended the creation of a Commission on Sustainable Development, and new co-ordinating mechanisms among UN and other bodies. It proposed a Convention on Drought and Desertification (which was adopted in 1994), but could not agree on a possible international agreement on forests (which remains an unachieved goal for some states). It proposed two intergovernmental follow-up conferences, on 'straddling stocks' of marine living resources (a convention was adopted in 1995) and on the sustainable development of small island states. It endorsed a partnership role for all members of the international community (states, international organisations, non-state actors) in the development and implementation of law and policy on environment and development. And it established programme areas of variable quality and likely effect to cover virtually all human activity. Its contribution to international law can be considered at three levels. First, as a consensus document negotiated by the international community over a period of two years, it provides the only agreed global framework for the development and application of international legal instruments, including 'soft law' instruments, and the activities of international organisations. Secondly, limited parts of Agenda 21 might be considered to reflect rules of 'instant' customary law. Thirdly, it reflected a consensus on principles, practices and rules which might contribute to the development of new rules of conventional and customary law.

Agenda 21 comprises a Preamble (Chapter 1) and four sections. Section 1 (Chapters 2-8) addresses 'Social and Economic Dimensions'. The seven chapters in this section provide for national and international action in relation to international co-operation, poverty, consumption patterns, population, human health, sustainable human settlement and the integration of environment and development in decision-making. Section II (Chapters 9-22) is concerned with 'Conservation and Management of Resources for Development'. Its fourteen chapters address substantive issues for the protection and sustainable use of natural resources in various sectors:

- protection of the atmosphere (Chapter 9);
- planning and management of land resources (Chapter 10);
- deforestation (Chapter 11);
- desertification and drought (Chapter 12);

- sustainable mountain development (Chapter 13);
- sustainable agriculture and rural development (Chapter 14);
- conservation of biological diversity (Chapter 15);
- management of biotechnology (Chapter 16);
- protection of oceans, seas, coastal areas, and the protection, use and development of their living resources (Chapter 17);
- protection of the quality and supply of freshwater resources (Chapter 18);
- management of toxic chemicals (Chapter 19);
- management of hazardous wastes (Chapter 20);
- management of solid and sewage wastes (Chapter 21); and
- management of radioactive wastes (Chapter 22).

Section III (Chapters 23-32) provides for 'Strengthening the Role of Major Groups'. The section recognises that '[o]ne of the fundamental prerequisites for the achievement of sustainable development is broad public participation in decision-making', including new forms of participation. In a chapter devoted to each, it identifies key groups for the implementation of Agenda 21 and proposes their roles at the national and international levels: women; children and youth; indigenous people and their communities; non-governmental organisations; local authorities; workers and their trade unions; business and industry; the scientific and technological community; and farmers. Finally, Section IV (Chapters 33-40) identifies 'Means of Implementation'. The eight chapters in this section identify actions relating to financial resources and mechanisms (Chapter 33), technology transfer, co-operation and capacity-building (Chapter 34), science (Chapter 35), education, public awareness and training (Chapter 36), capacity-building in developing countries (Chapter 37), international institutional arrangements (Chapter 38), international legal instruments and mechanisms (Chapter 39), and information for decision-making (Chapter 40).

A comprehensive assessment of Agenda 21 lies beyond the scope of this chapter. The provisions of Section II, as well as those of Chapters 38, 39 and 40 on financial resources, technology transfer, institutions, legal instruments and mechanisms, and information and education may provide useful points of reference. Agenda 21 aims at developing the concept of the international law of sustainable development, and calls on competent intergovernmental and non-state actors to co-operate to provide governments and legislators, upon request, with an integrated programme of environment and development law (sustainable development law) services, carefully adapted to the specific requirements of the recipient legal and administrative systems.

Institutions

Chapter 38 of Agenda 21 proposes a framework for institutional arrangements to implement Agenda 21, and calls for the establishment of a new commission to ensure effective follow-up of UNCED, to enhance international co-operation and to rationalise the intergovernmental decision-making capacity for the integration of environmental and development issues. The underlying principles

to guide institutional arrangements, in the context of reform and revital-isation of the UN system, are an 'action- and result-oriented approach' based on 'universality, democracy, transparency, cost-effectiveness and accountability'. In fulfilling the task of integrating environment and development issues, institutional arrangements in the UN system are called upon: to ensure the implementation of Agenda 21; to adopt concrete programmes to strengthen co-operation and co-ordination; to strengthen institutional capabilities; to establish effective co-operation and exchange of information; to respond to continuing and emerging issues; and to ensure that any new institutional arrangements support revitalisation, clearly divide responsibilities, and avoid duplication. Specific proposals are made for the UN and its organs and bodies, as well as UN specialised agencies, related organisations and other relevant intergovernmental organisations, and regional and sub-regional organisations. Chapter 38 also identifies the need for partnership with nongovernmental organisations and calls for their 'expanded role'. The development of environmental law is addressed in two chapters: Chapter 8, Part B, deals with environmental law at the national level; and Chapter 39 deals with international law.

National law

Chapter 8 identifies limitations in legal and regulatory arrangements at the national level, and recognises that the enactment and enforcement of laws and regulations at the regional, national, state/provincial or local/municipal levels are 'essential for the implementation of most international agreements in the field of environment and development'. The survey of existing agreements undertaken in UNCED preparations indicated problems of compliance with international agreements; according to Chapter 8, this was due, in part, to the fact that law-making in many countries appeared to be 'ad hoc and piecemeal, or . . . not endowed with the necessary institutional machinery and authority for enforcement and timely adjustment'.

The basis for national legal and regulatory arrangements was summarised thus: it is essential to develop and implement integrated, enforceable and effective laws and regulations that are based upon sound social, ecological, economic and scientific principles. It is equally critical to develop workable programmes to review and enforce compliance with the laws, regulations and standards that are adopted. Technical support may be needed for many countries to accomplish these goals. Technical co-operation requirements in this field include legal information, advisory services, and specialised training and institutional capacity-building.

Three specific objectives are proposed to address international aspects:

1. The dissemination of information on effective legal and regulatory innovations;
2. Supporting country requests to modernise and strengthen the legal framework; and
3. Encouragingthe developmentand implementation ofnational,state, provincial and local programmes to assess and promote compliance and respond to non-compliance.

To give effect to these objectives, six activities are proposed:

1. Governments and international organisations are called upon to assess their laws and regulations and institutional and administrative machinery;
2. Judicial and administrative procedures should be established 'for legal redress and remedy of actions affecting environment and development that may be unlawful or infringe on rights under the law, and should provide access to individuals, groups and organisations with a recognised legal interest';
3. International organisations and non-governmental organisations should provide governments and legislators with an 'integrated programme of environment and development law (sustainable development law) services';
4. International and academic institutions should provide postgraduate programmes and in-service training facilities in environment and development law;
5. Countries should develop strategies to maximise compliance with their laws and regulations, with assistance from international organisations and other countries (including: enforceable laws incorporating sanctions designed to punish violations, obtain redress and act as deterrence; mechanisms for promoting compliance; collecting data; and involving individuals and groups in the development and enforcement of laws); and
6. Parties to international agreements should improve practice and procedures for collecting information on the legal and regulatory measures taken.

International law

Its provisions are limited compared to the specific proposals put forward in, *inter alia*, the Brundtland Report, the WCED Legal Principles, the Perspective 2000 Plan adopted by the UN General Assembly, and the WCN/UNEP/WWF document, *Caring for the Earth*. The UNCED Preparatory Committee had also examined areas for the further development of international environmental law, in light of the need to integrate environment and development and taking into account the needs and concerns of developing countries, and had before it the conclusions of the 1990 Siena Forum on International Law of the Environment, the Beijing Symposium on Developing Countries and International Environmental Law, the Report of the Meeting of Experts for the Review of the Montevideo Programme, and relevant comments by governments and international organisations in the context of the United Nations Decade of International Law.

The proposals in Chapter 39 are premised on: the need to clarify and strengthen the relationship between existing international agreements; the importance of participation from all countries; the need for technical assistance; the work of the International Law Commission; and the need for universality. The overall objective is:

to evaluate and to promote the efficacy of that law and to promote the integration of environment and development policies through effective international agreements or instruments taking into account both universal principles and the particular and differentiated needs and concerns of all countries.

Eight specific objectives are identified:

1. Addressing the difficulties which prevent some states, in particular developing countries, from participating in or implementing international agreements;
2. Setting priorities for future law-making at the global, regional or sub-regional level;
3. Promoting the participation of all countries in the negotiation, implementation, review and governance of international agreements;
4. Gradually promoting international environmental standards;
5. Ensuring effective, full and prompt implementation of legally binding instruments;
6. Improving the effectiveness of administrative arrangements;
7. Identifying and preventing conflicts; and

8. Providing for the identification, avoidance and settlement of international disputes in the field of sustainable development.

To the extent that the international community has a blueprint for the development of the international law of sustainable development (including international environmental law), this is it. Chapter 39 is short on substance, and there was no agreement on the need for a binding instrument of general application, although it was agreed that it would be useful to examine 'the feasibility of elaborating general rights and obligations of states . . . in the field of sustainable development'. Specific activities to be undertaken include: the review and assessment of the performance and effectiveness of agreements and priorities for future law-making on sustainable development; further consideration by the General Assembly of armed conflict and 'large-scale destruction of the environment that cannot be justified under international law'; and efforts to conclude a nuclear safety convention under the International Atomic Energy Agency (IAEA).

Chapter 39 also calls for the promotion and review of the effective, full and prompt implementation of international agreements (including by establishing efficient and practical reporting systems and enhancing the contribution of international bodies such as UNEP), and the provision of technical and financial assistance, particularly to developing countries, to ensure their effective participation. The measures proposed to ensure the avoidance and settlement of disputes call for further study and consideration of existing techniques, and are disappointing in the context of the more specific proposals which were put forward. Beyond UNCED: trends and directions

TheUNGeneralAssemblyadopted fivefollow-upresolutionsto UNCED.These established a negotiating committee to elaborate a convention on drought and desertification; conveneda globalconference on the sustainable development of small island states; noted the report of UNCED, endorsed the Rio Declaration and the Forest Principles and called for effective follow-up action and the implementation of all commitments, agreements and recommendations;established new institutional arrangements to follow up UNCED, including the Commission on Sustainable Development; and convened a conference on straddling and highly migratory fish stocks.

Since UNCED, a number of important new instruments have been adopted and the negotiation of others continues. There is no sign that the rate of legislative activity is dropping off. A treaty was signed to replace the 1972 Oslo Dumping Convention and the 1974 Paris LBS Convention, incorporating many of the principles (precaution, polluter-pays) and legal techniques (environmental impact assessment, access to information, economic instruments) which were endorsed at UNCED. In 1995, a global Agreement on Straddling Fish Stocks was adopted by parties to the 1982 UNCLOS. The parties to the 1969 CLC and the 1971 Fund Convention adopted 1992 Protocols which introduced significant legal changes; and the Council of Europe adopted a convention on civil liability for environmental damage which incorporates many of the recommendations on procedural matters referred to in the Rio Declaration, including access to information and national legal remedies.

The Kyoto Protocol to the 1992 Climate Change Convention was adopted in 1997, and the Biosafety Protocol to the 1992 Biodiversity Convention was adopted in 2000: both instruments reflect new thinking in the approach to international regulation and the role of various actors, including the private sector. In 1998, under the auspices of the UNECE, states adopted the Aarhus Convention, the first treaty to address in a comprehensive fashion the rights of participation reflected in Principle 10 of the Rio Declaration.

Other treaties whichhave beenadoptedinclude an IAEA nuclear safetyconvention; amendments to the 1960 and 1963 nuclear liability conventions; a convention on desertification and drought under the auspices of the General Assembly; an International Labor Organization convention on the prevention of industrial disasters; revisions to the 1985 SO_2 Protocol to the 1979 LRTAP Convention andtheadoptionof Protocols concerning other matters; aliability protocolto the 1989 Basel Convention; global conventions on chemicals and pesticides and on persistent organic pollutants; and a convention on liability for hazardous andnoxious substances under the auspices of the International Maritime Organization. Important new treaties have also been adopted in relation to international watercourses, at the global, regional and bilateral levels.

International organisations have continued to address a wide range of environmental issues. Recent developments include: the maintenance by the International Whaling Commission of its moratorium on commercial whaling;the maintenance of the prohibition on trade in African elephant ivory; further adjustments and amendments to the Montreal Protocol bringing forward the phaseout of certain substances and adopting a non-compliance procedure which provides for sanctions; the adoption of the EC's Sixth Environmental Action Programme; and the OSPAR Commission Decisions on reprocessing activities. In the meantime, the International Law Commission has concluded its work on state responsibility, and transformed its work on liability for injurious consequences arising out of acts not prohibited by international law.

The decade since UNCED has been notable for the significant increase in international litigation on international environmental issues, reflecting a willingness on the part of states to bring international claims and a growing recep-tiveness on the part of the courts to give effect to environmental considerations. The International Court of Justice has addressed the environment in three important cases, including the dispute between Hungary and Slovakia concerning theGabcikovo-Nagymarosproject on theDanubeRiver.

Importantdecisions have been handed down by other international courts and tribunals, including the WTO Appellate Body, the International Tribunal for the Law of the Sea, the European Court of Human Rights, and international arbitral tri-bunals. As increased attention is given to compliance with environmental obligations, states have also established new non-compliance mechanisms.There is also considerable evidence that national courts are increasingly willing to apply international environmental obligations.

World Summit on Sustainable Development

To mark the tenth anniversary of UNCED, the World Summit on Sustainable Development (WSSD) was held in Johannesburg in September 2002. The WSSD did not adopt any conventions or a statement of principles, and was generally focused on the eradication of poverty.

The Johannesburg Declaration on Sustainable Development notes that the global environment continues to suffer, but proposes no specific actions beyond a general commitment to sustainable development. The WSSD Plan of Implementation is long on general commitments and aspiration, but short on specific actions to be taken. Such soft targets and timetables as are proposed are intended to build on post-UNCED achievements and expedite the realisation of UNCED's goals. Among the relatively more specific undertakings are commitments to:

- halve, by 2015, the proportion of the world's people whose income is less than US$1 a day and the proportion of people who suffer from hunger;
- halve, by 2015, the proportion of people without access to safe drinking water;
- halve, by 2015, the proportion of people who do not have access to basic sanitation;
- encourage and promote the development of a ten-year framework of programmes to accelerate the shift towards sustainable consumption and production;
- diversify energy supply and substantially increase the global share of renewable energy sources in order to increase its contribution to total energy supply;
- establish domestic programmes for energy efficiency with the support of the international community, and accelerate the development and dissemination of energy-efficiency and energy-conservation technologies, including the promotion of research and development;
- aim, by 2020, to use and produce chemicals in ways that do not lead to significant adverse effects on human health and the environment;

- promote the ratification and implementation of relevant international instruments on chemicals and hazardous waste, including the 1998 Chemicals Convention so that it can enter into force by 2003 and the 2001 POPs Convention so that it can enter into force by 2004;
- encourage countries to implement the new globally harmonised system for the classification and labelling of chemicals as soon as possible, with a view to having the system fully operational by 2008;
- develop integrated water resources management and water efficiency plans by 2005;
- encourage the application by 2010 of the ecosystem approach for the sustainable development of the oceans;
- on an urgent basis and where possible by 2015, maintain or restore depleted fish stocks to levels that can produce the maximum sustainable yield;
- put into effect the FAO international plans of action for the management of fishing capacity by 2005, and to prevent, deter and eliminate illegal, unre-ported and unregulated fishing by 2004;
- establish by 2004 a regular process under the UN for the global reporting and assessment of the state of the marine environment;
- eliminate subsidies that contribute to illegal, unreported and unregulated fishing and to over-capacity;
- achieve, by 2010, a significant reduction in the current rate of loss of biological diversity;
- adopt new measures to strengthen institutional arrangements for sustainable development at international, regional and national levels;
- enhance the role of the Commission on Sustainable Development, including through reviewing and monitoring progress in the implementation of Agenda 21 and fostering the coherence of implementation, initiatives and partnerships.

A potentially more useful indicator of future international legal developments are reflected in the revisions to the Montevideo Programme. A first revision had been completed by government experts from eighty-one countries (with input from observers from one country, one national liberation movement and twelve international organisations, but no non-governmental organisations) in September 1992.

This was endorsed by the UNEP Governing Council in May 1993. A second revision - the Programme for the Development and Periodic Review of Environmental Law for the First Decade of the Twenty-first Century - was completed by government experts from seventy countries (with input from observers, a national liberation movement and international organisations, but no non-governmental organisations) in October 2000.

The Programme is divided into three parts. Part I addresses the effectiveness of environmental law, and focuses on:

- achieving effective implementation of, compliance with and enforcement of environmental law;
- strengthening the regulatory and institutional capacity of developing countries to develop and implement environmental law;
- strengthening measures to prevent environmental damage, and to mitigate such damage when it occurs;
- improving the effectiveness of measures and methods for avoiding and settling international environmental disputes;
- strengthening and further developing international environmental law, building on the existing foundations;
- promoting appropriate harmonised approaches to the development and implementation of environmental law and promoting co-ordination between relevant institutions;
- improving decision-making in environmental matters through increased transparency, access to information and public participation;
- improving the development, content, effectiveness and awareness of environmental law through the use of new and existing information technology; and

- improving the effectiveness of environmental law through the application of innovative approaches.

Part II seeks to enhance conservation and management, in particular by:

- enhancing the conservation, protection, integrated management and sustainable use of freshwater resources, both ground and surface water;
- improving the management, conservation and sustainable use of coastal and marine resources and ecosystems;
- improving the conservation, rehabilitation and sustainable use of soils;
- enhancing the conservation and sustainable use of all types of forests;
- enhancing the conservation of biological diversity, the sustainable use of its components, and the fair and equitable sharing of benefits arising out of the utilisation of genetic resources;
- strengthening and expanding existing, and developing new, legal instruments to prevent, reduce and control environmental pollution, to minimise the generation of wastes and to achieve their safe disposal, and to achieve the environmentally sound and safe management of hazardous substances;
- improving the sustainability of ecosystems through adequate patterns of production and consumption; and
- improving the ability of the international community to prevent and respond to environmental emergencies arising from man-made and natural disasters.

Part III addresses the relationship between environmental issues and other fields, and focuses on three areas:

- securing environmental protection objectives in international trade, investment and financial laws and policies in order to achieve sustainable development;
- promoting the integration of the environmental dimension into traditional concepts of international and national security; and

- reducing the harmful effects of military activities on the environment and encouraging a positive role for the military sector in environmental protection.

FROM EARLY FISHERIES CONVENTIONS TO THE CREATION OF THE UNITED NATIONS

Early attempts to develop international environmental rules focused on the conservation of wildlife (fisheries, birds and seals) and, to a limited extent, on the protection of rivers and seas. International legal developments followed the research efforts of scientists in the late eighteenth and nineteenth centuries, including: the work of Count Buffon which contrasted the appearance of inhabited life with uninhabited life; the studies by Fabre and Surrell of flooding, siltation, erosion and the division of watercourses brought about by deforestation in the Alps; and the conclusions of de Saussure and von Humboldt that deforestation had lowered water levels of lakes in the Alps and in Venezuela. By the mid-eighteenth century, the relationship between deforestation and the drying-up of water basins was widely observed. In the island of Ascension,

> there was an excellent spring situated at the foot of the mountain originally covered with wood; the spring became scanty and dried up after the trees which covered the mountain had been felled. The loss of the spring was rightly ascribed to the cutting down of the timber. The mountain was therefore planted anew. A few years afterwards the spring reappeared by degrees, and by and by flowed with its former abundance.

Concern for flora and fauna coincided with industrialisation and the use of mineral resources. This led to the adoption of early environmental legislation at the national level.

The adoption of treaties was *ad hoc*, sporadic and limited in scope. Bilateral fisheries conventions were adopted in the mid-nineteenth century to halt over-exploitation. Examples include a convention to conserve oysters by prohibiting fishing outside certain dates, and instruments to protect fisheries, usually in rivers or lakes or in or around territorial waters, from over-exploitation. The first whaling convention was adopted in 1931. Migratory birds also required international co-operation to ensure their conservation. In 1872, Switzerland proposed an international regulatory commission for the protection of birds. This led to consideration of the matter by the non-governmental International Ornithological Congress and the creation in 1884 of an International Ornithological Committee, which formulated a treaty proposal, and the adoption in 1902 of the Convention to Protect Birds Useful to Agriculture. The Convention relied upon regulatory techniques still used today, such as the grant of absolute protection to certain birds, a prohibition on their killing or the destruction or taking of their nests, eggs or breeding places, and the use of certain methods of capture or destruction. The 1902 Birds Convention allowed exceptions, such as scientific research and repopulation, which continue to be reflected in more modern instruments, such as the 1979 Berne Convention and the 1992 Biodiversity Convention. 1916 saw the adoption of the first bilateral treaty for the protection of migratory birds. The founding in 1922 of the International Committee (later Council) for Bird Protection (later Preservation) (ICBP) reflected the recognition that substantive rules needed to be accompanied by new institutional arrangements. The ICBP was created to strengthen links between American and European bird protection groups, and its aim of encouraging 'transnational co-ordination rather than international integration' reflected a reluctance to go too far in impinging upon the sovereignty of states.

The first treaty aimed at the protection of wildlife in a particular region was the 1900 Convention Destine´e a' Assurer la Conservation des Diverses Espe'ces Animales Vivant a' l'Etat Sauvage en Afrique qui sont Utiles a' l'Homme ou Inof-fensive. It sought to ensure the conservation of wildlife in the African colonies of European states, including the use of trade restrictions on the export of certain skins and furs, reflecting a desire to combine regulatory techniques with economic incentives. The 1900 Convention was replaced by the 1933 Convention on the Preservation of Fauna and Flora in their Natural State, which was itself superseded by a new instrument in 1968 following the attainment of independence by these former colonial territories of Africa. Like other early conventions, the 1933 Convention did not create any institutional arrangements for administering its provisions, monitoring compliance or ensuring implementation. During this first period, the only other region to adopt a treaty for the protection of wildlife was the Americas.

It was not only fisheries and wildlife that attracted the attentions of the international legislators. The 1909 Water Boundaries Treaty between the United States and Canada was the first to commit its parties to preventing pollution,and under the auspices of its International Joint Commission a draft Treaty on Pollution Prevention was drawn up in 1920, but not adopted. Another draft instrument prepared in this period, also not adopted, sought to prevent oil pollution of the seas. Treaties were adopted to limit the spread of phylloxera and epizootic diseases, and to prevent damage from corrosive and poisonous substances. Developments relating to the creation of international environmental organisations were limited. The first international institution to address nature protection arose from the 1909 meeting ofthe International Congressfor the Protection of Nature, in Paris, which proposed the creation of an international nature protection body. In 1913, an Act of Foundation of a Consultative Committee for the International Protection of Nature was signed in Berne by seventeen countries, with the task of collecting, classifying and publishing information on the international protection of nature. The outbreak of the First World War laid the Commission to rest. Rudimentary international organisations were created at this time to address locust infestation and contagious animal diseases.

It is evident that many of the developments during this period were inspired by the efforts of private individuals, scientists and environmental organisations in Europe and the United States. Lawyers were also active: in 1911 the Institut de Droit International, a private association of lawyers, adopted International Regulations Regarding the Use of International Watercourses for Purposes Other than Navigation. Although these were not binding, they declared that 'neither [riparian] state may, on its own territory, utilise or allow the utilisation of the water in such a way as seriously to interfere with its utilisation by the other state or by individuals, corporations, etc. thereof'.

During this period, two environmental disputes were submitted to international arbitration.Both awards set forth principles which influenced subsequent developments and included regulatory provisions governing the conduct of future activities. In the *Pacific Fur Seal Arbitration,* the dispute between the United States and Great Britain concerned the latter's alleged over-exploitation of fur seals in areas beyond national jurisdiction. The award rejected the argument that states had the right to assert jurisdiction over natural resources outside their jurisdiction to ensure their conservation, and set forth regulations for the 'proper protection and preservation' of fur seals outside jurisdictional limits.

The regulations reflected earlier treaty provisions, and provided a basis for a convention prohibiting pelagic sealing in the North Pacific Ocean and the importation of sealskins. The episode provided early evidence of the potential for disputes over valuable natural resources lying beyond the national jurisdiction of any state, as well as evidence of the role international law might play in resolving disputes and establishing a framework for the conduct of activities.

The second arbitral award of this period is the better known. The *Trail Smelter* case arose out of a dispute between the United States and Canada over the emission of sulphur fumes from a smelter situated in Canada which caused damage in the state of Washington. The Tribunal applied the principle that under international law 'no state has the right to use or permit the use of its territory in such a manner as to cause injury by fumes in or to the territory of another or the properties or persons therein, when the case is of serious consequence and the injury is established by clear and convincing evidence'.The award of the Tribunal and its finding on the state of international law on air pollution in the 1930s has come to represent a crystallising moment for international environmental law which has influenced subsequent developments in a manner which undoubtedly exceeds its true value as an authoritative legal determination.

These two arbitral awards, together with the treaties and organisations which were brought into being, established early foundations. Institutional arrangements to address environmental matters were limited, and international rules were sparse in terms of both the subject matter they addressed and the regions they covered. However, there was a growing awareness that the exploitation of natural resources could not occur on an unlimited basis, that industrialisation and technological developments brought with them pollution and associated problems, and that international measures were needed to address these matters.

FROM THE CREATION OF THE UNITED NATIONS TO STOCKHOLM: 1945–1972

The second phase in the development of international environmental law began with the creation of the UN and its specialised agencies in 1945. It was a period characterised by two features: international organisations at the regional and global level began to address environmental issues; and the range of environmental concerns addressed by international regulatory activity broadened to include afocus on thecausesof pollutionresulting fromcertain ultra-hazardous activities. A third feature was the limited recognition of the relationship between economic development and environmental protection.

Despite attempts by certain individuals to push conservation onto the international agenda following the Second World War, the UN Charter did not include provisions on environmental protection or the conservation of natural resources. Nevertheless, the UN's purposes include the achievement of international co-operation in solving international problems of an economic, social, cultural or humanitarian character, and this has provided the basis for the subsequent environmental activities of the UN. No environment or nature conservation body was established among the specialised agencies. However, the constituent instruments of the Food and Agriculture Organization (FAO) and the United Nations Educational, Scientific and Cultural Organization (UNESCO) included provisions with an environmental or conservationist aspect, and the instrument establishing the General Agreement on Tariffs and Trade (GATT) permits certain measures relating to 'the conservation of exhaustible natural resources' as exceptions to the rules establishing free trade obligations.

In October 1948, governments and non-governmental actors established the first major international organisation to address environmental issues. A conference convened with the assistance of UNESCO, which was attended by representatives of eighteen governments, seven international organisations and 107 national organisations, established the International Union for the Protection of Nature (IUPN), to promote the preservation of wildlife and the natural environment, public knowledge, education, scientific research and legislation.

The IUCN is a unique organisation whose members are governments and nongovernmental actors, and which has played an important role in developing treaties to protect wildlife and conserve natural resources.

UNCCUR

The seeds of intergovernmental environmental action were sown in 1947 by the UN, with the Economic and Social Council (ECOSOC) resolution convening the 1949 United Nations Conference on the Conservation and Utilisation of Resources (UNCCUR). The origins of this resolution have been traced to the initiative of Presidents Franklin D. Roosevelt and Harry S. Truman. The resolution reflected an awareness of the need for international action to establish a balanced approach to the management and conservation of natural resources. The resolution emphasised the importance of the world's natural resources and their importance to the reconstruction of devastated areas; it also recognised the need for the 'continuous development and widespread application of the techniques of resource conservation and utilisation'. The resolution determined the competence of the UN over environmental matters and ultimately resulted in the 1972 Stockholm Conference and the 1992 UNCED, as well as other UN action on the environment.

UNCCUR provided a modest start. It had a limited scope, having been convened to exchange information on 'techniques in this field, their economic costs and benefits, and their interrelations' and being devoted to the exchange of ideas and experience. It had no mandate to adopt any recommendations. Held from 17 August to 6 September 1949 in New York State, it was attended by over 1,000 individuals from more than fifty countries, some 500 having been selected by the UN Secretary General upon the nomination of governments, non-governmental organisations and the Preparatory Committee. UNCCUR addressed six issues: minerals, fuels and energy, water, forests, land, and wildlife and fish. The main topics addressed included:

- the world resource situation;
- a world review of critical shortages;
- the interdependence of resources;
- the use and conservation of resources;
- the development of new resources by applied technology;
- education for conservation;
- resource techniques for less developed countries; and
- the integrated development of river basins.

If UNCCUR's accomplishments were limited, the topics were similar to those addressed at UNCED nearly half a century later. Even at this early stage, the relationship between conservation and development was a central theme, with discussions focusing on the relationship between conservation and use, on the need to develop standards to ensure conservation and on the relationship between conservation and development.

Following the 1949 UNCCUR, environmental action by the UN and its specialised agencies addressed issues relating to the conservation of flora and fauna. In 1954, the General Assembly convened a major Conference on the Conservation of the Living Resources of the Sea, which led to the conservation rules adopted in the 1958 Geneva Conventions. The major new development was the attention given by the General Assembly to the effects of atmospheric nuclear tests and oil pollution.

The fact that these subjects were debated, and resolutions adopted, signalled a shift in emphasis, away from the protection of flora and fauna and towards international action addressing products and processes associated with industrial and military activity. With hindsight, it is easy to see how significant these developments were, although at the time it was probably not foreseeable that the implications of intergovernmental environmental action would be far-reaching. In 1955, the General Assembly adopted the first of a number of resolutions on the use of atomic energy and the effects of atomic radiation, which led to the adoption of the Test Ban Treaty in 1963, and provided the political context for Australia and New Zealand to bring actions before the International Court of Justice (ICJ) calling on France to stop all atmospheric nuclear tests.

In 1954, under the auspices of the International Maritime Organization (IMO), the first global convention for the prevention of oil pollution was adopted (building on the text of the earlier drafts of 1926 and 1935), to be followed fifteen years later by treaties permitting intervention to combat the effects of oil pollution, establishing rules of civil liability for oil pollution damage and creating an oil pollution compensation fund. These were adopted in response to specific incidents resulting in large-scale oil pollution which caused damage to the marine environment and to people and property. Other global conventions were the 1958 High Seas Fishing and Conservation Convention which established innovative provisions on conservation of marine living resources, and the 1958 Convention on the High Seas which committed contracting parties to preventing oil pollution and the dumping of radioactive wastes. The 1971 Ramsar Convention was the first environment treaty to establish rules addressing the conservation of a particular type of ecosystem.

At this time, notable regional developments were occurring to prohibit or regulate activities previously beyond the scope of international law. The 1959 Antarctic Treaty committed parties to peaceful activities in that region, and prohibited nuclear explosions or the disposal of radioactive waste. The United Nations Economic Commission for Europe (UNECE) promulgated harmonising regulations on emissions from motor vehicles, and the Committee of Ministers of the Council of Europe adopted the first international act dealing with general aspects of air pollution. In 1967, the European Community (EC) adopted its first environmental act, on the packaging and labelling of dangerous goods, despite the absence of express environmental provisions in the 1957 Treaty of Rome. In relation to wildlife conservation, the 1968 African Nature Convention went beyond the limited approach to conservation of fauna and flora by aiming at the 'conservation, utilisation and development of soil, water, flora and fauna resources in accordance with scientific principles and with due regard to the best interests of the people'. In early 1972, shortly before the Stockholm Conference, the Oslo Dumping Convention became the first treaty to prohibit the dumping of a wide range of hazardous substances at sea. During this period, treaties sought to protect the quality of rivers and, under the auspices of the International Labor Organization (ILO), the quality of the working environment.

Other developments were noteworthy. In 1949, the International Court of Justice (ICJ) confirmed 'every state's obligation not to allow knowingly its territory to be used for acts contrary to the rights of other states', a *dictum* which was to contribute significantly to the emergence of Principle 21 of the Stockholm Conference. In 1957, in the *Lac Lanoux Arbitration*, the Tribunal affirmed principles concerning limitations on the right of states in their use of shared rivers and informing the meaning of co-operation in international law.However, the substantive commitments adopted in these treaties were not accompanied by the adoption of guiding principles of general application. What was looming, however, was the broader issue of the relationship between environment and development, which had been identified by the 1949 UNCCUR; in 1962, the General Assembly adopted a resolution on the relationship between economic development and environmental protection.

By 1972, there was, therefore, an emerging body of international environmental rules at the regional and global levels, and international organisations were addressing international environmental issues. Limitations on the right of states to treat their natural resources as they wished were being established.

Nevertheless, these treaty and institutional developments were developing in a piecemeal fashion, and the lack of co-ordination hampered efforts to develop a coherent international environmental strategy. Moreover, no international organisation had overall responsibility for co-ordinating international environmental policy and law, and few had a specific environmental mandate. International procedures for ensuring the implementation of, and compliance with, international environmental standards were virtually non-existent. The regulatory techniques available for addressing a growing range of issues were limited, and no rules had yet been developed on procedural obligations, such as environmental impact assessment or the dissemination of and access to environmental information. The 1972 Stockholm Conference must be seen in this context.

The 1972 Stockholm Conference can be traced to an Intergovernmental Conference of Experts on the Scientific Basis for Rational Use and Conservation of the Resources of the Biosphere convened by UNESCO in 1968 (the 1968 Biosphere Conference). The Conference considered the impact of human activities on the biosphere, including the effects of air and water pollution, overgrazing, deforestation and the drainage of wetlands, and adopted twenty recommendations reflecting themes adopted at the 1972 Stockholm Confer-ence. The scale of the task facing the international community was reflected in the final report of the 1968 Biosphere Conference:

Until this point in history the nations of the world have lacked considered, comprehensive policies for managing the environment. Although changes have been taking place for a long time, they seem to have reached a threshold recently that has made the public aware of them. This awareness is leading to concern,to therecognitionthat to a large degree, man now hasthe capability and the responsibility to determine and guide the future of his environment, and to the beginnings of national and international corrective action . . . It has become clear, however, that earnest and bold departures from the past will have to be taken nationally and internationally if significant progress is to be made.

The 1972 United Nations Conference on the Human Environment

Report of the UN Conference on the Human Environment, Stockholm, 5–16 June 1972, UN Doc. A/CONF.48/14/Rev.1; W. Kennett, 'The Stockholm Conference on the Human Environment',

48 *International Affairs* 33 (1972); A. C. Kiss and J. D. Sciault, 'La Conference des Nations Unies sur l'Environnement', AFDI 603 (1972); A. C. Kiss and J. D. Sciault, 'Post Stockholm: Influencing National Environmental Law and Practice Through International Law and Policy', 66 *Proceedings of the American Society of International Law* 1 (1972); L. Sohn, 'The Stockholm Declaration on the Human Environment', 14 *Harvard International Law Journal* 423 (1973); A. Kiss, 'Dix Ans Apre`s Stockholm, Une Dece´nnie de Droit International de l'Environnement', 28 AFDI 784 (1982); A. Kiss, 'Ten Years After Stockholm: International Environmental Law', 77 *Proceedings of the American Society of International Law* 411 (1983).

The Stockholm Conference was convened in December 1968 by the United Nations General Assembly. This followed the adoption in July 1968 of a resolution, first proposed by Sweden, noting 'the continuing and accelerating impairment of the quality of the human environment', and recommending that the General Assembly consider the desirability of convening a UN Conference. The Conference was held in Stockholm on 5–16 June 1972, under the chairmanship of Maurice Strong, a Canadian, and was attended by 114 states and a large number of international institutions and non-governmental observers. The Conference adopted three non-binding instruments: a resolution on institutional and financial arrangements, a Declaration containing twenty-six Principles, and an Action Plan containing 109 recommendations. The Conference did not adopt any binding obligations and formal decisions had to await the twenty-seventh session of the UN General Assembly the following autumn. The Conference was generally considered to have been successful, largely because the preparatory process had allowed agreement to be reached on most issues prior to the Conference. According to one commentator, 'Stockholm enlarged and facilitated means toward international action previously limited by inadequate perception of environmental issues and by restrictive concepts of national sovereignty . . . There were significant elements of innovation in (1) the redefinition of international issues, (2) the rationale for co-operation, (3) the approach to international responsibility, and (4) the conceptualisation of international organisational relationships.' Although the infusion of new international law was not dramatic, trends underway before Stockholm relating to marine pollution, transboundary air and water pollution, and the protection of endangered species were reinforced by the Stockholm resolutions. From a legal perspective, the significant developments were the recommendations for the creation of new institutions and the establishment of co-ordinating mechanisms among existing institutions (the Action Plan), the definition of a framework for future actions to be taken by the international community (the Recommendations), and the adoption of a set of general guiding principles (the Principles).

The recommendation on institutional and financial arrangements proposed that action be taken by the UN General Assembly to establish four institutional arrangements: an intergovernmental Governing Council for Environmental Programmes to provide policy guidance for the direction and co-ordination of environmental programmes; an Environment Secretariat headed by an Executive Director; an Environment Fund to provide financing for environmental programmes; and an inter-agency Environmental Co-ordinating Board to ensure co-operation and co-ordination among all bodies concerned in the implementation of environmental programmes in the United Nations system. The Action Plan comprised 109 recommendations. These were generally accepted by consensus, and reflected an agenda which identified six main subject areas:

1. planning and management of human settlements for environmental quality;
2. environmental aspects of natural resources management;
3. identification and control of pollutants and nuisances of broad international significance;
4. educational, informational, social and cultural aspects of environmental issues;
5. development and environment; and
6. international organisational implications of action proposals.

The Action Plan included proposals on environmental assessment (by the establishment of Earthwatch, which was to include a Global Environmental Monitoring System (GEMS) and an International Referral System (subsequently INFOTERRA)); on natural resources management; and on supporting measures related to training and education and the provision of information. Consensus was virtually complete, although some reservations were made. The United Stateswould not accept the principle of additionality, accordingto which an increase in its foreign aid budget would be required to cover costs imposed by environmental protection measures on development projects (Recommendation 109), and Japan refused to observe the recommendation calling for a ten-year moratorium on commercial whaling (Recommendation 33).

The Declaration of Principles for the Preservation and Enhancement of the Human Environmentwas based on a draft Declaration preparedby the Prepara-toryCommittee.Itwas intended toprovide'acommonoutlookand... common principles to inspire and guide the peoples of the world in the preservation and enhancement of the human environment'. The twenty-six Principles reflected a compromise between those states which believed it should stimulate public awareness of, and concern for, environmental issues, and those states which wanted the Declaration to provide specific guidelines for future governmental and intergovernmental action.

From a legal perspective, the most relevant provisions are Principles 24, 21, 22 and 23. Principle 24 called for international co-operation 'to effectively control, prevent, reduce and eliminate adverse environmental effects resulting from activities conducted in all spheres, in such a way that due account is taken of the sovereignty and interests of all states'. Principle 21 affirmed the responsibility of states to ensure that activities within their jurisdiction or control do not cause damage in another state or beyond national jurisdiction, such as in outer space or on the high seas. This responsibility is said to extend also to activities under a state's 'control', such as those carried out by its nationals or by or on ships or aircraft registered in its territory.

Principle 22 required states to co-operate in developing international environmental law. This is a substantially weakened version of an earlier proposal, which would have required states to pay compensation for all environmental damage caused by activities carried on within their territory. The earlier proposal failed because of concerns that it implied acceptance of a no-fault or 'strict' standard of liability for environmental harm. Certain states made clear their view that liability to pay compensation would only exist where there had been negligence attributable to the state concerned. Principle 23 foresaw a limited role for international regulation and suggested that certain standards would 'have to be determined nationally' on the basis of the value systems applying in each country and their social costs, and in accordance with the need for different environmental standards in different countries. The Stockholm Principles are weak on techniques for implementing environmental standards, such as environmental impact assessment, access to environmental information and the availability of administrative and judicial remedies. Principle 24 simply calls for international organisations to play a co-ordinated, efficient and dynamic role.

The other Stockholm Principles were couched in non-legal language. Principle 1 linked environmental protection to human rights norms, stating that man has 'the fundamental right to freedom, equality and adequate conditions of life, in an environment of a quality that permits a life of dignity and well-being, and he bears a solemn responsibility to protect and improve the environment for present and future generations'. Other Principles can be grouped into themes. Principles 2, 3 and 5 set forth general guidelines for the natural resources of the earth to be safeguarded for the benefit of present and future generations, and for the maintenance, restoration and improvement of vital renewable resources and the non-exhaustion of non-renewable resources. Principles 4, 6 and 7 identified specific environmental threats, recalling the special responsibility of man to safeguard and wisely manage the heritage of wildlife and habitat, halt the discharge of toxic and other substances and heat which cause serious or irreversible damage to the ecosystem, and prevent pollution of the seas or harm to living resources and marine life. Principles 8–15 addressed issues which reflected the relationship between development and the environment: they recognised the relationship between economic and social development and environmental quality; they called for 'accelerated development' through the transfer of financial and technological assistance and stable and adequate prices for commodities and raw materials; and they supported an integrated and co-ordinated approach to rational development planning which is compatible with protecting and improving the human environment. Principles 16–20 recognised the need for appropriate demographic policies; supported the development of national institutions to manage environmental resources; called for the application of science and technology; and encouraged education and scientific research and development.

The draft Declaration prepared by the Preparatory Committee had included a third important legal principle, originally entitled 'Principle 20', which would have provided that: relevant information must be supplied by states on activities or developments within their jurisdiction or under their control whenever they believe, or have reason to believe, that such information is needed to avoid the risk of significant adverse effects on the environment in areas beyond their national jurisdiction.

This Principle was not agreed at the Conference following the objections of a number of developing states, which maintained that the obligation to consult might be abused by developed states to impede development projects. As will be seen, this requirement is now recognised by the International Law Commission, and by many conventions, as a basic requirement.

Stockholm follow-up

The Report of the Stockholm Conference was considered by the UN General Assembly at its twenty-seventh session, which adopted eleven resolutions. Resolution 2994 (XXVII) noted with satisfaction the Conference Report. Resolution 2995 (XXVII) was a partial revival of the Preparatory Committee's original 'Principle 20', providing that technical information on proposed works should be supplied to other states where there is a risk of significant transboundary environmental harm, but that this information should be received in good faith and not used to delay or impede development of natural resources. Resolution 2996 (XXVII) affirmed that Resolution 2995 was not to be construed as limiting Principles 21 and 22 of the Stockholm Declaration, and Resolutions 2997 to 3004 addressed institutional and financial arrangements for international environmental co-operation, including the creation of the United Nations Environment Programme.

CONCLUSIONS

First, the focus on implementation means that international environmental law will increasingly be concerned with procedural, constitutional and institutional issues: environmental impact assessment; access to and dissemination of environmental information; techniques of law-making and issues of international governance, including accountability and transparency in decision-making; the participation or representation of the different members of the international community in the international legal process; new compliance mechanisms (including appropriate national judicial and administrative remedies), and new techniques of regulation (including economic instruments).It is apparent that over the past decade the rules of international law have become increasingly complex and technical, as environmental considerations are increasingly addressed in economic and other social fields, in particular human rights. Secondly, as environmental issues are increasingly integrated into aspects of economic and development institutions and law (in particular trade, development lending and intellectual property), the field in which international environmental law has developed will continue to broaden, creating new challenges for the subject and for lawyers and others involved in its development and application. While UNCED and its follow-up(the WorldSummit on Sustainable Development) have not provided a clear sense of direction as to likely future developments, one feature emerges as international environmental law moves into its next phase: international environmental law is no longer exclusively concerned with the adoption of normative standards to guide behaviour, but increasingly addresses techniques of implementation which are practical, effective, equitable and acceptable to most members of the international community.

3

International Society Law and Sustainable Development

INTRODUCTION

The International Law Commission (ILC) was established by the General Assembly in 1947 to promote the 'progressive development of international law and its codification'. Since 1981, it has had thirty-four members, who are persons of recognised competence in the field of international law elected by the UN General Assembly (the original membership of fifteen was raised to twenty-one in 1956 and to twenty-two in 1961).

Since 1949, the ILC has worked on more than thirty topics. Apart from its important contribution to the development of general aspects of international law, including the law of treaties, state responsibility, and treaties between states and international organisations and between two or more international organisations, the ILC has also addressed environmental issues and contributed significantly to the development of international environmental law.

ENVIRONMENT AND INTERNATIONAL LAW: DEFINING TERMS

International environmental law comprises those substantive, procedural and institutional rules of international law which have as their primary objective the protection of the environment. Dictionaries define 'environment' as 'the objects or the region surrounding anything'. Accordingly, the term encompasses both the features and the products of the natural world and those of human civilisation. On this definition, the environment is broader than, but includes, 'nature', which is concerned only with features of the world itself. 'Ecology', on the other hand, is a science related to the environment and to nature which is concerned with animals and plants, and is 'that branch of biology which deals with the relations of living organisms to their surroundings, their habits and modes of life'. The 'ecosystem' is 'a unit of ecology . . . which includes the plants and animals occurring together plus that part of their environment over which they have an influence'.

The legal definition of the 'environment' and related concepts is important at two levels. At a general level, it defines the scope of the legal subject and the competence of, say, international organisations. Thus, the failure of the 1946 International Whaling Convention to define the term 'whale' has led to protracted disputes over whether the International Whaling Commission has competence over dolphins; and the text of CITES was unclear as to whether its provisions applied to artificially propagated plants grown under controlled conditions in a 'non-natural environment' More specifically, the definition of the 'environment' assumes particular significance in relation to efforts to establish rules governing liability for damage to the environment.

Legal definitions of the 'environment' reflect scientific categorisations and groupings, as well as political acts which incorporate cultural and economic considerations. A scientific approach will divide environmental issues into 'compartments'. These include the atmosphere, atmospheric deposition, soils and sediments, water quality, biology and humans. Scientific definitions are transformed by the political process into the legal definitions found in treaties; although 'environment' does not have a generally accepted usage as a term of art under international law, recent agreements have consistently identified the various media included in the term.

The approaches to defining the 'environment' do nevertheless vary. Early treaties tended to refer to 'flora and fauna' rather than the environment, thus restricting the scope of their application. Article XX(b) and (g) of the General Agreement on Tariffs and

Trade (GATT) refers not to the environment but to 'human, animal or plant life or health' and to the 'conservation of exhaustible natural resources', and these terms are considered by some to have limited the scope of permissible exceptions to the rules of free trade, particularly in the context of the narrow construction given to the terms used by GATT Dispute Settlement Panels. Although the 1972 Stockholm Declaration does not include a definition of the environment, Principle 2 refers to the natural resources of the earth as including 'air, water, land, flora and fauna and . . . natural ecosystems'. The Stockholm Declaration also recognises, as the Preamble makes clear, that the environment of natural resources should be distinguished from the man-made environment, which includes in particular the living and working environment. The 1982 World Charter for Nature similarly does not define the 'environment', but addresses the need to respect nature through principles which are applicable to all life forms, habitats, all areas of the earth, ecosystems and organisms, and land, marine and atmospheric resources.

Those treaties which do refer to the environment and seek to include some form of working definition tend to adopt broad definitions. Under the 1974 Nordic Convention, 'environmentally harmful activities' are those which result in discharges 'into water courses, lakes or the sea, and the use of land, the sea bed, buildings or installations'. Under the 1977 ENMOD Convention, 'environmental modification' refers to changing the 'dynamics, composition or structure of the earth, including its biota, lithosphere, hydrosphere and atmosphere, or of outer space'. As used in the 1979 LRTAP Convention, the environment includes 'agriculture, forestry, materials, aquatic and other natural ecosystems and visibility'. Under the 1991 Espoo Convention and the 1992 Watercourses Convention, the 'environment', which is defined in terms of impacts, includes 'human health and safety, flora, fauna, soil, air, water, climate, landscape and historical monuments or other physical structures or the interactionamong these factors'. In similar terms, the 1991 Antarctic Environment Protocol protects the climate and weather patterns; air and water quality; atmospheric, terrestrial (including aquatic), glacial or marine environments; fauna and flora; and areas of biological, scientific, historic, aesthetic or wilderness significance. Under EC law, the environment comprises 'the relationship of human beings with water, air, land and all biological forms'. EC Council Directive 85/337 (as amended by Directive 97/11), on environmental impact assessment, includes in the scope of information to be provided the likely effect of projects on human beings, fauna and flora, soil, water, air, climate and the landscape, and material assets and cultural heritage. The 1990 EC Directive on freedom of access to information on the environment includes information on the state of 'water, air, soil, fauna, flora, land and natural sites', and the 2000 Directive on eco-labelling establishes an 'Indicative Environmental Matrix' which requires pollution and contamination in eleven environmental fields to be taken into account (air, water, soil, waste, energy savings, natural resources consumption, global warming prevention, ozone layer protection, environmental safety, noise, and biodiversity) when deciding whether to grant an eco-label to a particular product. Other agreements which use the term 'environment' do not define it. The 1982 United Nations Convention on the Law of the Sea does not define 'marine environment', although it appears to include ecosystems, habitats, threatened or endangered species and other forms of marine life, and atmospheric pollution.

More specific international legal terms are being used and are subject to carefully negotiated definition. Recent examples include definitions of biological resources, the climate system, and the ozone layer. Other terms frequently used in international agreements relating to environmental matters and for which specific legal definitions have been established include 'pollu-tion', 'conservation', 'damage', adverse effects' and 'sustainable use' or 'management'.

Its draft articles on the legal regime of the high seas and territorial waters led to the development of the 1958 Geneva Conventions, which include provisions which have influenced the development of environmental law. The ILC's draft articles on the Law of the Non-Navigational Uses of International Watercourses, completed in 1994, led to the adoption of the 1997 Watercourses Convention. In 2001, the ILC adopted Draft Articles on the

Responsibility of States for Internationally Wrongful Acts and Draft Articles on the Prevention of Transboundary Harm from Hazardous Activities.In 2002, the ILC decided to resume work on the liability aspects of the longstanding topic of International Liability for Injurious Consequences Arising out of Acts Not Prohibited by International Law, and established a new project on Shared Natural Resources.

UN COMMISSION ON SUSTAINABLE DEVELOPMENT

In 1992, pursuant to its mandate in Agenda 21, the General Assembly and ECOSOC established the UN Commission on Sustainable Development (CSD). The CSD comprises representatives of fifty-three states elected by ECOSOC with due regard to equitable geographical distribution, and on the basis of representation at a high level including ministerial participation.

Other member states of the UN and its specialised agencies and other observers of the UN are able to participate as observers, and international organisations (including the EC) participate to assist and advise the Commission in the performance of its functions; non-governmental organisations are also entitled to 'participate effectively' in the Commission's work and contribute to its deliber-ations. The CSD is assisted by a secretariat based in New York and meets annually in New York. The Commission makes recommendations to ECOSOC and, through it, to the General Assembly. The Commission's objectives are to ensure the effective follow-up of [UNCED], as well as to enhance international co-operation and rationalise the intergovernmental decision-making capacity for the integration of environment and development issues and to examine the progress of the implementation of Agenda 21 at the national, regional and international levels, fully guided by the principles of the Rio Declaration on Environment and Development and all other aspects of the Conference, in order to achieve sustainable development.

The CSD is the UN body primarily responsible for sustainable development issues and has ten enumerated environmental functions. From an international legal perspective, the most significant are those requiring it to monitor progress in the implementation of Agenda 21 and the integration of environmental and developmental goals; to consider information provided by governments, including periodic communications or reports; to consider information regarding the progress made in the implementation of environmental conventions, which is provided by relevant conferences of the parties; and to make recommendations to the General Assembly on the implementation of Agenda 21.

The Commission can 'receive and analyse relevant input from competent non-governmental organisations', a function representing a compromise between those states which sought to deny NGOs any role in the activities of the Commission, and those states which envisaged NGOs providing regular information, and even complaints, along the lines of the procedures established by the UN Human Rights Committee. In practice, the involvement of non-state actors is organised around the categories of 'major groups' recognised in Section III of Agenda 21.

The Commission is recognised as being open, transparent and accessible to non-state actors. The Commission's other functions include: reviewing progress towards the UN target of 0.7 per cent of the gross national product of developed countries for official development assistance; reviewing the adequacy of funding and mechanisms; enhancing dialogue with NGOs and other entities outside the UN system; and considering the results of reviews by the Secretary General of all the recommendations of UNCED.

The CSD divided its work programme into three areas: the first addresses financial resources and mechanisms, transfer of technology and other cross-sectoral issues; the second reviews the implementation of Agenda 21, taking into account progress in the implementation of relevant environmental conventions; and the third is a high-level meeting to consider the implementation of Agenda 21 on an integrated basis, to consider emerging policy issues, and to provide the necessary political impetus to implement the decisions and commitments of UNCED.

Since its first session, in June 1993, the Commission has organised its work around thematic clusters of topics and a multi-year thematic programme of work. The thematic clusters are based upon the various chapters of Agenda 21, and address the following themes:

- critical elements of sustainability;
- financial resources and mechanisms;
- education, science, transfer of environmentally sound technologies, cooperation and capacity-building;
- decision-making structures;
- the roles of major groups;
- health, human settlement and freshwater;
- land, desertification, forests and biodiversity;
- atmosphere, oceans and all kinds of seas; and
- toxic chemicals and hazardous wastes.

Under the multi-year thematic programme of work, the CSD has annually reviewed various aspects of these clusters, on the basis of information submitted by governments in the form of periodic communications or national reports. These reports are used by the secretariat to prepare analytical reports comprising an annual overview report on the progress made in the implementation of Agenda 21, and thematic reports corresponding to the Agenda 21 sectoral clusters in accordance with the multi-year programme of work. The information provided by governments includes the following:

- policies and measures adopted to meet the objectives of Agenda 21;
- institutional mechanisms to address sustainable development issues;
- assessments of progress to date;
- measures taken and progress achieved to reach sustainable production and consumption patterns and lifestyles, to combat poverty and to limit population growth;
- the impact of environmental measures on the national economy;
- experience gained and progress in strategies to improve social conditions and environmental sustainability;
- specific problems and constraints encountered;

- the adverse impact on sustainable development of trade-restrictive and dis-tortive policies, and measures and progress in making trade and environment mutually supportive;
- assessments of capacity;
- assessments of needs and priorities for external assistance;
- implementation of Agenda 21 commitments related to finance;
- assessments of the effectiveness of activities and projects of international organisations; and
- other relevant environment and development activities.

WSSD reviewed the functioning of the Commission and concluded that, although its original mandate remained valid, the Commission needed to be strengthened and more emphasis needed to be placed on reviewing and monitoring the implementation of Agenda 21 and on fostering the coherence of implementation, initiatives and partnerships. To this end, WSSD recommended that the Commission should limit the number of issues addressed in each session and limit negotiations to every two years.

GOVERNANCE: STATES, INTERNATIONAL ORGANISATIONS AND NON-STATE ACTORS

A wide range of actors participate in those aspects of the international legal order which address environmental issues, including the negotiation, implementation and enforcement of international environmental agreements. Apart from state delegations, which play the central role, a visitor to ozone or climate change negotiations would find international organisations and non-state actors actively involved. International environmental law is characterised by this phenomenon which, with the possible exception of the human rights field, renders it unique. Various reasons explain this state of affairs. States are involved because they are still the pre-eminent international legal persons.

International organisations participate because they have been created by states to address particular environmental issues. Of the various non-state participants, the scientific community is involved because, to a great extent, international environmental law is driven by scientific considerations; business is involved because of the significant implications which decisions taken at the global level can now have even for individual companies; and environmental non-governmental organisations (NGOs) are involved because their membership increasingly drives them into the international arena as the distinction between local, national and global issues disintegrates.

The participation of non-state actors in international environmental law has an established history, and is now widely encouraged and accepted.

The various actors have different roles and functions, both as subjects and objects of international environmental law, including: participating in the law-making process; monitoring implementation, including reporting; and ensuring implementation and enforcement of obligations. The role of each actor turns upon its international legal personality and upon the rights and obligations granted to it by general international law and the rules established by particular treatiesandother rules.TheRio Declaration and Agenda 21, aswell as an increasing number of international environmental agreements, support an expanded role for international organisations and non-state actors in virtually all aspects of the international legal process. States

OECD, *Transfrontier Pollution and the Role of States* (1981); T. M. Franck, *The Power of Legitimacy Among Nations* (1990); R. Jennings and A. Watts, *Oppenheim's International Law* (1992, 9th edn), chapter 2 (especially pp. 110–26); B. Simma, 'From Bilateralism to Community Interest in International Law', 250 RdC 217 (1994); U. Beyerlin, 'State Community Interests and Institution Building in International Environmental Law', 56 Zao¨RV 602 (1996); P. Daillier and A. Pellet, *Droit International Public* (2002, 7th edn), 407–514.

States are the primary subjects of international law. This remains the case in spite of the incursions made by international organisations into previously sovereign spheres of activity and the expanded role of non-state actors. It is still states which create, adopt and implement international legal principles and rules, establish international organisations, and permit the participation of other actors in the international legal process. There are currently 191 member states of the UN, another five states which are not members and numerous entities which do not possess the full characteristics of statehood, including dependent territories and non-self-governing territories. The role played by the 191 UN member states in the development and application of international law depends on the subject being addressed and on the relationship of their vital interests to that subject, and on a complex blend of economic, political, cultural, geographical and ecological considerations. Broadly speaking, states are divided by international, legal and institutional arrangements into developed countries, developing countries, and economies in transition. Developed countries include the thirty member states of the OECD. The twenty-seven states which previously formed part of the 'Soviet bloc' are generally referred to as 'economies in transition'.

The rest of the world, comprising some 134 states, are the developing states which form the Group of 77. The Group of 77 often works as a single negotiating bloc within the framework of the UN, although in relation to environmental matters their perspectives vary widely. Within the UN system, states are also arranged into regional groupings, usually for the purpose of elections to UN bodies. The five groupings are: the Latin American and Caribbean Group; the African Group; the Asian Group; the Western European and Others Group; and the Central and Eastern European Group (although this grouping is increasingly less tenable with the prospect of EC membership for seven states in 2004). Frequently in environmental negotiations these distinctions tend to break down as states pursue what they perceive to be their vital national interests, including their strategic alliances, which may be unrelated to environmental matters. The UNCED negotiations – and more recently those relating to the 2000 Biosafety Protocol – have illustrated the extent of the differences which existed between and among developed states and developing states on particularly contentious issues: atmospheric emissions, production and trade in living modified organisms, conservation of marine mammals, protection of forests, institutional arrangements and financial resources. International organisations

National Academy of Sciences, *Institutional Arrangements for International Environmental Co-operation* (1972); J. Hargrove (ed.), *Law, Institutions and the Global Environment* (1972) (especially A. Chayes, 'International Institutions for the Environment'); J. Schneider, *World Public Order of the Environment: Towards an International Ecological Law and Organisation* (1979); R. Boardman, *International Organisation and the Conservation of Nature* (1981); E. Ostrom, *Governing the Commons: The Evolution of Institutions for Collective Action* (1990); 'Institutional Arrangements', in 'Developments – International Environmental Law', 104 *Harvard Law Review* 1484 at 1580 (1991); P. Thacher, 'Multilateral Co-operation and Global Change', 44 *Journal of International Affairs* 433 (1991); UNCED, *International Institutions and Legal Instruments* (Research Paper No. 10, 1991); A. Boyle, 'Saving the World: Implementation and Enforcement of International Environmental Law Through International Institutions', 3 *Journal of Environmental Law* 229 (1991); L. A. Kimball, *Forging International Agreement: Strengthening Inter-Governmental Institutions for Environment and Development* (1992); L. A. Kimball, 'Towards Global Environmental Management: The Institutional Setting', 3 *Yearbook of International Environmental Law* 18 (1992); H. French, *After the Earth Summit: The Future of Global Environmental Governance* (1992); P. Haas, R. Keohane and M. Levy (eds.), *Institutions for the Earth: Sources of Effective Environmental Protection* (1993); J. Werksman (ed.), *Greening International Institutions* (1996); N. Desai, 'Revitalizing International Environmental Institutions: The UN Task Force Report and Beyond', 40 *Indian Journal of International Law* 455 (2000); P. Sands and P. Klein, *Bowett's Law of International Institutions* (2001, 5th edn).

International organisations involved in environmental law are established at the global, regional, sub-regional and bilateral levels. Almost all international organisations today have some competence or responsibility for the development, application or enforcement of international environmental obligations, including functions related to standard-setting. The decentralised nature of international organisations in the environmental field makes it difficult to assess their role by reference to any functional, sectoral or geographic criteria. They can be divided into three general categories: global organisations associated with the UN and its specialised agencies; regional organisations outside the UN system; and organisations established by environmental and other treaties. Within these categories, there are of course overlaps, since many of the organisations established in the third category were created by acts of the UN or its specialised agencies. History of international organisational arrangements

The role of international organisations has developed in a somewhat *ad hoc* manner. Early environmental agreements did not generally establish standing bodies to administer, or ensure implementation of, their provisions. Since 1945, the number of international environmental organisations has flourished, and they have usually been established at the sub-regional, regional or global level either to deal with specific environmental issues or, as is more often the case, by formally or informally adapting existing organisations to endow them with competence in the area of environmental issues. The Stockholm Conference and UNCED provided opportunities to establish more orderly and coherent arrangements for international organisations in addressing environmental matters. The Stockholm Declaration recognised that the growing global and regional environmental problems required 'extensive co-operation among nations and action by international organisations in the common interest'. Its Principle 25 called on states to 'ensure that international organisations play a co-ordinated, efficient and dynamic role for the protection and improvement of the environment'. Following the Stockholm Conference, the UN General Assemblyestablished theUnited Nations EnvironmentProgramme (UNEP),an environment secretariat and fund, and an Environment Co-ordination Board to co-ordinate UN environment activities.

Between Stockholm and UNCED, the environmental activities of global and regional organisations proliferated, and many new organisations were created by environmental treaties and acts. The proliferation did not occur in the context of a coherent strategy, and there was little effort to ensure effective co-operation or co-ordination between them. Moreover, significant gaps existed, and many activities considered to be particularly harmful to the environment remained outside the scope of formal international institutional authority. Activities relating to the energy, mining and transport (other than air transport) sectors are examples of areas for which no single UN body yet has overall responsibility. The Brundtland Report recognised the gaps and in 1989a group oftwenty-fourdeveloped anddevelopingstates adoptedthe Hague Declaration calling for the development of a new institutional authority, within the framework of the UN, with responsibility for preserving the earth's atmo-sphere. The Hague Declaration even called for decisions of the new institutional authority to be subject to control by the International Court of Justice. UNCED reflected the unwillingness of states to institute such far-reaching changes.

UNCED

The UN General Assembly recognised the gaps, overlapping activities and lack of co-ordination in international environmental arrangements. In 1990, UNCED was called upon to review and examine the role of the UN system in dealing with the environment, to promote the development of regional and global organisations, and to promote international co-operation within the UN system in monitoring, assessing and anticipating environmental threats.

During the UNCED negotiations, many proposals were put forward by states, international organisations and non-governmental actors. Three main issues needing international attention were identified: the role of institutions for environment and development within the UN system; institutional follow-up arrangements after UNCED, especially regarding Agenda 21; and the relationship of the UN system to other institutions in the field of environment and development. During the UNCED negotiations, specific institutional proposals related to five functions and responsibilities: functions related to technical and operational matters; responsibilities for policy-making; co-ordinating functions; responsibilities for financial matters; and functions relating to the administration and implementation of international law. Proposals on technical and operational functions focused on UNEP, the development of regional institutions in the UN system, and new technical functions, particularly environmental assessment, early warning and emergency response, and energy management.

Chapter 38 of Agenda 21 proposed the framework for institutional arrangements. The underlying principles and tasks to guide such arrangements were identified in chapter 2 above. With regard to specific institutions, UNCED proposed the establishment of a UN Commission on Sustainable Development and the further development of UNEP and the United Nations Development Programme (UNDP).

It affirmed the central role of the UN General Assembly and the Economic and Social Council (ECOSOC), and provided limited guidance on co-operative mechanisms between UN bodies, and between UN bodies and regional organisations and international financial organisations. Overall, it appears that UNCED missed the opportunity to set in motion a wholesale and effective review of activities and operations. UN General Assembly Resolution 47/191 (1992) endorsed the Agenda 21 recommendations on international institutional arrangements to follow up on UNCED and took the following decisions:

- requested ECOSOC to set up a high-level Commission on Sustainable Development;
- requested all UN specialised agencies and related organisations of the UN system to strengthen and adjust their activities, programmes and plans in line with Agenda 21;
- invited the World Bank and other international, regional and sub-regional financial and development institutions, including the Global Environment Facility, to submit regularly to the Commission on Sustainable Development reports on their activities and plans to implement Agenda 21;
- requested UNEP, UNDP, the United Nations Conference on Trade and Development (UNCTAD), the UN Sudano-Sahelian Office and the regional economic commissions to submit reports of their plans to implement Agenda 21 to the Commission on Sustainable Development; and

- endorsed the view of the UN Secretary General concerning the establishment of a High Level Advisory Board.

UNCED received its first major review at the World Summit on Sustainable Development (WSSD) in Johannesburg in 2002. The main outcomes relating to the institutional framework to support sustainable development were recommendations to:

- adopt new measures to strengthen institutional arrangements for sustainable development at international, regional and national levels;
- facilitate and promote the integration of the environmental, social and economic dimensions of sustainable development into the work programmes of UN regional commissions;
- establish an effective, transparent and regular inter-agency co-ordination mechanism on ocean and coastal issues within the UN system;
- enhance the role of the Commission on Sustainable Development, including through reviewing and monitoring progress in the implementation of Agenda 21 and fostering coherence of implementation, initiatives and partnerships; and
- take immediate steps to make progress in the formulation and elaboration of national strategies for sustainable development and begin their implementation by 2005. The function and role of international organisations

International organisations perform a range of different functions and roles in the development and management of international legal responses to environmental issues which are of a judicial, legislative or administrative nature. The function of each organisation depends upon the powers granted to it by its constituent instrument as subsequently interpreted and applied by the practice of the organisation and the parties to it. Apart from very specific functions required of some particular organisations, international organisations perform five main functions.

First, they provide a forum for co-operation and co-ordination between states on matters of international environmental management. The participation of states in the activities of international organisations is the principal means for consultation and the informal sharing of ideas and information which contribute towards building an international consensus for regional and global action. Thus, the formal negotiation of the 1992 Climate Change Convention followed extensive 'consciousness-raising' activities by a number of international organisations, including the UN General Assembly, the World Health Organization (WHO), the World Meteorological Organization (WMO) and the Intergovernmental Panel on Climate Change (IPCC), as well as the less formal settings of the World Climate Conferences held in 1979 and 1990. International organisations thus contribute to developing the international agenda on environmental matters, broadening the participation of interested states, and encouraging technical research and development. Such organisations also play an important role in liaising with non-state actors.

The second function of international organisations is more formal, and relates to the provision of information. International organisations receive and disseminate information, facilitate information exchange, and provide for formal and informal consultation between states, and between states and the organisation. They also act as a conduit for notification of emergencies and other urgent matters. In the case of certain highly developed organisations, such as the EC Commission and various international human rights bodies, the information function may include a formal fact-finding role.

A third function of international organisations is to contribute to the development of international legal obligations, including 'soft law'. This function may take place informally, where the organisation acts as a catalyst for the development of legal and other obligations outside the organisation itself. Alternatively, it may take place formally and within the organisation, where the organisation adopts acts and decisions which can create legal obligations or which may contribute to the subsequent development of legal obligations. International organisations develop policy initiatives and standards, may adopt rules which establish binding obligations or reflect customary law, and can establish new and subsidiary institutional arrangements. Once environmental and other standards and obligations have been established, institutions increasingly play a role in ensuring implementation of and compliance with these standards and obligations. Assisting in implementation takes a number of forms. It may be limited to receiving information from parties or other persons on an informal and *ad hoc* basis, or it may entail the regular receipt and consideration of reports or periodic communications from parties to international environmental treaties as a means of reviewing progress in implementation. Assisting in implementation also takes place through the provision of advice on technical, legal and administrative or institutional matters. Under the 1987 Montreal Protocol, the parties seek to ensure implementation through the work of a non-compliance procedure including an Implementation Committee; and the 1992 Climate Change Convention provides for the establishment of a Subsidiary Body for Implementation to assist the conference of the parties in the assessment and review of the implementation of the Convention. There are now a growing number of such institutional arrangements, as described in chapter 5 below.

A fifth function of international institutions is to provide an independent forum, or mechanism, for the settlement of disputes, usually disputes between states. This may occur through the work of bodies with general competence, such as a conference or meeting of the parties to an environment agreement, adopting an authoritative interpretation of a provision, or by the reference of an issue to a body created specifically to assist in dispute settlement through a judicial or quasi-judicial function, such as the International Court of Justice, the International Tribunal for the Law of the Sea, the European Court of Justice, human rights courts, or WTO Dispute Settlement Panels. Finally, some organisations are granted enforcement or compliance functions. To date, the only institution which has been granted extensive powers and international legal personality to engage in enforcement activities is the EC Commission, which has brought more than two hundred cases to the European Court of Justice against member states alleging non-compliance with their environmental obligations.

Global organisations

United Nations (www.un.org)

TheUN,itsspecialisedagencies,andsubsidiary bodies, organs and programmes are the focal point for international law and institutions in the field of the environment. The UN Charter does not expressly provide the UN with competence over environmental matters. The relevant purposes of the UN include the maintenance of international peace and security, the adoption of measures to strengthen universal peace, and the achievement of co-operation in solving international economic, social, cultural or humanitarian problems. Since the late 1960s, however, the practice of the organisation through its principal organs, in particular the General Assembly and the Economic and Social Council (ECOSOC), has been to interpret and apply these broad purposes as including the protection of the environment and the promotion of sustainable development. The UN is the principal forum for global environmental law-making and has played a central role in the development of international environmental law, its universal character making it the only 'appropriate forum for concerted political action on global environmental problems'. Apart from the Secretariat, the UN has five principal organs: the General Assembly, the Security Council, ECOSOC, the Trusteeship Council and the International Court of Justice.Each organ has, to differing degrees, addressed international environmental issues.

Co-ordination From 1977 until recently, co-ordination between the various UN organs and bodies at the Secretariat level took place under the Administrative Committee on Co-ordination (ACC) (co-ordination at the political level is a responsibility of ECOSOC), which was established in 1946 to supervise the implementation of the agreements between the UN and the specialised agencies and to ensure that the activities of the various bodies are co-ordinated. The ACC comprised the heads of the specialised agencies and related bodies and organs who met several times a year under the chairmanship of the Secretary General. Together with an inter-agency board of Designated Officials on Environmental Matters, the ACC deliberated and adopted recommendations on the co-ordination of all environment-related programmes which are carried on by the participating agencies and bodies, and prepared an annual report to the UNEP Governing Council.

In October 1992, an Inter-Agency Committee on Sustainable Development (IACSD) was established to make recommendations to the ACC and to improve co-operation and co-ordination between the various UN bodies and organs on issues related to sustainable development, including environmental matters. The IACSD, attended by the senior officials of UN bodies most closely involved in the issues, was established to rationalise subsidiary mechanisms for co-ordination, allocate and share responsibilities for implementing Agenda 21, monitor financial matters, and assess reporting requirements. In December 1992, the UN Secretary General established a new Department for Policy Co-ordination and Sustainable Development (DPCSD) in the

Department of Economic and Social Development which provided support to ECOSOC and to the Commission on Sustainable Development. This was later consolidated with other departments to form the Department of Economic and Social Affairs which continues to act as the central co-ordinating mechanism for policy and programme development on sustainable development issues, including co-operative relationships with international organisations, NGOs, the academic community and the corporate sector. Agenda 21 recognised the important role of the Secretary General, and the need for the further development of the co-ordination mechanism under the ACC.

The operation of the ACC has recently been reformed as part of the Secretary General's wider reform efforts. The ACC has been renamed the UN System Chief Executives Board for Co-ordination (CEB), a title which is intended to emphasisethehigh-levelnature ofthebodyand theshiftto amorecollegial body whose participants share a collective responsibility over an integrated system. The reforms have also involved a transformation of the subsidiary structures. The previous multi-layered and rigid arrangements of inter-agency committees have been transformed and streamlined into two high-level committees, the High Level Committee on Programmes and the High-Level Committee on Management, complemented by flexible 'networks' of specialists in different areas of common concern, along with time-bound task-oriented inter-agency arrangements. These changes have involved the abolition of the previous subsidiary bodies, including the IACSD, and its subcommittees. The exact shape of future inter-agency co-ordination in the area of sustainable development has been caught up in the recommendations of the WSSD and their implementation by the General Assembly, but it is interesting to note that, in one area at least, the shift from standing committees has been resisted: the WSSD recommended the establishment of an effective, transparent and regular inter-agency co-ordination mechanism on ocean and coastal issues within the United Nations system, presumably to replace the abolished ACC Sub-Committee on Oceans and Coastal Areas.

UN GENERAL ASSEMBLY

The UN General Assembly, which is the principal policy-making organ on UNCED follow-up, has the power to discuss any questions or matters within the scope of the UN Charter, to make recommendations to the member states or to the Security Council on any such questions or matters, and to promote international co-operation in the political, economic, social, cultural, educational and health fields and the progressive development of international law and its codification.

Although it does not have a specific environmental mandate, its role over the past two decades has led to its being identified by Agenda 21 as 'the principal policy-making and appraisal organ' on UNCED follow-up, having a regular review function with the possibility of convening an overall review and appraisal of Agenda 21 no later than 1997. This review was conducted by a Special Session of the General Assembly convened in June 1997 (UNGASS-19), which produced a Programme for the Further Implementation of Agenda 21. The Programme of Implementation adopted by the WSSD affirmed the need for the General Assembly to adopt sustainable development as a key element of the overarching framework for United Nations activities and its role in giving overall political direction to the implementation of Agenda 21 and its review.

Although its resolutions are not formally binding, the General Assembly has taken decisionswhich havecreatednewbodies, convenedconferences,endorsed principles and substantive rules, and recommended actions. Its contribution to the development of international environmental law is not to be underestimated. The General Assembly has long been involved in natural resource issues: the 1962 resolution on permanent sovereignty over natural resources was a landmark instrument in the development of international law, and has continued to influence debate and practice on the nature and extent of limitations imposed on states for environmental reasons. It was only in the late 1960s, however, that the General Assembly began to address the protection of the environment and the conservation of natural resources, and since 1968 it has adopted a large number of resolutions contributing directly or indirectly to the development of substantive legal obligations and new institutional arrangements.

The General Assembly's early interest in environmental matters related to the protection of the marine environment, the relationship between environment and development, and co-operation on shared natural re-sources. The General Assembly convened the 1972 UN Conference on the Human Environment, and created UNEP later that year. Other bodies created by the General Assembly include the United Nations Development Programme (UNDP), the International Law Commission, UNCED and the Commission on Sustainable Development. Other relevant bodies established by the UN, which are conspicuous by their more limited actions, include the Committee on the Development and Utilisation of New and Renewable Sources of Energy. More recently, and at a more informal level, the General Assembly has also created the Open-Ended Informal Consultative Process on Oceans and the Law of the Sea established on the recommendation of the Commission on Sustainable Development to facilitate the General Assembly's annual review of ocean affairs.

Amongst the General Assembly resolutions on broad principles are those: declaring the historical responsibility of states for the preservation of nature;noting the 1978 UNEP draft Code of Conduct; adopting the 1982 World Charter for Nature; requesting the UN Secretary General to prepare and regularly update a consolidated list of products whose consumption or sale has been banned, withdrawn, severely restrictedornot approved by governments;endorsing the Brundtland Report; and seeking to improve co-operation in the monitoring and assessment of environmental threats. The General Assembly has also convened UNCED, the negotiations of the framework Convention on Climate Change, the Convention on Drought and Desertification, the negotiations leading to the 1995 Straddling Stocks Agreement, and, more recently, the WSSD. In 1997, it adopted the Watercourses Convention. The General Assembly has only on a few occasions adopted resolutions on substantive matters, examples being the recommendation that moratoria should be imposed on all large-scale pelagic driftnet fishing on the high seas by the end of 1993, and support for the precautionary approach to the conservation, management and exploitation of straddling fish stocks and highly migratory fish stocks. The General Assembly's 1994 request for an advisory opinion on the legality of the use of nuclear weapons resulted in the ICJ affirming the existence UNEP was established in 1972 by General Assembly Resolution 2997 following the Stockholm Conference, and it has played a significant catalytic role in the development of treaties and soft law rules. It is based in Nairobi and comprises a Governing Council of fifty-eight members elected by the General Assembly (which meets bi-annually at the headquarters in Nairobi and reports to the General Assembly through ECOSOC) and an Environment Secretariat headed by the UNEP Executive Director. Following UNCED and WSSD, it remains the only UN body exclusively dedicated to international environmental matters. Its constituent instrument commits it to promote international environmental co-operation; to provide policy guidance for the direction and co-ordination of environmental programmes within the UN system; to receive and review reports from UNEP's Executive Director on the implementation of the UN's environment programmes; to review the world environment situation; to promote scientific knowledge and information and contribute to technical aspects of environmental programmes; and to maintain under review the impact of national and international environmental policies on developing countries. Despite its limited status as a UN programme (rather than a specialised agency or body) and its limited financial resources, few observers would dispute that UNEP has made an important contribution to the development and application of international environmental law. UNEP promoted the Regional Seas Programme, which now includes more than thirty environmental treaties and numerous regional Action Plans, including the Zambezi Agreement and Action Plan, and has been responsible for the development of several global environmental treaties, including the 1985 Vienna Convention and 1987 Montreal Protocol (Ozone), the 1989 Basel Convention (Hazardous Waste), the 1992 Biodiversity Convention, the 2000 Biosafety Protocol, and the 2001 POPs Convention. UNEP provides secretariat functions to these treaties and performs a supportive role in relation to several others including the 1998 Chemicals Convention (with FAO).

UNEP has also been responsible for sponsoring numerous soft law instruments, including the 1978 draft Principles on shared natural resources, offshore mining and drilling; and instruments on land-based marine pollution; the management of hazardous wastes; environmental impact assessment; and the international trade in chemicals.UNEP has focused attention on the inadequacy of existing international legal instruments in the field of the environment and has sought to further develop international environmental law in a variety of ways. Among its most important initiatives has been the regular convening of the experts group which led to the Programme for the Development and Periodic Review of Environmental Law (Montevideo Programme). This formed the basis for many of its activities in the field of environmental law over the following decade.

Resolutions of the UNEP Governing Council guide the development of UNEP's contribution to international law. UNEP Governing Council resolutions are supplemented by the activities of the Environmental Law Branch of the Division of Policy Development, which publishes the *Register of International Treaties and Other Agreements in the Field of the Environment*. The Division of Environmental Policy Implementation is responsible for issues relating to compliance and enforcement. UNEP also participates in the Global Environmental Monitoring System (GEMS) and collaborates in the operation of INFOTERRA. UNEP has also established, on an experimental basis, the UN Centre for Urgent Environmental Assistance, focusing on assessment of and responses to man-made environmental emergencies.

Although UNEP was not significantly strengthened by UNCED, its increasingly focused and enhanced role is reflected in the decision granting it co-management responsibilities, with UNDP and the World Bank, of the Global Environment Facility. The need to enhance and strengthen the policy and co-ordinationroleof UNEP wasrecognisedbyUNCEDin Chapter 38of Agenda21.

The priority areas for UNEP set out in Agenda 21 include: strengthening its 'catalytic role', through the development of techniques such as natural resource accounting and environmental economics; promoting environmental monitoring and assessment; co-ordinating scientific research; disseminating information and raising general awareness; further developing international environmental law, including promoting implementation and co-ordinating functions; further developing environmental impact assessment; and providing technical, legal and institutional advice. UNEP's present priorities include: environmental information, assessment and research, including environmental emergency response capacity and strengthening of early warning and assessment functions; enhanced the co-ordination of environmental conventions and development of policy instruments; fresh water; technology transfer and industry; and support to African states.

UN DEVELOPMENT PROGRAMME (WWW.UNDP.ORG)

The UN General Assembly established the UN Development Programme (UNDP) in 1965. It is the principal channel for multilateral technical and investment assistance to developing countries. It is active in all economic and so-cialsectors andhas addressed environmentalissuessince theearly 1970s. UNDP receives voluntary contributions from participating states, as well as donor co-financing, and additional finance from the business sector, foundations and NGOs, and in 2002 had a total budget of approximately US$2.58 billion. The role of UNDP in environmental programmes has been strengthened by its participation in the management of important programmes and institutions, such as the Tropical Forestry Action Plan and the Global Environment Facility. In 2001, UNDP adopted major reforms which realigned its global network around six thematic practice areas, including energy and environment, the focus of which is on building developing country capacity to protect natural resources wisely, acquire them affordably and use them sustainably. UNDP's role is to help developing countries strengthen their capacity to deal with these challenges at global, national and community levels, seeking out and sharing best practices, providing policy advice and linking partners through practical pilot projects on the ground. UNDP's work in this area is supported by two trust funds: the Energy for Sustainable Development Trustfund and the Environment Trustfund. UNDP also administers several special-purpose funds which are relevant to environmental matters, and is particularly active in translating international efforts into grass-roots programmes and activities.

OTHER SUBSIDIARY BODIES ESTABLISHED BY THE GENERAL ASSEMBLY

The General Assembly has established numerous other bodies with less direct responsibility for environmental issues. The UN Conference on Trade and Development (UNCTAD) was established by the General Assembly in 1964 as one of its organs. UNCTAD's functions include promoting international trade with a view to accelerating the economic growth of developing countries, and formulating and implementing principles and policies on international trade and the related problems of economic development. The eighth session of UNCTAD, held in 1992, adopted A New Partnership for Development: The Cartagena Commitment', which commits UNCTAD to a programme of ensuring that growth and development, poverty alleviation, rural development and

the protection of the environment are 'mutually reinforcing'. UNCTAD has convened international commodity conferences which have led to the negotiation and adoption of international agreements on individual commodities, under the Integrated Programme for Commodities. The Bangkok Declaration and Programme of Action, adopted in February 2000 at the tenth session of UNCTAD, provide the main thrust for the current work of UNCTAD, as the focal point for the integrated treatment of development and the interrelated issues of trade, finance, investment, technology and sustainable development. The Bangkok Programme of Action made a number of specific recommendations on the focus of UNCTAD's work on trade and the environment.Other bodies created by the General Assembly which play a role in international environmental issues include: the United Nations Institute on Training and Research (UNITAR), whose role is to carry out training programmes and initiate research programmes; the UN Population Fund, which promotes awareness of the social, economic and environmental implications of national and international population problems; the Committee on Peaceful Uses of Outer Space (COPUOS) to review international co-operation in peaceful uses of outer space and study associated legal problems; the Scientific Committee on Effects of Atomic Radiation (UNSCEAR) to consider the effects of radiation levels and radiation on humans and their environment; and the United Nations Human Settlements Programme, known as UN-Habitat, which has a mandate to promote sustainable human settlements development in all countries with due regard for the carrying capacity of the environment in accordance with the Habitat Agenda adopted at the Habitat II Conference held in Istanbul in 1996. Additionally, several human rights treaties have established committees to monitor implementation which report on their activities to parties and to the General Assembly. Of particular relevance to environmental matters are the Human Rights Committee (established under the 1966 International Covenant on Civil and Political Rights) and the Committee on Economic, Social and Cultural Rights (established under the 1966 International Covenant on Economic, Social and Cultural Rights). In November 2002, the Committee on Economic, Social and Cultural Rights issued a 'General Comment recognising access to safe drinking water and sanitation as a human right, which stresses that water is a limited natural resource and a public commodity fundamental to life and health'. Economic and Social Council (ECOSOC)

The Economic and Social Council (ECOSOC), which has fifty-four members serving three-year terms, has competence over international economic, social, cultural, educational and health issues, and related matters. Although it does not have an express mandate over environmental issues, it has addressed a broad range of topics which are directly related to the environment. ECOSOC makes recommendations with respect to the General Assembly, to the UN members and to specialised agencies, and it can also prepare draft conven-tions. ECOSOC has responsibility for co-ordinating the activities of specialised agencies, including UNEP and the CSD, and obtaining regular reports from them. This co-ordinating function was underlined by UNCED which called for ECOSOC to assist the General Assembly by 'overseeing system-wide co-ordination, overview on the implementation of Agenda 21 and making rec-ommendations'.

ECOSOC has contributed to the development of international environmental law. In 1946, it convened the 1949 UN Scientific Conference on the Conservation and Utilisation of Resources (UNCCUR), the predecessor to the Stockholm and Rio Conferences. It receives the reports of the UNEP Governing Council and the CSD, which are passed on to the General Assembly. Since it does not have any committees which focus exclusively on the environment, it has not itself served as a forum for important decisions on these matters. It has, however, established subsidiary bodies relevant to the environment.

The five Regional Economic Commissions, established under Article 68 of the UN Charter, have contributed significantly to the development of international environmental law. Under the auspices of the UN Economic Commission for Europe (UNECE), regional treaties have been adopted on: transboundary air pollution; environmental impact assessment; industrial accidents; protection of watercourses; and public access and participation in environmental decision making. The UNECE Group of Senior Advisers to UNECE Governments on Environmental and Water Problems has also adopted numerous recommendations on water issues and biodiversity conservation, as well as a draft UNECE Charter on Environmental Rights and Obligations. In 1995, the UNECE ministers adopted the Environmental Programme for Europe, the first attempt to set long-term environmental priorities at the pan-European level and to make Agenda 21 more operational in the European context. It covers a broad range of issues and contains some 100 recommendations.

The other UN Regional Economic Commissions are responsible for Asia and the Pacific (ESCAP), Africa (ECA), Latin America and the Caribbean (ECLAC) and West Asia. Although the Regional Economic Commissions have not yet promoted the negotiation of international environmental agreements, they play some role in developing 'soft' instruments and the regional preparatory arrangements for international conferences and meetings.

ECOSOC recently established the UN Forum on Forests with a mandate to promote the management, conservation and sustainable development of all types of forests and to strengthen long-term political commitment to this end. Over the first five years of its operation, in addition to its more generalised activities, the Forum is to work on a mandate for developing a legal framework for all types of forests.

Other relevant ECOSOC subsidiary bodies include: the newly established Permanent Forum on Indigenous Issues, an expert advisory body with a mandate to consider indigenous issues relating to economic and social development, culture, the environment, education, health and human rights; the Commission on Population and Development; the Commission on Social Development; the Commission on Human Rights; the Committee on Energy and Natural Resources for Development; and the Standing Committee for Development Policy. The now-disbanded Commission on Transnational Corporations carried out useful work examining the relationship between transnational corporations and international environmental obligations. Security Council

The Security Council, which has primary responsibility in the UN system for the maintenance of international peace and security, has only recently addressed international environmental issues. Its five permanent members and ten members elected for a period of two years can adopt legally binding resolutions which give it the potential to develop a significant role.

The Security Council's first foray into environmental affairs was in 1991, when it adopted a resolution holding Iraq liable for, *inter alia,* damage to the environment resulting from the invasion of Kuwait. In the following years it met for the first time at the level of heads of government or state, and adopted adeclaration which affirmed that 'non-military sources of instability in the economic, social, humanitarian and ecological fields have become threats to peace and security'. In recognising the link between environment and security, the Security Council has opened the door to further consideration of significant environmental matters, and over time it is increasingly likely that the Council will address issues relating to environmental emergencies and their consequences. More recently, the Security Council has addressed the link between the illegal exploitation of natural resources and armed conflict in Africa. Trusteeship Council

The Trusteeship Council assists the Security Council and the General Assembly in performing the UN's functions under the International Trusteeship System of Chapter XII of the UN Charter. The Trusteeship Council has one administering power (US) and four non-administering powers (China, France, Russia and the United Kingdom). Its basic objectives include the promotion of political, economic, social and educational advancement of the inhabitants of trust territories, without specifying environmental objectives. Although the Trusteeship Council has not played a direct role in the development of international environmental law, its obligation to respect these basic objectives provides a role in natural resource issues, including conservation.

The role of the Trusteeship Council was therefore indirectly at issue in the case concerning *Certain Phosphate Lands in Nauru,* where Nauru asked the ICJ to declare Australia's responsibility for breaches of international law relating to phosphate mining activities, including, *inter alia,* breaches of Article 76 of the UN Charter and the Trusteeship Agreement between Australia, New

Zealand and the United Kingdom.

As the number of international trusteeships has steadily declined, alternative functions for the Trusteeship Council have been proposed. One idea, put forward by President Gorbachev of the Soviet Union in 1990, was to expand the trusteeship function to include responsibility for environmental protection in areas beyond national jurisdiction, the global commons. Although the suggestion received widespread attention, it was rejected at UNCED, and has not since been revived.

INTERNATIONAL COURT OF JUSTICE (www.icj-cij.org)

The environmentally-related activities of the International Court of Justice (ICJ) are considered in more detail in chapter 5 below. Through its judgments and advisory opinions, the ICJ has contributed to the development of international environmental law through general principles and rules elaborated in non-environmental cases and in cases concerned directly with environmental issues. Recent cases raising significant environmental issues include those relating to *Certain Phosphate Lands in Nauru*, the *Gabcikovo-Nagymaros Project*

(Hungary/Slovakia), the *Advisory Opinion on the Legality of the Use or Threat of Nuclear Weapons* and the *Request for an Examination of the Situation in Accordance with Paragraph 63 of the Court's Judgment of 20 December 1974 in the Nuclear Tests (New Zealand* v. *France)*. In July 1993, the ICJ established a seven-member Chamber for Environmental Matters, in view of the developments in the field of environmental law and protection which had taken place in the past few years.

United Nations specialised agencies and related organisations

The UN specialised agencies and related international organisations were established before environmental matters became an issue for the international community. It is therefore not surprising that none was designed to deal with, or given express competence over, environmental matters, and that consequently the environment has tended to play a somewhat peripheral role in their affairs. Since the specialised agencies were designed to deal with issues of concern to the international community in the post-war period, there are numerous significant gaps in their competence, including in particular energy, mining and transport matters.

FOOD AND AGRICULTURE ORGANIZATION (www.fao.org)

The Food and Agriculture Organization (FAO), which is based in Rome, was established in 1945 to collect, analyse, interpret and disseminate information on nutrition, food and agriculture (including fisheries, marine products, forestry and primary forest products), to promote national and international action, and to provide technical and other assistance. The FAO is the only specialised agency with an environmental mandate in its constitution, namely, to promote the 'conservation of natural resources and the adoption of improved methods of agricultural production'.

The FAO Conference and Council may initiate and approve conventions and agreements on food and agriculture,and the FAO has developed soft law, including the operation with WHO of the World Food Programme, the operation of a Global System on Plant Genetic Resources, and the adoption and operation of the 1985 International Code of Conduct on the Distribution and Use of Pesticides.

The FAO also established (with WHO) the *Codex Alimentarius* Commission (discussed below). Additionally, the FAO has sponsored numerous international treaties and created a number of international organisations in, for example, the fields of fisheries, plant protection, forest research and locust control. It has addressed forest issues, and in 1985 established the Tropical Forestry Action Plan. The FAO convenes international conferences which have led to the adoption and development of international action plans and strategies, some of which have subsequently led to binding international obligations. Examples include the 1981 World Soil Charter, the 1984 World Soil Policy and Plan of Action, the 1991 Strategy and Agenda for Action for Sustainable Agriculture and Rural Deveiopment, and the 1995 World Food Summit. Recent international plans of action of importance to the environment are the 1999 Plans of Action on seabirds, sharks and fishing capacity and the 2001 Plan of Action on illegal unreported and unregulated fishing.

United Nations Education and Scientific Organization

The United Nations Education and Scientific Organization (UNESCO), which is based in Paris, was established in 1945 to contribute to peace and security by promoting international collaboration through education, science and culture, including the conservation and protection of historic and scientific monuments and recommending necessary international conventions. UNESCO played a role in convening and hosting the 1948 UNCCUR and has established institutions and programmes such as the Intergovernmental Oceano-graphic Commission in 1960, and the Man and the Biosphere Programme (under which the 1985 Action Plan for Biosphere Reserves was adopted).

UNESCO was responsible for the adoption of, and performs secretariat functions for, the 1971 Ramsar Convention, the 1972 World Heritage Conven-tion and the 2001 Convention on the Protection of Underwater Cultural Heritage.

International Maritime Organization

The International Maritime Organization (IMO, formerly known as the Intergovernmental Maritime Consultative Organisation) is based in London and was established in 1948. Its objectives, which originally did not refer to marine pollution, include: the provision of machinery for co-operation among governments on regulation and practice relating to technical matters of all kinds affecting shipping engaged in international trade; encouraging the general adoption of the highest practical standards in matters concerning maritime safety; and ensuring the efficiency of navigation and the prevention and control of marine pollution from ships. IMO activities relating to marine pollution are mainly carried out through the Legal Committee and the Marine Environment Protection Committee (MEPC), established by the IMO Assembly in 1975. The MEPC has broad powers to consider any matter to do with the prevention and control of marine pollution from ships, including the power to propose regulations and develop recommendations and guidelines. The IMO has supported the negotiation and conclusion of a number of important environmental treaties, for which it provides secretariat functions. These relate to oil pollution, pollution from ships, civil liability and compensation for oil pollution damage, and emergency preparedness. The IMO also acts as Secretariat to the 1972 London Convention and has contributed to soft law by adopting non-binding guidelines, standards and codes relating to maritime safety and the protection of the marine environment.

International Labor Organization

The purposes of the International Labor Organization (ILO), which is based in Geneva and was originally established in 1919, include the protection of workers against sickness, disease and injury arising out of employment, and the adoption of humane conditions of labour. To this end, the ILO has adopted a number of conventions which set international standards for environmental conditions in the workplace, including occupational safety and health as well as numerous non-binding recommendations and guidelines.

World Meteorological Organization

The World Meteorological Organization (WMO) was established in 1947 and is based in Geneva. Its purposes are: to facilitate worldwide co-operation in meteorological observation and hydrological and other geophysical observations related to meteorology; to promote the establishment and maintenance of meteorological centres and the rapid exchange of meteorological information; to promote the standardisation and uniform publication of observations and statistics; and to encourage research and training.

The WMO operates the World Weather Watch, the World Climate Programme and the Atmospheric Research and Environment Programme. The World Climate Programme supports the Global Climate Observing System (GCOS) which is sponsored jointly by the WMO, UNESCO's International Oceanographic

Commission, UNEP and the ICSU. In 1988, the WMO, with UNEP, established the Intergovernmental Panel on Climate Change (IPCC), an intergovernmental body providing scientific, technical and socio-economic advice on climate change issues, and has contributed to the establishment of the legal regimes for ozone depletion, climate change and transboundary atmospheric pollution. The Atmospheric Research and Environment Programme incorporates the Global Atmosphere Watch (GAW) and is the vehicle for the WMO's involvement in the GCOS.

International Civil Aviation Organization

The International Civil Aviation Organization (ICAO), based in Montreal, was established in 1947. Its objectives include the promotion of safe, efficient and economical air transport and generally the development of all aspects of international civil aeronautics. To that end, it has adopted several relevant instruments, including international standards and recommended practices on aircraft engine emissions and on noise pollution.

World Health Organization

The World Health Organization (WHO) was established in 1946 to ensure 'the attainment by all peoples of the highest possible level of health'. It is based in Geneva. The WHO Assembly can adopt conventions or agreements for any matters within the competence of the organisation, as well as regulations on sanitary and quarantine requirements, and on the standards, advertising and labelling of biological, pharmaceutical and similar products placed on international markets.

It may also make recommendations, and non-binding standards have been adopted for drinking water and air quality. In 1990, the WHO established the WHO Commission on Health and Environment which played a key role in ensuring that environmental health considerations were incorporated in Agenda 21. In 1993, the WHO Assembly requested an Advisory Opinion from the International Court of Justice on the legality of nuclear weapons use, in the context of its work on the effects of nuclear weapons on health and the environment.

The WHO administers the Food Standard Programme with the FAO, which is administered by the *Codex Alimentarius* Commission. The *Codex Alimentarius* Commission was established in 1963 with the purposes of making proposals to the FAO and the WHO on all matters relating to the implementation of the Joint FAO/WHO Food Standards Programme, the purpose of which are: to protect the health of consumers and to ensure fair practices in the food trade; to promote the co-ordination of all food standards work undertaken by international governmental and non-governmental organisations; to guide the preparation of and finalise standards and, after acceptance by governments, to publish them in a *Codex Alimentarius* either as regional or worldwide standards; and to amend published standards in the light of de-velopments. Over 160 states are members of the Commission, which has adopted commodity standards and general standards for a very large number of foodstuffs, including in relation to additives, pesticide residues and labelling. In varying degrees, the *Codex* standards are recognised and applied in international trade regimes, including by the WTO, NAFTA, the EC, APEC and MERCOSUR.

International Atomic Energy Agency (www.iaea.org)

The International Atomic Energy Agency (IAEA), which is based in Vienna, was established in 1956 to develop the peaceful uses of atomic energy. The IAEA is autonomous and not formally a specialised agency of the United Nations, but sends reports to the General Assembly and other UN organs. It is the only member of the UN 'family' dedicated to the energy sector, although its dual promotional and regulatory function appears anomalous. Under the 1963 Treaty on the Non-Proliferation of Nuclear Weapons, the IAEA has responsibilities for safeguarding nuclear materials in non-nuclear weapon states parties to it. The IAEA has also sponsored, and provides secretariat functions for, international conventions relating to liability, the protection of nuclear material, nuclear accidents, and the safety of nuclear installations. The IAEA has also adopted numerous non-binding standards and recommendations on basic safety standards relating to, *inter alia*, radioactive discharges into the environment and the disposal and transboundary movement of radioactive wastes.

The World Bank (comprising the International Bank for Reconstruction and Development (IBRD), the International Development Association (IDA) and the International Finance Corporation (IFC)), the IMF and the WTO are central players in international environmental law. They and their activities are considered in chapters 19 and 20 below.

CO-OPERATIVE ARRANGEMENTS

Apart from the subsidiary bodies of the specialised agencies which are referred to above, two others bodies merit special mention on account of their contribution to the negotiation and adoption of international legal instruments: the Joint Group of Experts on Scientific Aspects of Marine Pollution (GESAMP) and the Intergovernmental Panel on Climate Change (IPCC).GESAMP (which is jointly run by the UN, UNEP, FAO, UNESCO, WHO, WMO, IMO and IAEA) has a mandate to conduct research and carry out assessments on the state of the marine environment, and to make appropriate recommendations, and has produced numerous reports since 1982. The IPCC was established to assess the available scientific information on climate change, to assess the environmental and socio-economic impacts of climate change, and to formulate response strategies. Its efforts are organised under three working groups (Science, Impact and Adaptation, and Mitigation) and a task force (on National Greenhouse Gas Inventories). It has produced three Assessment Reports on Climate Change (1990, 1995 and 2001), contributing to the ongoing intergovernmental negotiations around the 1992 Climate Change Convention and its 1997 Kyoto Protocol, and a number of special reports on particular aspects, such as aviation and land-use.

OTHER GLOBAL INSTITUTIONS

Beyond the activities of the UN and specialised agencies, in law of the sea matters, the 1982 UN Convention on the Law of the Sea (UNCLOS) established two new international institutions which address environmental aspects of the law of the sea. These are the International Tribunal for the Law of the Sea (ITLOS), which has already made a significant contribution to maritime environmental law, and the International Seabed Authority, which has recently promulgated regulations which establish environmental conditions for deep sea-bed prospecting.

Regional and sub-regional organisations

Regional organisations outside the UN system also play a growing role in the development of international environmental law. In application of the principle that different environmental standards could be applied to different geopolitical regions, the role of regional organisations is likely to increase significantly. They are frequently able to provide the flexibility needed to accommodate special regionalconcerns, as was recognisedby theBrundtland Report'scall for regional organisations to do more to integrate environmental concerns into their activities. As the regional rules of international environmental law and institutional arrangements are particularly well developed in the Antarctic and in the European Communities, organisations related to those developments are considered in more detail in chapters 14 and 15 below.

Some international organisations are not regional, in a strict geographic sense, and are not UN agencies, bodies or programmes. These include the Commonwealth Secretariat, the Organization of the Islamic Conference, the League of ArabStates whose members are in Africa and Asia, and the Organization of Petroleum Exporting Countries. Although each maintains an interest in environmental matters, none has adopted rules of international environmental law or ensured their enforcement, although they provide assistance to states on environmental matters.

EUROPE AND THE OECD

In the European context, apart from the EU, three organisations play an important role in the development of regional rules: the Council of Europe, the Organization for Economic Co-operation and Development (OECD) and the Conference on Security and Co-operation in Europe (CSCE). More recently, the European Bank for Reconstruction and Development (EBRD) has emerged as an innovative contributor to European environmental law and policy; it is noteworthy, in a broader global context, as the first multilateral development bank to have a constituent instrument which expressly requires it to fulfil environmental protection and sustainable development objectives. OECD (www.oecd.org)

The OECD (formerly the Organization for European Economic Co-operation, OEEC) was established in 1960 to promote policies designed to achieve in its member countries the highest sustainable economic growth, sound economic expansion in the process of economic development, and the expansion of world trade. Seven of its thirty members are not European states. In 1974, the members of the OECD established an International Energy Agency, the Nuclear Energy Agency having been established in 1957.

The OECD Convention does not specify environmental protection among its functions, but the organisation began to address environmental issues in 1970 following the decision to create an Environment Committee as a subsidiary body to the Executive Committee, which is itself subordinate to the OECD Council. The OECD became involved in environmental issues for three reasons. First, certain environmental issues were recognised to be intrinsically international; secondly, differences among member countries' environmental standards were considered to have implications for trade and economic and political relations; and, thirdly, it was felt that some member countries might be insufficiently prepared to address certain environmental problems.

The OECD Council may adopt two types of act: decisions, which are binding on its members; and recommendations, which are non-binding. Both acts are usually adopted with the support of all members. Since 1972, the OECD Council has adopted a large number of environmental measures, and has promulgated a treaty on liability for nuclear damage. These environmental acts have influenced the development of national environmental legislation in the member countries, and have often provided a basis for international environmental standards and regulatory techniques in other regions and at the global level. The OECD Council has frequently been at the forefront of developments in international environmental policy, focusing on the relationship between economic and environmental policies; defining and endorsing the 'polluter-pays' principle; providing early support for the development and use of environmental assessment techniques;

promoting economic instru-ments; endorsing the use of integrated pollution prevention and control; using pollutant release and transfer registers; and 'greening' public procurement. The OECD Council has also supported the broad use of techniques for ensuring the availability of environmental information, and for developing co-operation on transfrontier pollution. Substantive issues have also been addressed, and the OECD Council has developed a broad range of decisions or recommendations on many sectors of environmental protection, including air quality, water quality, energy, waste, chemicals,noise, tourism and multinational enterprises.

Council of Europe (www.coe.int)

The Council of Europe was established in 1949 to achieve greater unity between members 'for safeguarding and realising their ideals and principles which are their common heritage and facilitating their economic and social progress'.The Council of Europe now has forty-one members across the whole of Europe. Withoutan explicit environmental mandate, the Council of Europe has adopted a number of acts and policies relating to environmental protection through its organs, the Committee of Ministers and the Consultative Assembly. The Parliamentary Assembly has adopted many non-binding recommendations on environmental issues. The Council of Europe's contributions include several treaties: apart from an early environmental treaty restricting the use of detergents, the Council of Europe has adopted treaties on: the protection of animals; the protection of archaeological heritage; the conservation of wildlife; transfrontier co-operation; civil liability for environmental damage; the protection of the environment through criminal law; and landscape. The European Convention on Human Rights and the European Social Charter, both of which have contributed to environmental jurisprudence and policy, were also adopted under the auspices of the Council of Europe.

Organization for Security and Co-operation in Europe (www.osce.org)

The Final Act of the 1975 Conference on Security and Co-operation in Europe (CSCE) encompassed co-operation on the protection and improvement of the environment, and the institutions established thereunder may accordingly address matters relating to the environment. The 1990 Charter of Paris for a New Europe affirmed the close relationship between economic liberty, social justice and environmental responsibility. In 1994, the CSCE was renamed the OSCE, and its institutions now comprise a Ministerial Council, a Senior Council,aPermanentCouncil, anda Conflict PreventionCentre. So far,these institutions do not appear to have been apprised of a security issue arising out of an environmental conflict, although there was some suggestion that the dispute between Hungary and Slovakia over the Gabcikovo-Nagymaros Project might be referred to CSCE procedures.

AFRICA

The principal African organisation which addresses environmental matters is the African Union (formerly the Organization of African Unity (OAU)), which was established in 1963 to promote the unity and solidarity of African states and to co-ordinate co-operation to achieve a better life for the peoples of Africa.To that end, the OAU has supported the adoption of a treaty on the conservation of nature and natural resources, and a treaty on the trade in and management of hazardous waste. The OAU also sponsored the 1981 African

Charter on Human Right and Peoples' Rights and the 1991 African Economic Community, both of which have environmental provisions. Apart from the UN Economic Commission for Africa, other organisations having environmental responsibilities and activities include the African Development Bank, the ArabBank for Economic Development in Africa, the Economic Community of Central African States, the Economic Community of West African States, and the Intergovernmental Authority on Drought and Development.

The Southern African Development Community was established in 1992 and has adopted protocols on shared watercourses, wildlife conservation and law enforcement. Regional bodies have also been established to manage shared natural resources.

AMERICAS AND THE CARIBBEAN

The Organization of American States (OAS), whose purposes include promoting the economic, social and cultural development of its members, has played a limited role in international environmental law. As the successor organisation to the Pan American Union, the OAS has responsibility for the dormant 1940 Western Hemisphere Convention, and has been responsible for the adoption of just one convention, with passing relevance for environmental protec-tion. Other organisations with a higher environmental profiie include the Inter-American Development Bank, the Caribbean Development Bank, the Central American Commission on Environment and Development, and the American Convention on Human Rights, which is the only such instrument to state expressly that people have a right to a clean and healthy environment.Neither the Caribbean Community nor the Organization of Eastern Caribbean States has played a particularly active role, save in the field of fisheries. Regional free trade agreements have played a catalytic role in developing regional rules of environmental protection, particularly the Canada–United States Free Trade Agreement and the North American Free Trade Agreement. At the bilateral level, the Canada–United States International Joint Commission, established in 1909, is significant, and important bilateral arrangements also exist between Mexico and the United States. Asia

Asia has taken only limited measures towards establishing regional environmental organisations. Given the rapid industrialisation which is occurring in many countries in the region, the important role of Japan, and the size and significance of China and India, shared environmental problems and the need to conserve natural resources will inevitably lead to the creation of such organisations. In the short term, developments are likely to focus on giving existing organisations greater environmental competence, and on the relationship between economic commitments (free trade and investment) and environmental standards.

One of the few regional organisations to have already made a significant contribution is the Association of South East Asian Nations (ASEAN), under whose auspices the 1985 ASEAN

Convention was adopted. The Asian Development Bank integrates environmental considerations into its decision-making process, and the South Asian Association for Regional Co-operation (SAARC) may ultimately be granted a role in the development of regional rules.

Regional organisations in Oceania are more active, including in the negotiation of multilateral environmental agreements. The South Pacific Commission has promulgated at least two treaties for the protection of natural resources. At the annual meetings of the South Pacific Forum, regional and global environmental issues are high on the agenda, and the Forum has taken decisions which led to the negotiation and adoption of a nuclear free zone treaty and the prohibition of driftnet fishing. The South Pacific Regional Environment Programme (SPREP) became an independent and autonomous regional organisation in 1991, and has recently adopted an Action Strategy for Nature Conservation in the Pacific Islands Region.

Organisations established by environmental treaties

The third type of organisation is that established by environmental treaty, most of which establish institutional arrangements for their implementation, development and review. The institutional arrangements have a variety of names and forms, and have not attracted a great deal of scholarly or practical attention. They range from the standing Commission established by the 1992 OSPAR Convention (replacing the Commissions established by the 1972 Oslo Convention and the 1974 Paris Convention), to the *ad hoc* conferences or meetings of the parties to a wide range of agreements.

Each treaty organisation will also have a secretariat. These institutional arrangements are, in effect, international organisations. They have international legal status, rules of procedure and membership, and have enumerated powers relating to decision-making and dispute settlement and, occasionally, enforcement powers.

A large number of treaty organisations are highly active and have made significant contributions to the development of international environmental law, much of which is not collectively well documented and assessed. The reporting arrangements established under the Commission on Sustainable Development should have provided an opportunity for improved co-ordination of the activities of these organisations and the consequential rationalisation.

A detailed list of these organisations is beyond the scope of this section: where appropriate, they are identified in relevant sections of the book. As will be seen, they may, through their acts, impose obligations on states which range from the legally binding to recommendations with no legal consequences. Certain treaty organisations at the regional and global level are, or are likely to become, noteworthy in respect of particular environmental issues, and these are listed below.

Atmosphere Transboundary air pollution

- 1979 LRTAP Convention (and Protocols), Executive Body (meets annually)

Ozone

- 1985 Vienna Convention, conference of the parties (as necessary)
- 1987 Montreal Protocol, meetings of the parties (at regular intervals)

Climate change

- 1992 Climate Change Convention and 1997 Kyoto Protocol, Conference of the Parties (every year unless decided otherwise)

Oceans and seas General

- UNEP Regional Seas Conventions, various
- 1974 Baltic Convention, Helsinki Commission (at least annually)
- 1982 UNCLOS, Assembly of the International Sea-Bed Authority (annually)
- 1992 OSPAR Convention, OSPAR Commission (at regular intervals)

Dumping

- 1972 London Convention, consultative meetings (annually)

Pollution from ships

- MARPOL 1973/78, IMO Assembly (annually)

Compensation and liability

- 1992 Oil Pollution Fund Convention, Assembly and Executive Committee (annually/at least every two years)

Freshwaters

- 1963 Rhine Convention, International Commission
- 1992 Watercourses Convention, meeting of the parties (at least every three years)

Biological diversity General

- 1979 Berne Convention, Standing Committee
- 1992 Biodiversity Convention and 2000 Biosafety Protocol, conference of the parties (at regular intervals)

Trade in endangered species

- 1973 CITES, conference of the parties (at least once every three years, in practice every two years)

Wetlands

- 1971 Ramsar Convention, conferences (as necessary)

Whales

- 1946 International Whaling Convention, Commission (meets annually)

Migratory species

- 1979 Bonn Convention, conference of the parties (at least every three years)

Fisheries

- 1949 Tropical Tuna Convention, Commission
- 1952 North Pacific Fisheries Convention, Commission (annually)
- 1966 Atlantic Tuna Convention, Commission (every two years)

- 1969 South East Atlantic Convention, Commission (at least every two years)
- 1973 Baltic Fishing Convention, Commission (every two years unless decided otherwise)
- 1978 Northwest Atlantic Fisheries Convention, General Council of the Northwest Atlantic Fisheries Organisation (annually)
- 1979 South Pacific Forum Fisheries Agency, Committee (annually)
- 1980 North-East Atlantic Fisheries Convention, Commission (annually unless decided otherwise)
- 1980 Convention for the Conservation of Antarctic Marine Living Resources, Commission (annually)
- 1982 North Atlantic Salmon Conservation Organization, Council (annually)

World heritage

- 1972 World Heritage Convention, World Heritage Committee

Waste: 1989 Basel Convention, conference of the parties (at regular intervals) 1991 Bamako Convention, conference of the parties (at regular intervals)

Chemicals: 1998 Chemicals Convention, conference of the parties (at regular intervals) 2001 POPs Convention, conference of the parties (at regular intervals)

ENVIRONMENTAL IMPACT ASSESSMENT, ACCIDENTS

1991Espoo Convention, meeting of the parties (as necessary)

1992Industrial Accidents Convention, conference of the parties (annually)

Public participation

1998 Aarhus Convention, meeting of the parties (at least once every two years)

War and environment

1977 ENMOD Convention, conference of the parties (usually every five years)

Non-state actors

P. Lowe and J. Goyder, *Environmental Groups in Politics* (1983); M. Bettati and P. Dupuy (eds.), *Les ONG et le droit international* (1986); R. Branes Ballesteros, *Aspectos institucionales y juridicos del medio ambiente, includia la participacion de las organizaciones no gubernamentales en la gestion ambiental* (Inter-American Development Bank, 1991); M. Garner, 'Transnational Alignment of Non-Governmental Organisations for Global Environmental Action', 24 *Vanderbilt Journal of Transnational Law* 653 (1991); S. Charnovitz, 'Two Centuries of Participation: NGOs and International Governance', 18 *Michigan Journal of International Law* 183 (1997); P. Sands, 'International Law, the Practitioner and Non-State Actors', in C. Wickremasinghe (ed.), *The International Lawyer as Practitioner* (2000).

Non-state actors have played a central role in developing international environmental law. They remainhighly influential.Sincethe latter half ofthe nineteenth century, the scientific community and environmental groups have mobilised the forces of public opinion, and have sought to contribute to the progressive development of international law.

The corporate sector has also fought to ensure that its voice is heard, especially as international rules expand and touch directly upon industrial and other economic activities. At the international level, non-state actors play a formal role in several ways. They identify issues requiring international legal action; they participate as observers in international organisations, and in treaty negotiations; and they participate, formally and informally, in the national and international implementation of principles and rules adopted at the regional and global levels.

Over the past two decades, six categories of non-state actors have emerged as important actors: the scientific community; non-profit-making environmental groups and associations (NGOs);

private companies and business concerns; legal organisations; the academic community; and individuals. The Rio Declaration and Agenda 21 affirm the important partnership role of nongovernmental organisations and call for their 'expanded role'. Agenda 21 declared that:

> [t]he organisations of the United Nations system and other intergovernmental organisations and forums,bilateral programmes and the private sector as appropriate, will need to provide increased financial and administrative support for non-governmental organisations and their self-organised networks, in particular those based in developing countries, contributing to the monitoring and evaluation of Agenda 21 programmes, and provide training for non-governmental organisations . . . to enhance their partnership role in programme design and implementation.

Agenda 21 also calls on the UN system, including international finance and development agencies and all intergovernmental organisations, to take measures to enhance the contribution of non-governmental organisations to 'policy design, decision-making, implementation and evaluation at the individual agency level, in inter-agency discussions and in United Nations conferences'.This objective is to be achieved by, *inter alia*: augmenting their role as partners in project and programme implementation; ensuring their participation in the processes to review and evaluate the implementation of Agenda 21; providing them with access to accurate and timely data and information; and providing them with increased administrative and financial support. Agenda 21 urges governments to take similar measures at the national level and to take: any legislative measures necessary to enable the establishment by nongovernmental organisations of consultative groups, and to ensure the right of non-governmental organisations to protect the public interest through legal action.

Non-state actors have for many years been able to participate as observers in the activities of international organisations, such rights being granted expressly in the treaty establishing the organisation, or by its rules of procedures, or by practice. The 1992 OSPAR Convention included, for the first time, a treaty provision for observers which does not distinguish between states, international governmental organisations and non-governmental organisations with respect to the conditions of the granting of observer status, save that the nongovernmental organisations must carry out activities which are related to the Convention. Moreover, once observer status has been granted, each observer appears to have identical rights, namely, to present to the Commission any information or reports relevant to the objectives of the Convention but not the right to vote. Even more far-reaching is the 1998 Aarhus Convention which, no doubt because of its subject matter, entitles non-governmental organisations to participate in the meeting of the parties and – uniquely – to nominate candidates for election to the Convention's implementation committee.

Scientific community

Often, the driving force behind international environmental law is science, a feature which distinguishes this from other areas of public international law where developments are frequently initiated by political, economic or commercial imperatives. The important place for science introduces an objective element over which governments have less control. As one commentator has noted, this has two effects: the 'environmental movement has been powerfully affected by the consequences of science misused to the detriment of the living world, but even more importantly by what advancing science has revealed about the structure and process of nature'. Non-state actors rely upon scientific evidence generated from different sources, including that which emerges from international processes such as the IPCC and GESAMP, from government departments, and from non-state sources. The last-mentioned have long played a role in the development of international environmental law. Early efforts leading to international legal developments include the work of individual members of the scientific community in the eighteenth century and the scientific congresses of the late nineteenth century. Today the principal co-ordinating force for the non-governmental activities of individual researchers and academics, and university and commercial research centres and institutes is the International Council of Scientific Unions (ICSU), a co-ordinating federation of twenty or so constituent unions. ICSU committees address particular issues, of which the following are among the more influential: the Scientific Committees on Oceanic Resources (SCOR, 1957), on Space Research (COSPAR, 1958) on Antarctic Research (SCAR, 1958) and on Problems of the Environment (SCOPE, 1969). SCOPE serves as a non-governmental, interdisciplinary and international council of scientists, and provides advice for governments and non-governmental bodies on environmental problems. It is often through the activities of environmental organisations that this scientific work is brought to the attention of governments and international organisations, supporting calls for further international action and providing the basis for political lobbying in intergovernmental negotiating fora.

Environmental and developmental organisations

Internationally, a number of environmental and developmental organisations have played a particularly important role in developing international environmental law. The International Union for the Conservation of Nature (IUCN), established in 1948, has developed policy initiatives and has prepared texts of draft instruments which have served as the basis for the negotiation of the 1971 Ramsar Convention, the 1973 CITES and the 1992 Biodiversity Convention. Together with UNEP and WWF, IUCN was also instrumental in drawing up the 1980 World Conservation Strategy and the 1990 World Conservation Strategy II. WWF, Greenpeace and Friends of the Earth are other international non-governmental organisations which have played an active role in developing treaty language and other international standards, and in acting as watchdogs in the implementation of treaty commitments, together with groups such as

Oxfam and Action Aid. This extends to the filing of international cases, where rules permit, or intervening as *amicus curiae*. Grassroots environmental and consumer organisations have also influenced the development of international environmental law, including through domestic litigation. Often, they participate in global networks which focus on specific issues, such as the Climate Action Network and the Pesticides Action Network; similar global networks have been established to address environmental issues relating to matters such as the GATT Uruguay Round and NAFTA, as well as policies and projects funded by the multilateral development banks. At UNCED, a large group of non-governmental organisations prepared their own draft treaties on a range of international legal issues relating to sustainable development.

Legal groups

Private groups and associations of lawyers have long played a role in the progressive development of international environmental law. Since the Institut de Droit International adopted its 1911 Resolution on International Regulations Regarding the Role of International Watercourses for Purposes Other Than Navigation, it and the International Law Association have developed model international rules on a range of environmental issues, including trans-boundary water resources and atmospheric pollution. The IUCN Environmental Law Centre and the IUCN Commission on Environmental Law have prepared important draft treaties which have formed the basis of formal negotiations. Other private organisations contributing significantly to the field includeenvironmentallaw groupsbasedintheUnited States,suchastheNatural Resources Defense Council (NRDC), Earthjustice and the Environmental Defense Fund (EDF), which play an advocacy role in the development of international environmental law. The International Council on Environmental Law and university-based organisations, such as the Foundation for International Environmental Law and Development (FIELD) at University College London, and theCenter for International EnvironmentalLaw (CIEL) in WashingtonDC, have provided international legal assistance to developing countries and nongovernmental organisations. Many national academic institutions have also contributed to the domestic implementation of international environmental obligations.

Corporate sector

In the private sector, associations such as the International Chamber of Commerce and the Business Council for Sustainable Development have sought to ensure that the interests of the business community are taken into account. To that end, they, and others, have developed proposals for the development of international environmental law, such as the Business Charter on Sustainable Development, the Declaration of the World Industry Conference on Environmental Management (WICEM II) and the Valdez Principles (in the United States). In 2000, the UN established a Global Compact as a 'voluntary corporate citizenship initiative' intended to provide 'a contextual framework to encourage innovation, creative solutions, and good practices among participants'. The Global Compact commits its corporate participants to adhere to nine principles, of which three relate to the environment and commit businesses to:

- support a precautionary approach to environmental challenges;
- undertake initiatives to promote greater environmental responsibility; and
- encourage the development and diffusion of environmentally friendly technologies.

The WSSD Plan of Implementation commits states to 'enhance corporate environmental and social responsibility and accountability' including actions at all levels to encourage industry: [t]o improve social and environmental performance through voluntary initiatives, including environmental management systems, codes of conduct, certification and public reporting on environmental and social issues, taking into account such initiatives as the International Organization for Standardization (ISO) standards and Global Reporting Initiative guidelines on sustainability reporting, bearing in mind Principle 11 of the Rio Declaration.

The corporate sector also participates as observers in international legal negotiations where it is perceived that issues affecting their interests are likely to be legislated on. At negotiations relating to the 1987 Montreal Protocol, the 1992 Climate Change Convention and the 2000 Biosafety Protocol, among others, individual companies, trade associations and other industry groups have been particularly active. Their participation reflects the growing relevance of public international law to the business community. Transnational corporations have also been the subject of international regulatory efforts in relation to activities which may entail harmful consequences. The OECD Guidelines for multinational enterprises were introduced in 1976 as the first internationally agreed

framework for co-operation in the field of international direct investment and multinational enterprises, and updated most recently in 2000. Part V of the 2000 Guidelines (on the environment) provides that:

Enterprises should, within the framework of laws, regulations and administrative practices in the countries in which they operate, and in consideration of relevant international agreements, principles, objectives, and standards, take due account of the need to protect the environment, public health and safety, and generally to conduct their activities in a manner contributing to the wider goal of sustainable development.

Individuals and indigenous communities

Individual citizens have traditionally expressed their involvement in the development and application of international environmental law through the activities of environmental organisations. However, the growing relationship between human rights and environmental discourse at the international level has led to individuals having recourse to international human rights norms and procedures including, where available, the right to complain to international bodies. International law also increasingly recognises the special interests and rights of indigenous communities, for example in relation to land rights and traditional knowledge associated with the conservation of biodiversity.As citizens of nation-states, individuals are responsible for the implementation

of international obligations; their role will be enhanced if they are able to report violations by governments of international legal obligations to environmental organisations, to national public authorities and, in the case of the EC and international human rights organisations, to international organisations. It is in regard to the latter that individuals have acquired rights under international law: the increased availability of complaint procedures – such as the Inspection Panel of the World Bank and the non-compliance mechanism established under the 1998 Aarhus Convention – provides formal mechanisms.

Potentially important developments took placeat UNCED, asreflected in the Rio Declaration, which recognises the rights of individual citizens to participate in decision-making processes, to have access to information, and to have access to judicial and administrative remedies. Principle 10 of the Rio Declaration provides that:

[e]nvironmental issues are best handled with the participation of all concerned citizens, at the relevant level. At the national level, each individual shall have appropriate access to information concerning the environment that is held by public authorities, including information on hazardous materials and activities in their communities, and the opportunity to participate in decision-making processes. States shall facilitate and encourage public awareness and participation by making information widely available. Effective access to judicial and administrative proceedings, including redress and remedy, shall be provided.

Although Principle 10 is not binding *per se*, it has provided an international benchmark against which the compatibility of national standards can be compared. Building on the human rights model, these developments foresee the creation of a new range of procedural rights which may be granted to individuals by international law, and which would be exercisable at the national and, possibly, international levels. Principle 10 has inspired the adoption of the first international convention – the 1998 Aarhus Convention – to require parties to guarantee the rights of access to information, public participation in decision-making and access to justice in environmental matters, and to promote the Convention's principles in international environmental decision-making and within international organisations. Article 6 of the Convention requires parties to inform the public concerned – early in the decision-making process – of proposed activities listed in Annex I to the Convention and other activities which may have a significant effect on the environment, and to ensure early public participation in decision-making. The right to participate includes access to information relevant to decision-making (subject to certain exceptions), the right to submit comments, information, analyses or opinions considered relevant, the requirement that account is taken of the outcome of the public participation, and the requirement to inform the public of the decision. These rights are to apply equallyin respectof thereconsideration orupdating of operating conditions.Article 7 obliges parties to enable the public to participate in the preparation of plans and programmes relating to the environment within a 'transparent and fair framework'. Article 8 requires parties to 'strive to promote' public participation during the preparation of executive regulations and other generally applicable, legally binding rules that may have a significant effect on the environment.

Article 9 governs access to justice. In respect of the right to environmental information, parties must provide access to remedies before a court or other independent and impartial body established by law. In respect of decisions, acts or omissions subject to Article 6, parties must ensure that a member of the public having a sufficient interest or maintaining impairment of a right has access to a review procedure or a court of law or other independent and impartial body established by law to challenge its substantive and procedural legality.

The Convention provides that 'sufficient interest' and 'impairment of a right' are to be determined in accordance with national law and are to be consistent with the objective of giving the public concerned wide access to justice, and that non-governmental organisations meeting certain requirements will be deemed to have a sufficient interest. In respect of decisions, acts or omissions subject to other relevant provisions of the Convention (i.e. Articles 7 and 8) the matter is governed by national law. Further, in accordance with criteria (if any) laid down in national law, members of the public are to have access to administrative or judicial procedures to challenge acts or omissions by private persons and public authorities which contravene national law relating to the environment. All of the procedures are to provide adequate and

The media

Whilst the contribution of the media to international environmental law should not be overstated, there is little doubt that it plays an important informal role in various aspects of international environmental law. The media is able to place a spotlight on particular international legal issues which excite public interest and which can serve to change the public (or private) position of states. The media also provides an opportunity for governments to make statements which may have legal consequences. In the *Nuclear Tests* cases, the International Court of Justice held that it did not have to decide on the Australian and New Zealand claims, after the French Prime Minister made a statement at a press conference that France no longer intended to conduct atmospheric nuclear tests after 1974. Conclusions

The discussion in this chapter confirms that 'relationships among global, regional, national and local organisations – governmental and non-governmental – are an expanding webof international governance that will grow increasingly interconnected in the future'. The discussion indicates that the range of actors involved in the development and application of international environmental law is broad and that the involvement of non-state actors is recognised as legitimate, and is increasingly being encouraged, at both national and international levels. International law has three interrelated challenges: first, to ensure that all states are able to participate in the response of the international community to the growing range of environmental challenges which require an international legal response; Secondly, to strengthen the role of international organisations, and their effectiveness, by rationalising their activities and endowing them with increased functions; and, thirdly, to ensure that the role of non-state actors is properly harnessed, by providing them with sufficient international status to participate effectively in the international legal process and to make the link that governments and international organisations seem to find so difficult: translating global obligations into domestic action and implementation.

These three challenges are closely interconnected, and each will require the further elaboration of rules of participation and procedure; the amendment of the constitutions of most international organisations; and a rethink about the limits of sovereignty. Beginning with the participation of states, it has become ever clearer that most developing states are not able to participate as fully and effectively in the law-making process as they should, because they frequently have insufficient financial and human resources. This is not a comment on their lack of insight, ability, inspiration or commitment; it simply reflects the explosion in the number of centres of international environmental legislation which has occurred in the past twenty years. Without effective participation in the law-making process, there can be little expectation that countries, particularly developing countries, will be able to translate their international commitments into domestic action. International law is increasingly complex and technical, both to negotiate and to apply, and significant effort needs to be made to develop the human capacities, including developing international legal knowledge.

The UNCED process made an important start by ensuring that the funds were available to allow most developing countries at least to attend the negotiations, and it is a testament to their skills that they achieved as much as they did without the resources available to other, more affluent countries.

The process of rationalisation of the activities of international organisations is closely linked to the effective participation of states. The proliferation of organisations, including treaty-based environmental organisations, has brought with it a proliferation of secretariats, most of which would be able to function far more efficiently if they could share experiences and expertise. Rationalisation would allow the functions of the organisations and the secretariats to be more efficiently undertaken, and might then provide them with a stronger basis to engage in the sorts of activities which are clearly needed, for which they are well equipped, and which they should be undertaking: preparing documentation, synthesising national implementation reports, encouraging compliance, conducting verification and sponsoring new agreements. Many international organisations already rely heavily on the efforts and activities of non-state actors, either informally or formally. These actors need to be given a strengthened role, and as implementation and enforcement becomes increasingly important their participation in the process as observers could be supplemented by allowing them to provide information of a general nature or, more specifically, on non-compliance by states with their international obligations. This has now happened under the non-compliance procedure of the 1998 Aarhus Convention. The model provided by the human rights field is a useful one which could be further extended into the environmental field.

INTERNATIONAL LAW-MAKING AND REGULATION

This chapter identifies the sources of international legal obligation in the field of the environment, and the regulatory techniques used to give effect to these obligations. International law is traditionally stated to comprise 'the body of rules which are legally binding on states in their intercourse with each other'. These rules derive their authority, in accordance with Article 38(1) of the Statute of the International Court of Justice (ICJ), from four sources: treaties, international custom, general principles of law, and subsidiary sources (decisions of courts and tribunals and the writings of jurists and groups of jurists). It is to these sources that the ICJ would look in determining whether a particular legally binding principle or rule of international environmental law existed. The list of sources identified in Article 38(1) does not wholly reflect the sources of obligation, broadly understood, which have arisen in international environmental law. A list of sources of international environmental law is more properly reflected in the list proposed by the International Law Commission (ILC) in 1989, which included those identified in Article 38(1) as well as binding decisions of international organisations, and judgments of international courts or tribunals.

Beyond these sources of 'hard law', which establish legally binding obligations, there are also so-called rules of 'soft law', which are not binding *per se* but which in the field of international environmental law have played an important role; they point to the likely future direction of formally binding obligations, by informally establishing acceptable norms of behaviour, and by 'codifying' or possibly reflecting rules of customary law. It is also worth recalling that, although the rules of public international law primarily govern relations between states, it is now widely accepted that states are no longer the only subjects of international law, and that the rules of international law can, and do, impose obligations upon other members of the international community, in particular international organisations and, to a more limited extent, non-state actors, including individuals and corporations.

The traditional sources of international law, together with acts of international organisations and taking account of hard and soft law, have given rise to a large body of international legal obligations which relate, directly or indirectly, to the protection of the environment. These have arisen without a central legislative authority: the international law-making function is decentralised and fragmented. Accordingly, the rules and principles of international environmental law which have developed at the global, regional and bilateral levels comprise a complex network of bilateral and multilateral legal relations. With the exception of some of the general rules and principles identified in chapter 6 below, and the particular rules established by each individual treaty, there exists no 'level playing field' which subjects all states and other members of the international community to identical standards. As treaties increasingly apply differentiated standards, the precise rules applicable to any state will depend on the treaties to which it is a party, and the acts of international organisations and the customary and other rules which are binding upon it. Disparities exist between countries and groups of countries, regions and sub-regions, and within regions and sub-regions.

UNCED attempted to propose a rationalisation of the law-making process by allocating particular functions to the regional and global levels, and by seeking to specify the roles of regional and global international organisations. The effort was not successful, having failed to address the root causes of legal and institutional fragmentation, although it did focus attention on the limitations of the existing international law-making process in the field of environment and development. Three limitations of an institutional or procedural nature dominate:

- the need to improve the mechanisms for identifying critical issues and legislative priorities;
- the need to ensure that all relevant actors participate in the law-making process (in particular, developing countries), including the negotiation, implementation, review and governance of international environmental. agreements; and
- rationalising the law-making process by improving co-ordination between international organisations, including those established by environmental agreements.

These limitations are reflected in most activities relating to treaty-making and acts of international organisations, although they may also be relevant to developing rules of customary law which can be subjected to 'consciously directed adjustment' even if they are not as 'easily and unambiguously manufactured'. Treaties

The main collections of treaties are the *Consolidated Treaty Series* (C. Parry (ed.), 1648-1918); the *League of Nations Treaty Series* (205 volumes, 1920-46); and the *United Nations Treaty Series* (since 1946). Relevant national collections include the *United Kingdom Treaty Series* (since 1892), the *European Communities Treaty Series* (since 1974) and the United States' *Treaties and Other International Agreements Series* (13 volumes, 1776-1949 and annually thereafter). Apart from the collections of international environmental treaties cited in the 'Further reading' section in chapter 1 (especially those edited by Burhenne and by Ruster and Simma), important environmental treaties are regularly reproduced in *International Legal Materials.*

A. D. McNair, *The Law of Treaties* (1961, revised edn); S. Rosenne, *The Law of Treaties* (1970); E. D. Brown, 'The Conventional Law of the Environment', 13 *Natural Resources Journal203 (1973);T.O.* Elias, *The Modern Law of Treaties* (1974); I. M. Sinclair, *The Vienna Convention on the Law of Treaties* (1984, 2nd edn); P. Reuter, *Introduction to the Law of Treaties* (English trans., 1989); T. Gehring, 'International Environmental Regimes: Dynamic SectoralLegal Systems',1 *Yearbook of International Environmental Law* 35 (1990); D. Caron, 'Protection of the Stratospheric Ozone Layer and the Structure of International Environmental Law-making', 14 *Hastings. International and Comparative Law Review* 755 (1991); A. Flournay, 'Legislative Inaction: Asking the Wrong Questions in Protective Environmental Decisionmaking', 15 *Harvard Environmental Law Review* 327 (1991); A. Aust, *Modern Treaty Law and Practice* (2000).

Treaties (also referred to as conventions, accords, agreements and protocols) are the primary source of international legal rights and obligations in relation to environmental protection. A treaty can be adopted bilaterally, regionally or globally, and is defined by the 1969 Vienna Convention on the Law of Treaties (1969 Vienna Convention) as 'an international agreement concluded between states in written form and governed by international law, whether embodied in a single instrument or in two or more related instruments and whatever its particular designation'. At the heart of this definition is the idea that the instrument is intended to create international legal rights and obligations between the parties. Whether an instrument is intended to create such binding obligations will usually be clear from its characteristics and the circumstances in which it was adopted. The 1972 Stockholm Declaration, the 1978 UNEP Draft Principles of Conduct, the 1982 World Charter for Nature, the 1992 Rio Declaration and the 2002 WSSD Plan of Implementation were not intended to create legal rights and obligations; the fact that they are not treaties, however, does not preclude the possibility that they may reflect rules of international law or contribute to the development of such rules, other than by operation of treaty law.

Numerous attempts have been made to classify treaties in one form or another, such as whether they are bilateral or multilateral, or of general or universal effect. These efforts frequently have not shed a great deal of light on the practical consequences of a particular treaty. Certain treaties nevertheless have greater authority than others, and may assume the quality of 'law-making treaties' in the sense that they have been concluded for the purpose of laying down general rules of conduct among a large number of states. Factors which are relevant in assessing the authority of a treaty include: the subject-matter it addresses; the number and representativity of states participating in its negotiation, and signing it or becoming parties; the commitments it establishes; and practice prior to and following its entry into force. In relation to environmental obligations, certain treaties of potentially global application might be considered to have 'law-making' characteristics, particularly where they have attracted a large number of ratifications. These include the 1946 International Whaling Convention, the 1963 Test Ban Treaty, the 1971 Ramsar Convention, the 1972 London Convention, the 1972 World Heritage Convention, MARPOL 73/78, the 1973 CITES, the 1982 UNCLOS, the 1985 Vienna Convention, the 1987 Montreal Protocol (as amended), the 1989 Basel Convention and the 1995 Straddling Stocks Agreement. The 1992 Climate Change Convention and the 1992 Biodiversity Convention can also be considered 'law-making' treaties since their provisions lay down basic rules of general conduct, as may the 1998 Chemicals Convention and the 2001 POPs Convention after they have come into force.

Regional arrangements and treaties can also have a general law-making role for those regions; examples include the UNEP Regional Seas Conventions, the 1992 OSPAR Convention, the 1959 Antarctic Treaty and the rules of EC environmental law.

The number of treaties relating to the environment has increased dramatically in the past two decades. UNEP's 1989 Register of Environmental Agreements listed a total of 139 treaties. The emergence and rapid recent development of international environmental law is evidenced by the number of treaties adopted in each decade of this century: according to the UNEP Register, the number of such treaties was six by 1950, eighteen in the 1950s and twenty-six in the 1960s. The 1970s saw a jump, following the Stockholm Conference, to forty-seven treaties, and a further forty-one treaties in the 1980s. The table of treaties in this book reflects a similar rate of increase during the 1990s and into the opening years of the twenty-first century.

To the UNEP Register list of treaties must be added those treaties which were not adopted primarily to address environmental issues but which nevertheless establish environmental obligations. Primary examples include agreements relating to trade and other international economic matters, such as the GATT/WTO, regional free trade agreements, the EC Treaty, the agreements establishing the World Bank and the regional multilateral development banks, and the multilateral development assistance agreements such as the 1989 Lome´ Convention.

To this list might now also be added bilateral and other agreements relating to the protection of foreign investments. Additionally, there also exists a huge body of bilateral environmental agreements which have contributed significantly to the development of international environmental law. More than 2,000 such treaties have apparently been adopted since the mid-eighteenth century.

Environmental treaties

Environmental treaties share the same general characteristics as other treaties, and are subject to the general rules reflected in the 1969 Vienna Convention and customary law. Nevertheless, certain special features exist, even if a standard format has not yet emerged. When regulating regional or global environmental problems, a framework treaty is frequently adopted. This sets out general obligations, creates the basic institutional arrangements, and provides procedures for the adoption of detailed obligations in a subsequent protocol. Frequently, a framework agreement or protocol will have one or more annexes or appendices, which include scientific, technical or administrative provisions (such as dispute settlement or information exchange), but which might also list the species, substances or activities which are regulated, or the parties to which one or more substantive obligations will apply. This three-tiered approach (framework agreement, protocol, annex/appendices) introduces flexibility by allowing legal amendments or other changes in accordance with political, scientific or economic developments.

The treaty-making process

The adoption and entry into force of an environmental treaty is preceded by a series of steps which will frequently take place over a lengthy period of time. Once two or more states have identified an environmental issue as requiring international legislation, they will identify the forum or institution to serve as a legislative forum. If the subject is already covered by a framework treaty, the new legal obligation could be developed in a protocol or by amendments to an existing protocol; in such cases, the appropriate forum will be the conference of the parties or equivalent institution established by the framework agreement. If the international legislation can appropriately be dealt with by an international act other than a treaty, it may be addressed simply by a binding decision, or resolution, or other act of an international organisation or the conference of the parties of an environmental treaty. If a new treaty is required, the states involved will need to determine which organisation shall conduct the negotiation of the treaty. This decision can be controversial. Thus, although the 1992 Biodiversity Convention was negotiated under the auspices of UNEP, developing countries insisted thatthe UN General Assembly, rather than UNEP, be responsible for the Climate Change Convention. Thiswas duetothe view that developing countries were better represented in the UN General Assembly than at UNEP and better able to participate in negotiations. Similar considerations lay behind the failure of the UN General Assembly in December 1992 to agree whether the UN Commission on Sustainable Development should meet in Geneva (where many developing countries are not represented) or New York (where all developing countries are represented), or in both places.

Once the forum for negotiations is agreed, that body will establish a negotiating process. This could be anything from an informal *ad hoc* group of governmental experts (such as was established by the UNEP Governing Council for what became the 1985 Vienna Ozone Convention), to a formal institutional structure (such as the Intergovernmental Negotiating Committee for a Framework Convention on Climate Change (INC/FCCC), established by UN General Assembly Resolution 44/212). Similar arrangements apply in the negotiation of protocols under framework agreements. An alternative approach is for an international organisation to establish a subsidiary body to 'prepare' a text for consideration and adoption by an Intergovernmental Diplomatic Conference (such as the establishment by the Governing Body of the IAEA of a Standing Committee on Nuclear Liability to prepare draft amendments to the 1963 Vienna Convention).

Negotiations may be open-ended in time or established for a limited period. Examples of the former include the negotiations of the 1985 Vienna Convention (which took place over five years) and the 1982 UN Convention on the Law of the Sea (UNCLOS) (which took nearly twenty years). On the other hand, formal negotiations of the 1992 Climate Change Convention and the 1992 Biodiversity Convention were concluded in just fifteen months, the negotiators having been asked to prepare a text in time for signature at UNCED. Once the draft text has been negotiated, it will be adopted and opened for signature. It will then enter into force in accordance with its provisions on entry into force. The 1969 Vienna Convention and legal issues relating to treaties

The international law of treaties is governed by customary law, the 1969 Vienna Convention and the 1986 Vienna Convention. The 1969 Vienna Convention, large parts of which reflect rules of customary international law, provides the basis for considering many of the legal issues which arise in relation to treaties. With respect to 'environmental' treaties, certain legal issues merit particular attention: these include: the effect of treaties on third parties; the proper approach to interpreting the terms of a treaty; the consequences of conflict between two or more treaties; the legal effect of reservations and interpretative declarations; and the legal effect, if any, of unratified treaties. Each of these issues raises complex legal points, the resolution of which will always turn on the particular facts of a matter. Accordingly, the discussion which follows should be considered as introductory.

Interpretation

The techniques used to interpret treaties and other international acts can have important practical consequences. A restrictive approach to interpretation will limit the scope and effect of a rule, whereas a broad approach may identify an obligation where none was thought to exist. Most environmental treaties include definitions of some of the key words or phrases used in the treaty, but invariably there will be words for which states could not reach an agreed definition or for which no definition was thought necessary at the time of ne-gotiation. Different treaties may define the same word or words differently.The rules governing the interpretation of treaties are set out in Articles 31 and 32 of the 1969 Vienna Convention. Article 31 establishes the primary rule that a treaty is to be interpreted 'in good faith in accordance with the ordinary meaning to be given to the terms of the treaty in their context and in the light of its object and purpose'. From this general approach certain consequences follow.

A person seeking to rely on a special meaning for the terms of a treaty, as opposed to the ordinary meaning, will have to prove that special meaning. The context of a treaty includes the whole of its text, the preamble, annexes and, in the case of at least two environmental treaties, footnotes. Any agreement made between all the parties in connection with the conclusion of the treaty and any instrument made by one or more parties relating to the conclusion of the treaty and accepted by the other parties as such are included in understanding the treaty's context. Examples of the latter include a protocol adopted after the conclusion of a framework treaty. In relation to environmental treaties, this happens frequently and is usually specifically provided for in the treaty, and a protocol may incorporate certain parts of a framework treaty. Finally, apart from the context, Article 31(3) of the 1969 Vienna Convention provides that account is also to be taken of certain factors which are extrinsic to the treaty: subsequent agreement between the parties regarding the interpretation or application of the treaty; subsequent practice in application of the treaty which establishes the agreement of the parties regarding its interpretation; and any relevant rules of international law applicable in the relations between the parties.

A notable development in recent years has been the willingness of international courts charged with the interpretation and application of an international agreement to have regard to rules of international environmental law arising outside the treaty which is being interpreted. Related to this approach is the recognition by the ICJ that it is appropriate, in interpreting and applying environmental norms, including those reflected in treaties, to have regard to new norms and standards which may have been developed in the period after a treaty has been adopted:

Such new norms have to be taken into consideration, and such new standards given proper weight, not only when States contemplate new activities but also when continuing with activities begun in the past.

If the application of the approach laid down by Article 31 produces a result which is not clear or which is ambiguous, Article 32 allows recourse to be had to supplementary means of interpretation, which may also be used to confirm a meaning already established. The principal supplementary means are the *travaux pr´eparatoires* of a treaty, including the minutes of formal negotiations, reports of sessions, and prior drafts of a text. Other supplementary means include the circumstances of a treaty's conclusion, and the application of certain principles of interpretation, such as *in dubio mitius*, and *expressio unius est exclusio alterius*. The reliance on supplementary means of interpretation at a later date means that states will ensure during the negotiation of a text that they are alert to the possible consequences of adding or removing language, or of opposing or failing to oppose language. In the negotiation of recent instruments, such as the Climate Change Convention and the Biodiversity Convention, the number of states involved was so large that it proved impossible to keep detailed formal records of all aspects of proceedings, although informal records may be kept. This will make recourse to *travaux pr´eparatoires* less feasible.

In practice, international bodies which are required to interpret and apply the language of a treaty apply widely differing approaches. One example of a 'restrictive' approach to treaty interpretation is the GATT Panel decision in the yellow-fin tuna dispute between Mexico and the United States, where the Panel interpreted Article XX(b) and (g) of the GATT to exclude the possibility of allowing an importer to take into account the environmental effects of a process leading to a product's final state when considering whether a product's import could be prohibited. An example of a more 'expansive' approach to treaty interpretation is the holding by the European Court of Justice (ECJ) that environmental protection was one of the EU's 'essential objectives', even in the absence of any express reference to environmental protection in the original Treaty of Rome. Entry into force Treaties provide expressly for the circumstances in which they will enter into force. This is usually upon ratification by a certain number of states. In the field of environmental law, global treaties have tended to require a low number of ratifications for entry into force. In some instances, entry into force depends upon the participation of certain states or states representing a certain percentage of a particular activity. Examples include the 1971 Oil Pollution Fund Convention (entry into force upon ratification by eight states importing 750 million tons of contributing oil), the 1987 Montreal Protocol (entry into force upon eleven ratifications representing at least two-thirds of the 1986 estimated global consumption of substances controlled by the Montreal Protocol) and the 1997 Kyoto Protocol (entry into force upon ratification by fifty-five states, incorporating developed states accounting for 55 per cent of total carbon dioxide emissions from developed states as at 1990).

Establishing a link between entry into force and the participation of particular states or all states which negotiated the agreement is designed to ensure the fullest participation of key states. However, it is liable to make entry into force hostage to the decision of just one or two states, as has happened with the 1984 Protocols to the Oil Fund Convention and the Civil Liability Convention. Other environmental agreements which have not entered into force because of the participation requirements include the 1985 ASEAN Agreement and the 1988 CRAMRA. Concerns about delay and the difficulty of agreeing applicable criteria prevented the participation of certain states or categories of states from being required in the Climate Change Convention. No agreement could be reached on which greenhouse gases or their proportions should establish a threshold for entry into force.

As environmental agreements increasingly affect national economic interests, and where a large number of states have been involved in the negotiation process, the number of states required to ratify to bring a treaty into force has increased. The Biodiversity Convention and the Climate Change Convention respectively require the ratification of thirty and fifty states. UNCLOS, which required sixty ratifications, only entered into force twelve years after its conclusion. Treaties which have not entered into force may nevertheless have certain legal consequences. Under the 1969 Vienna Convention, signatory states must refrain from acts which would defeat the objects and purposes of the treaty they have signed (unless they have indicated an intention not to become a party), and, partly with this in mind, arrangements have been made to allow for the provisional application of a treaty or part of a treaty, prior to its entry into force. Moreover, a treaty which has not yet entered into force may also contribute to the development of customary international law, or reflect in clearer terms pre-existing customary international law.

Reservations and interpretative declarations

Most recent international environmental agreements do not allow reserva-tions. A few are silent on the matter, and some permit reservations only in strict accordance with specific provisions of the treaty. The general tendency to prohibit the use of reservations is intended to avoid a proliferation of bilateral legal relations. There are two principal reasons for this in the environmental field. First, many environmental treaties are framework agreements providing general structures and guidelines, rather than specific commitments with implications for a particular activity or practice. Secondly, where a treaty does deal with particularly sensitive or controversial matters, especially where important economic interests are involved, the negotiated text will often represent a series of delicate compromises which would be undermined by allowing one or more states to opt out of certain provisions. Flexibility is intended to be built into the text itself. Reservations or other forms of opt-out are usually permitted in respect of 'secondary legislation', such as an act adopted by the institutions established under an environmental agreement. Examples include the reservations entered by the former Soviet Union, Norway, Iceland and Japan to the 1983 International Whaling Convention moratorium on commercial whaling, and the reservation originally entered by the United Kingdom to the decision at CITES to uplist the African elephant from Appendix II to Appendix I and exclude for a limited period the operation of the decision to the territory of Hong Kong. Where reservations are either expressly allowed or not prohibited, either for treaties or acts of institutions adopted under treaties, customary international law and the 1969 Vienna Convention provide certain guidance on the conditions in which they will be permitted. Parties are free to object to reservations which have been entered, which usually happens when the reservation is considered to be incompatible with the objects and purposes of the treaty or another rule of international law.

The trend towards limiting the permissibility of reservations has not prevented states, when signing or ratifying environmental treaties, from entering statements or 'interpretative declarations' explaining an understanding of a particular provision. Recent examples include: the declaration by the then Federal Republic of Germany to the 1989 Basel Convention; the declaration entered by four small island states (Fiji, Kiribati, Nauru and Tuvalu) to the 1992 Climate Change Convention; and the declaration entered by the United Kingdom in respect of the 1992 Biodiversity Convention. The legal effect of such interpretative declarations remains an open question for which there are no settled general rules. On the other hand, some treaties expressly require declarations to be entered in respect of procedural matters or a choice among substantive options available under a treaty, or allow generally for declarations or statements. The majority are silent as to declarations.

Relations between international agreements

The proliferation of environmental treaties has raised the possibility of overlap or conflict between two or more treaties. This issue is particularly important for the relationship between the growing number of environmental treaties which prohibit trade in certain goods and the WTO, which seeks to restrict non-tariff barriers to trade, including national or, possibly, internationally agreed environmental protection measures. Potential conflict between environmental agreements also exists where regional and global agreements have been adopted for the same subject-matter, such as those for the protection of the marine environment (which might adopt different rules on the dumping of wastes)and the international trade in waste (which might regulate rather than prohibit such trade). The relationship between WTO rules and the 1987 Montreal Protocol illustrates the potential for conflict. Parties to the 1987 Montreal Protocol are under an obligation to prohibit the import of controlled substances from any state not party to the Protocol, a requirement which may conflict with earlier GATT obligations, if both the countries concerned were parties to the GATT. The 1990 amendments to the Protocol may be problematic, since they ban imports from third parties of products *containing* controlled substances (such as refrig-erators). In the event that a party to the Montreal Protocol were to ban the import of refrigerators containing CFCs from a third state, where both states were party to the GATT, which obligation would prevail?

Article 30 of the 1969 Vienna Convention sets forth rules governing the situation where states are parties to treaties relating to the same subject-matter (in this case, trade). Article 30(2) provides that, when a treaty specifies that it is subject to, or not incompatible with, an earlier or later treaty, then the provisions of the other treaty will prevail. Under Article 30(3), if all the parties to the earlier treaty are also parties to the later treaty, and the earlier treaty continues in force, then only those provisions of the earlier treaty which are compatible with the later treaty will apply. Finally, Article 30(4) governs the likely situations when the parties to the later treaty do not include all the parties to the earlier treaty. It provides that (a) as between states party to both treaties the same rule applies as in Article 30(3); and (b) as between a state party to both treaties and a state party to only one of the treaties, the treaty to which both states are parties governs their mutual rights and obligations.

The application of Article 30(4) would appear to lead to the following result: in the event of a conflict between the GATT (signed in 1947) (assuming that its obligations are to be considered treaty obligations) and the 1987 Montreal Protocol, where two states are parties to the GATT but only one state is a party to the Montreal Protocol, then the provisions of the GATT would appear to prevail, without taking into account any permissible exceptions under the GATT. However, if both states are parties to both instruments, then the later in time (the Montreal Protocol) will prevail. With the growing number of environmental agreements touching upon the same subject matter, the question has also arisen as to the conditions under which a party is entitled to invoke the dispute settlement provisions under one treaty as opposed to another. This may be a particularly complex issue where one treaty sets forth general rules and another more specialised rules, as is the case with the 1982 UNCLOS and more specific marine pollution or fisheries conservation agreements. The issue arose in the *Southern Bluefin Tuna* cases, which Australia and New Zealand chose to litigate under the 1982 UNCLOS rather than the (regional) 1993 Convention on the Conservation of Southern-Bluefin Tuna. Japan argued that the UNCLOS Annex VII arbitral tribunal did not have jurisdiction, on the grounds *inter alia* that the 1993 Convention governed the dispute and Article 16 of that Convention (on dispute settlement) excluded the application of the procedures on dispute settlement under Part XV of UNCLOS. By four votes to one, the UNCLOS arbitral tribunal accepted the argument: although Article 16 of the 1993 Convention did not expressly exclude any further procedure under Part XV of UNCLOS, the 'intent of Article 16 [was] to remove proceedings under that Article from the reach of the compulsory procedures of section 2 of Part XV of UNCLOS'.The award declining jurisdiction has not been received with broad approval.It should not be assumed that it will be followed, particularly having regard to the approach taken by the International Tribunal for the Law of the Sea (ITLOS) the following year in the provisional measures phase of the *MOX* case, which raised a related, but distinguishable, issue. The ITLOS rejected an argument by the United Kingdom to the effect that ITLOS did not have jurisdiction since the dispute was centred upon other conventions (and EC law) with their own dispute provisions, noting that: even if the OSPAR Convention, the EC Treaty and the Euratom Treaty contain rights or obligations similar to or identical with the rights or obligations set out in the Convention, the rights and obligations under those agreements have a separate existence from those under the Convention . . . the application of international law rules on interpretation of treaties to identical or similar provisions of different treaties may not yield the same results, having regard to, *inter alia*, differences in the respective contexts, objects and purposes, subsequent practice of parties and *travaux preparatoires.*

The approach maybe of particular importance for the interpretation and application of international environmental agreements, which often contain the same or similar language imposing substantive obligations, but which may have been negotiated or subsequently applied in a particular context.

Amendment

The need for expedited amendment processes for environmental agreements (to take into account changes of a scientific, economic or political nature) has led to the adoption of innovative approaches. Almost all environmental treaties make express provision for a formal amendment process by the adoption of a further treaty between the parties. Informal amendment may also take place orally or by tacit agreement of the parties, including decisions or acts of organs established under a treaty which may amount to a *de facto* amendment.

The provisions of the 1985 Vienna Convention and the 1987 Montreal Protocol illustrate new techniques, which have been subsequently followed. The 1985 Vienna Convention is a framework treaty with two annexes and provision for protocols. To date, the only protocol is the 1987 Montreal Protocol, which was amended and adjusted in 1990, 1992, 1997 and 1999. The 1985 Vienna Convention establishes the rules for its own amendment as well as that of any protocols: as a last resort, amendments to the 1985 Vienna Convention may be adopted by a 'three-fourths majority vote of the parties present and voting' at a meeting of the conference of the parties; amendments to protocols require only a 'two-thirds majority of the parties to that protocol present and voting' at a meeting of the parties to the protocol. The 1987 Montreal Protocol also provides an alternative to formal amendment by the adoption of 'adjustments and reductions' by the parties; adjustment may be made to the ozone-depleting potential of controlled substances identified in Annexes to the Protocol, as well as production or consumption levels of controlled substances. As a last resort, adjustments and reductions are adopted by a two-thirds majority of the parties present and voting which represent at least 50 per cent of the total consumption of the controlled substances, and these are binding on all parties without the possibility of objection. The Protocol also allows the parties to add or remove any substances from any Annex to the Protocol and decide on the mechanism, scope and timing of the control measures that should apply to such substances. Such decisions become effective provided they have been accepted by a two-thirds majority of the parties present and voting, without specifying the manner of acceptance or the effect of any objection of a party outside the two-thirds majority. Adjustments under Article 9 and decisions under Article 10 are made on the basis of assessments under Article 6. This procedure has been used to adopt adjustments at the second and fourth meetings of the parties to the Protocol. Amendments to the Annexes to the 1985

Vienna Convention or the 1987 Montreal Protocol are adopted in the same way as amendments to the Convention or Protocol. However, the procedure for entry into force of an Annex amendment differs: it requires a party which objects to such an amendment to opt out, by notifying the depositary within six months of its adoption, failing which it will bind any state which has not objected.

OTHER INTERNATIONAL ACTS

Other international acts include those adopted by international organisations (which may be binding or non-binding), and by states in the form of non-binding declarations or Action Plans. Non-binding acts are sometimes referred to as 'soft law'. Although not legally binding, they may contribute to the development of customary law or lead to the adoption of binding obligations by treaty or an act of an international organisation.

Acts of international organisations

Acts of international organisations, sometimes referred to as secondary legislation, provide an important source of international law: they may be legally binding*per se,* ortheymayamendtreaty obligations,or theymayauthoritatively interpret treaty obligations. Since binding acts of international organisations derive their legal authority from the treaty on which they were based, they can be considered as part of treaty law.

Many far-reachingdecisions affecting the useof natural resources resultfrom acts of international organisations. Examples include: the 1983 decision of the IWC to adopt a moratorium on commercial whaling; the 1985 resolution of the consultative meetingof theparties to the 1972 LondonConventionadopting a moratorium on the dumping of radioactive waste at sea; the 1989 decision by the CITES conference of the parties to ban the international trade in African elephant products; and the 1991 Security Council resolution reaffirming the liability of Iraq for the environmental damage caused by its unlawful invasion of Kuwait.

The legal effect of an act of an international organisation depends upon the treaty basis of the organisation, as the following examples illustrate. Usually, the treaty will specify the intended legal consequences. Under Article 25 of the UN Charter, UN General Assembly resolutions are 'only recommendatory', whereas resolutions of the Security Council are binding 'on all states'; Regulations, Directives and Decisions of the EU (the EC, ECSC and Euratom) are legally binding on member states and can create rights and obligations which are directly enforceable in the national legal systems of the member states.Acts of organisations established by environmental treaties may be binding or non-binding. Such institutions often have a choice. Thus, the IWC can adopt regulations which are 'effective' for parties not presenting an objection, or it can adopt recommendations which are not legally binding. The consultative meetings of the parties to the 1972 London Convention can amend the Annexes to the Convention, which enter into force either upon notification by a party or after a stated period of time, unless a party declares that it is not able to accept an amendment. The CITES conference of the parties adopts amendments to Appendices I and II to the Convention which 'enter into force' for all parties except those making a reservation. And the meeting of the parties to the 1987 Montreal Protocol may adopt amendments and adjustments which can bind even parties not accepting them. In each case, a majority of the parties to a treaty may adopt binding acts, although the minority is usually free to opt out. In other cases, an international organisation may adopt an act (which might be called a resolution, recommendation or decision), without a clear provision in the treaty establishing the legal consequences of that act. The legal effect of resolutions adopted under the 1972 London Convention is less clear (such as the resolution on the dumping of radioactive wastes at sea adopted by the ninth consultative meeting which agreed to a 'suspension of all dumping at sea of radioactive wastes and other radioactive matter'). Such resolutions, addressing substantive matters, are not binding *per se*, although they may contribute to the development of customary international law, or may set forth an authoritative interpretation of the international agreement under which it was adopted. Examples of such acts include the resolutions adopted by the Governing Council of UNEP which adopt or endorse principles, guidelines or recommended practices addressed to states and other members of the international community. The resolution or act could also bind those states supporting it through the operation of some general principle of law, such as the principle of estoppel. Where the act is an internal act of the organisation (adopting a budget or procedural rules, or establishing a subsidiary organ), the resolution may bind all members of the organisation as a matter of the internal law of the organisation.

A further issue is the legal effect, if any, of an act of one international organisation upon another, to the extent that it is arguable that there exists a 'common law of international organisations'. This would allow a measure, or interpretative act, adopted by one international organisation, to be relied upon by or have consequences for, another. The proliferation of international organisations addressing environmental issues increases the need for legal consistency and certainty. In practice, organisations do take account of each other's activities, in relation to both procedural and substantive matters, and precedents may be followed on an informal basis. Examples include: the emerging rules and practices governing the participation of non-state actors in the activities of international organisations; the definition of 'best available technology' adopted by the meeting of the parties to the 1974 Paris LBS Convention; and the definition of the 'precautionary principle' adopted by the parties to the 1976 Barcelona Convention or the 1974 Paris LBS Convention. Conference declarations and other acts Many intergovernmental conferences are convened every year to address environmental issuesandissueslinking environmentand development. Manyadopt declarations, statements orother non-binding acts, which may contribute to the development of international environmental law even if they are not binding as treaties or as formal acts of international organisations. The most important international conferences have been the 1949 UNCCUR, the 1972 Stockholm Conference, the 1992 UNCED and the 2002 WSSD. Each adopted non-binding acts, of which the Stockholm Declaration, the Rio Declaration and Agenda 21 include important elements which now reflect, or are contributing to the development of, customary international law. They continue to provide a significant influence on the development of new treaties and acts of international organisations.

Other conferences have addressed specific, or sectoral, issues. These too can contribute to the development of binding international rules over time. Examples of declarations which have influenced international legislation include the 1990 Ministerial Declaration of the Second World Climate Conference, the Declaration adopted by the 1990 UNECE Bergen Conference on Sustainable Development, and regional conferences on environment and development. These contributed to the consensus at UNCED and the negotiations of the Climate Change and Biodiversity Conventions. The 1992 Rio Declaration may be the single most significant such declaration, in terms of its contribution to the development of international environmental rules and jurisprudence. Other conference declarations have led to acts of international organisations which are then followed by the adoption of a new treaty rule incorporating in binding terms the original conference act or objective. One such example is the 1990 Third Ministerial Declaration on the North Sea, elements of which were incorporated into resolutions of the Commissions established under the 1972 Oslo and 1974 Paris Conventions, and are now reflected in the 1992 OSPAR Convention. A more recent example is the 1998 Sintra Ministerial Declaration on the prevention of pollution of the north-east Atlantic by radioactive substances.

Another act frequently adopted by international conferences (or by international organisations) is the 'Action Plan', which also frequently forms the basis or context for the subsequent adoption of treaty rules. Examples include: the Recommendations adopted by the 1972 Stockholm Conference; the various Regional Action Plans adopted under the UNEP Regional Seas Programme; Agenda 21; and the WSSD Plan of Implementation. Action Plans have also been adopted on a range of sectoral issues, such as water resources, drought and desertification, national parks, and the conservation of biodiversity.

CUSTOMARY INTERNATIONAL LAW

A. D'Amato, *The Concept of Custom in International Law* (1971); H. W. A. Thirlway, *International Customary Law and Codification* (1972); M. Akehurst, 'Custom as a Source of International Law', 47 BYIL 1 (1974–5); M. E. Villiger, *Customary International Law and Treaties* (1985); M. Mendelson, 'The Formation of Customary International Law', 272 RdC 155 (1998); International Law Association, *London Statement of Principles Relating to the Formation of General Customary International Law* (2000); I. Brownlie, 'A Survey of International Customary Rules of Environmental Protection', 13 *Natural Resources Journal* 179 (1973); P. M. Dupuy, 'Overview of Existing Customary Legal Regime Regarding International Pollution', in D. Magraw (ed.), *International Law and Pollution* (1991); D. Bodansky, 'Customary (and Not So Customary) International Environmental Law', 3 *Indiana Journal of Global Legal Studies* 105 (1995).

Customary law rules have played a secondary role in international environmental law, although they can establish binding obligations for states and other members of the international community and may be relied upon in the codification of obligations in treaties and other binding acts. The significance of custom lies in the fact that it creates obligations for all states (or all states within a particular region) except those which have persistently objected to a practice and its legal consequences. Moreover, a customary rule may exist alongside a conventional rule, can inform the content and effect of a conventional rule, and can give rise to a distinct cause of action for dispute settlement purposes. However, the process of developing rules of customary law cannot really be considered as part of a formal legislative process, and the existence of a customary rule may be difficult to prove. Proving customary international law requires evidence of consistent state practice, which practice will only rarely provide clear guidance as to the precise context or scope of any particular rule. Nevertheless, 'customary law can be somewhat shaped and directed, because the practices of states can be consciously affected by various international ac-tions', including the non-binding acts of international organisations and the intergovernmental statements and declarations discussed above. Article 38(1)(b) of the Statute of the International Court of Justice identifies the two elements of customary international law: state practice and *opinio juris*.

State practice

State practice is notoriously difficult to prove, and little empirical research has been carried out on state practice relating to international environmental obligations. State practice can be discerned from several sources, including: ratification of treaties; participation in treaty negotiations and other international meetings; national legislation; the decisions of national courts; votes and other acts in the UN General Assembly and other international organisations; statements by ministers and other governmental and diplomatic representatives; formal diplomatic notes; and legal opinions by government lawyers.Preparatory materials to these sources can also provide useful evidence of state practice. Other sources include the pleadings of states before national and international courts and tribunals, parliamentary debates, collections of diplomatic materials and the records and *travaux pr´eparatoires* of international conferences and treaty negotiations. Useful pleadings include those relating to the *Nuclear Tests* cases and the *Case Concerning Certain Phosphate Lands in Nauru*.

The pleadings in New Zealand's resumed *Nuclear Tests* case (1995), the ICJ's Advisory Opinion on the legality of the use of nuclear weapons and the *Gabcikovo-Nagymaros Project* case are also likely to repay careful consideration. It is important to bear in mind that the failure of a state to act can also provide evidence of state practice: mutual toleration of certain levels of pollution, or of activities which cause environmental degradation, can provide evidence that states accept such levels and activities as being compatible with international law.

For state practice to contribute to the development of a rule of law, the practice must be general, although this does not mean that it requires the participation of all states across the globe or in a particular region. The ICJ has stated that: it might bethat,evenwithout the passage of any considerable periodof time, a very widespread and representative participation in the convention might suffice of itself, provided it included states whose interests were specifically affected.

More recently, the ICJ deemed it sufficient that the conduct of states should, in general, be consistent with such rules, and that instances of state conduct inconsistent with a given rule should generally have been treated as breaches of that rule, not as indications of the recognition of a new rule.

In both cases, the ICJ was concerned with customary law arising in the context of treaty rules. The relationship between treaty and custom is close, often based upon elements of mutual interdependence. A treaty might codify or further develop a rule of customary law, as was the case in the 1982 UNCLOS. Alternatively, the conclusion and implementation of a treaty may reflect the existence of a rule of customary law. In the *North Sea Continental Shelf* cases, the ICJ found that state practice since the conclusion of the 1958 Geneva Convention on the Continental Shelf, including signature and ratification of the convention, could create a rule of customary law.

In the *Military and Paramilitary Activities* case, the ICJ again considered the relationship between treaties and custom, finding that multilateral conventions 'may have an important role to play in recording and defining rules deriving from custom. or indeed in developing them'. The frequent reference to, and incorporation of, Principle 21 of the Stockholm Declaration in the text of treaties is an example of treaties contributing to development of custom. In 1996, the

ICJ confirmed the customary status of the norm reflected in Principle 21,but without addressing the extent or uniformity of state practice. It appears to have taken a similarly flexible approach the following year, in its judgment in the *Gabcikovo-Nagymaros* case, where it cited with approval the principle of 'equitable utilisation' referred to in Article 5(2) of the 1997 Watercourses Convention. This suggests that in the environmental field the ICJ may well be conscious of the 'Herculean task' of deducing rules of customary international law directly from state practice, and will divine the existence of such rules by more flexible and pragmatic means.

Opinio juris

The second element of customary law, *opinio juris sive necessitatis*, requires evidence that a state has acted in a particular way because it believes that it is required to do so by law. The ICJ in the *North Sea Continental Shelf* cases identified the content and role of *opinio juris*:

> Not only must the acts concerned amount to a settled practice, but they must also be such, or be carried out in such a way, as to be evidence of a belief that this practice is rendered obligatory by the existence of a rule of law requiring it. The need for such a belief, i.e. the existence of a subjective element, is implicit in the very notion of the *opinio juris sive necessitatis*. The states concerned must therefore feel that they are conforming to what amounts to a legal obligation. The frequency, or even habitual character of the acts is not in itself enough. There are many intentional acts, e.g. in the field of ceremonial and protocol, which are performed almost invariably, but which are motivated only by considerations of courtesy, convenience or tradition, and not by any sense of legal duty.

Proving the existence of *opinio juris* will always be a difficult task, since it requires consideration of the motives underlying state activity. It has been suggested that it can be found from a number of sources, including: expressions of beliefs regarding acts of international organisations and other international meetings; statements made by representatives of states; and the conclusion of treaties. Given the difficulties of proving *opinio juris*, there is a certain attraction in the view of Sir HerschLauterpacht, who proposedthat the accurate principle consists in 'regarding all uniform conduct of Governments (or, in appropriate cases, abstention therefrom) as evidencing the *opinio necessitatis juris* except when it is shown that the conduct in question was not accompanied by any such intention'. Such an approach, which shifts the burden of proof but which is not universally shared, would make the acceptance of principles and rules set out in treaties more likely to contribute to the development of custom.

Treaties and custom

State practice in treaty-making and in accordance with obligations under treaties can contribute to the development of customary law. Moreover, as the ICJ recognised in the *Military and Paramilitary Activities* case, customary rules may emerge which are identical to those of treaty law, and which exist simultaneously with treaty obligations. In the *North Sea Continental Shelf* cases, the ICJ had to decide whether the principle of equidistance for delimitation of the continental shelf found in Article 6 of the 1958 Convention on the Continental Shelf constituted a rule of customary international law. The ICJ found that it was necessary to examine the status of a principle as it stood when a treaty was drawn up, as it resulted from the effect of the treaty, and in the light of state practice subsequent to the treaty. The ICJ held that at the time of its conclusion the principle set out in Article 6 of the 1958 Convention was a treaty rule and not regarded as *lege lata* or as an emerging rule of customary international law. The ICJ then considered whether the principle found in Article 6 had passed into the general *corpus* of international law, and was accepted as such by *opinio juris*, so as to be binding even for countries which were not parties to the Convention: such a process was 'a perfectly possible one which does from time to time occur, although it could not be a result lightly regarded as having been attained'. The ICJ identified the conditions to be fulfilled for a new rule of customary international law to be formed as a result of a treaty:

It would in the first place be necessary that the provision concerned should, at all events potentially, be of a fundamentally norm-creating character such as could be regarded as forming the basis of a general rule . . . With respect to the other elements usually regarded as necessary before a conventional rule can be considered to have become a general rule of international law, it might be that, even without the passage of any considerable period of time, a very widespread and representative participation in the convention might suffice of itself, provided it included that of states whose interests were specially affected.

In this case, the number of ratifications was respectable but insufficient. As to the time element:

> [a]lthough the passage of only a short period of time is not necessarily, or of itself, a bar to the formation of a new rule of customary international law on the basis of what was originally a purely conventional rule, an indispensable requirement would be that within the period in question, short though it might be, state practice, including that of states whose interests are specially affected, should have been both extensive and virtually uniform in the sense of the provision invoked; and should moreover have occurred in such a way as to show a general recognition that a rule of law or legal obligation is involved.

The ICJ held on the facts of the case that state practice was insufficient to transform the treaty obligation under Article 6 of the 1958 Convention into a customary obligation.

However, it should not be assumed that the mere fact that a large number of states are party to a treaty establishes a customary norm for all. For example, the ICJ declined to indicate that the rule prohibiting widespread and significant environmental harm in armed conflict reflected a customary rule. For environmental treaties, provisions of a fundamentally norm-creating character which are capable of being considered as rules of customary law include those of a substantive nature, as well as principles which inform and guide decision-making. Examples of substantive obligations reflected in many treaties include: Principle 21 of the Stockholm Declaration; the obligation to co-operate on environmental problems associated with shared natural resources the obligation to adopt general measures to protect the marine environment from significant damage; and the obligation to take measures to ensure the conservation of, and prevention of harm to, endangered species of flora and fauna.

More specific examples of treaty rules which can be considered as having a 'fundamentally norm-creating character' arguably include: the obligation to use a shared international watercourse in an 'equitable and reasonable' manner; the obligation not to dump high-level radioactive waste in the marine environment; the obligation not to engage in commercial whaling; and the general obligation of developed states to limit emissions of gases such as sulphur dioxide. Guiding principles which may, through treaty practice, reflect existing or emerging norms of customary law might include the polluter-pays principle, the principle of precautionary action, and the principle of common but differentiated responsibilities of developed and developing countries. Procedural obligations which may be binding under customary law, at least within certain regions, include consultation, the provision of information on the environment and the obligation to carry out an environmental impact assessment for activities likely to cause significant environmental damage.

Persistent objector

Since a rule of customary law may develop without the express or active support of all states in the international community, the silence or failure of a state to act will not necessarily prevent such a rule from becoming binding upon it, as is clear from the judgments of the ICJ in the *North Sea Continental Shelf* cases. However, a state can avoid being bound by a rule if it persistently objects to that rule. This was one of the issues in the *Anglo-Norwegian Fisheries* case, where the United Kingdom argued the unlawfulness of the Norwegian practice of drawing straight base-lines across the mouths of bays to measure the width of the territorial sea, and where both states accepted the existence of the 'persistent objector' principle. An example of persistent objection in the environmental field is provided by the clear and consistent objection of the United States to the view that the 'right to development' exists as a legal rule. Another example may perhaps be seen in the ICJ's 1996 opinion that environmental obligations under the 1977 Geneva

Protocol I did not, at least at that time, reflect customary law in view of the unwillingness of certain states to recognise the application of the Protocol to nuclear weapons. Closely related to the principle of the persistent objector is the operation of acquiescence, according to which the failure of a state to protest against the practice of other states over time will operate to limit or prevent a state from subsequently protesting against the fact that the practice is permitted as a matter of international law. The ICJ considered the principle of acquiescence in the *Anglo-Norwegian Fisheries* case, holding that the 'notoriety of the facts, the general toleration of the international community, Great Britain's position in the North Sea, her own interest in the question, and her prolonged abstention would in any case warrant Norway's enforcement of her system against the United Kingdom'. *Regional custom*

Rules of customary international law may also develop at the regional level. This was recognised by the ICJ in the *Asylum* case, holding that regional or local custom peculiar to Latin American states could be established where the rule invoked can be proved to be 'in accordance with a constant and uniform usage practised by the states in question'. This is important in the field of environmental protection, where global regimes have been the exception rather than the rule, and in respect of which some regions (Europe and the Antarctic) are particularly well developed. A regional approach allows flexibility in encouraging groups of countries to develop rules which reflect their particular interests, needs and capacities. The Pacific region has been particularly active in developing international treaty rules prohibiting the presence of radioactive materials and the use of driftnet fishing practices in the region, both of which may now reflect rules of customary law for that region. A similar conclusion may be drawn from state practice supporting efforts adopted by African states to limit and prohibit the import of hazardous and other waste onto the African continent, or in respect of certain mineral activities in the Antarctic.

GENERAL PRINCIPLES OF INTERNATIONAL LAW

B. Cheng, *General Principles of Law as Applied by International Courts and Tribunals* (1953); A. McNair, 'The General Principles of

Law Recognised by Civilised Nations', 33 BYIL 1 (1957); G. Herczegh, *General Principles of Law and the International Legal Order* (1969); E. Zoller, *La Bonne Foi en Droit International Public* (1977); M. Ake-hurst, 'The Application of General Principles of Law by the Court of Justice of the European Communities', 52 BYIL 29 (1981); B. Vitanyi, 'Les Positions Doctrinals Concernant le Sens de la Notion de "Principes Ge´ne´raux de Droit Reconnus par les Nations Civilise´es" ', 86 RGDIP 48 (1982)

The inclusion of 'general principles of law recognised by civilised nations' in Article 38 is widely believed to have been intended to allow the ICJ to consider and apply general principles of municipal law, and in practice they are occasionally relied upon when gaps need to be filled. The ICJ has only rarely relied on general principles, although other international tribunals, such as the ECJ, have relied on general principles of municipal law to assist in reaching conclusions.

The general principles relating to good faith in the exercise of rights and prohibitions on the abuse by a state of a right which it enjoys under international law have been invoked by the ICJ and arbitral tribunals which have considered international environmental issues. The principle of good faith appears to have been relied upon by the President of the Tribunal in the *Fur Seal Arbitration* in finding that the exercise of a right for the sole purpose of causing injury to another (abuse of rights) is prohibited. The award in the *Trail Smelter* case is also cited as an example of reliance upon the principle of good faith which governs the exercise of rights, to ensure that a proper balance is struck between a state's rights and obligations and a 'recognition of the interdependence of a person's rights and obligations'. The abuse of rights doctrine is also considered to provide the basis for the rule that a state must not interfere with the flow of a river to the detriment of other riparian states,and is related to the principle requiring respect for mutual interests which is now reflected in Principle 21 of the Stockholm Declaration and Principle 2 of the Rio Declaration, namely, *sic utere tuo ut alienum non laedas*. The principle of 'good faith' was relied upon by the ICJ in the *Nuclear Tests* cases to enable it to reach its conclusion on the legal effect of a French unilateral declaration that it would cease atmospheric nuclear tests. In recognising that unilateral declarations could have the effect of creating legal obligations which are binding 'if given publicly, and with an intent to be bound, even though not made within the context of international negotiations', the Court stated that:

> One of the basic principles governing the creation and performance of legal obligations, whatever their source, is the principle of good faith. Trust and confidence are inherent in international co-operation, in particular in an age when this co-operation in many fields is becoming increasingly essential. just as the very rule of *pacta sunt servanda* in the law of treaties is based on good faith, so also is the binding character of an international obligation assumed by unilateral declaration. Thus interested states may take cognisance of unilateral declarations and place confidence in them, and are entitled to require that the obligation thus created be respected.

The ICJ held that a number of communications made by senior government officers speaking for France created binding legal obligations for that country. States which make unilateral declarations may establish binding environmental obligations. Examples include: the declaration by the UK that it would cease to permit the disposal of sewage sludge in the North Sea by the end of 1998; the joint declaration by the EC and its member states that they would stabilise their emissions of carbon dioxide at 1990 levels by the year 2000; and the declaration by Japan that it would prohibit driftnet fishing by the end of 1993.

It is important to recall, however, that these and other such declarations need to be considered carefully, as they are often drafted to allow discretion in the act required by a state, or may only be intended to have political or domestic effects. Other 'general principles' which have relevance for environmental matters include: the obligation to make reparation for the breach of an engagement; the principle that a person may not plead his or her own wrong; the principle that no one may be a judge in his or her own suit; and 'elementary considerations of humanity' and 'fundamental general principles of humanitarian law'.

Equity

It is also important to consider the role of 'equity', which allows the international community to take into account considerations of justice and fairness in the establishment, operation or application of a rule of international law. In the *North Sea Continental Shelf* cases, the ICJ described the concept of equity as being a 'direct emanation of the idea of justice' and a 'general principle directly applicable aslaw'which should be applied as par to international law' to balance up the various considerations which it regards as relevant in order to produce an equitable result'.

In that case, the ICJ held there were no rigid rules as to the exact weight to be attached to each element in a case, and that equity was not an exercise of discretion or conciliation or the operation of distributive justice.The ICJ has linked equity with acquiescence and estoppel, and applied it to the conservation of fishery resources to achieve an 'equitable solution derived from the applicable law'.

Equity can therefore operate as a part of international law to inform the application of a particular rule. It may also be applied by the ICJ to decide a case *ex aequo et bono*, if the parties to a dispute agree, in application of Article 38(2) of the Statute of the Court, although no such judgment has yet been given by the ICJ.

As described in chapter 6 below, many environmental treaties refer to or incorporate equity or equitable principles. In applying equity in these treaties, it will be proper to establish its meaning in the context of its use in a particular treaty. Since, however, treaties rarely provide a working definition of equity, states, international organisations and international courts and tribunals may, ultimately, have to refer back to the general concept as interpreted and applied by the ICJ and other international tribunals.

SUBSIDIARY SOURCES

R. Jennings and A. Watts (eds.), *Oppenheim's International Law* (1992, 9th edn), vol. I; M. Shaw, *International Law* (1997, 4th edn); P. Daillier and A. Pellet, *Droit International Public* (2002, 7th edn);

I. Brownlie, *Principles of Public International Law* (2003, 6th edn); P.-M. Dupuy, *Droit International Public* (2002, 6th edn)

The main subsidiary sources are the decisions of courts and tribunals and the writings of jurists. The ICJ has only recently come to deal with the substantive aspects of international environmental protection: in the *Nuclear Tests* cases the dispute was settled by the ICJ before the merits could be addressed.

The ICJ has considered the conservation of fisheries resources (*Icelandic Fisheries* cases), guiding principles of general application (*Corfu Channel* case, *North Sea Continental Shelf* cases), the protection of the environment in times of war and armed conflict (Advisory Opinion on *The Legality of the Threat or Use of Nuclear Weapons*) and general norms of international environmental law and principles governing the law of shared watercourses (*Gabcikovo-Nagymaros* case).

Other international courts dealing with environmental issues are the European Court of Justice (which has been called upon to interpret and apply EC environmental law and international agreements such as 1973 CITES, the 1979 Berne Convention and the GATT), the European Court of Human Rights, the WTO Appellate Body and the International Tribunal for the Law of the Sea, as well as panels established under the Canada–US Free Trade Agreement.Awards of international arbitral tribunals have also contributed to the development of international environmental law.

Four stand out in particular: the 1893 decision in the *Pacific Fur Seals Arbitration*, the 1941 decision in the much cited *Trail Smelter* case, the 1957 award of the *Lac Lanoux Arbitration*, and the 2003 award in the *OSPAR Information* case. National courts and tribunals are increasingly faced with the task of interpreting international obligations in this field, and the jurisprudence of these tribunals is becoming an increasingly important source of reference in the development of international environmental law and policy.

The writings of jurists have played a less significant role in developing international environmental law. The *Trail Smelter* case relied on the writings of Professor Eagleton, and there is some evidence that international jurisprudence on environmental issues has been influenced byacademic and other writings.

Resolutions of groups of international jurists acting through the International Law Association and the Institut de Droit International have contributed in important ways to the development of subsequent treaty obligations, particularly in the field of water and atmospheric pollution, as will be seen in the chapters which follow.

4

Introduction to Regulatory Approaches

The principles and rules of international environmental law established by treaty and other sources of international law are applied to a range of regulatory techniques. These can be divided into two types: traditional forms of direct regulation (frequently referred to as 'command-and-control'), and techniques which make use of economic incentives (referred to as 'economic instruments'). Awareness of the limited effectiveness of international environmental regulation has resulted in numerous proposals for a new regulatory approach, referred to as integrated pollution prevention (or control), which aims to adopt a more comprehensive approach to regulation. It is beginning to gain favour at the national level and, at least in Europe, at the international level also.

The techniques relied upon are themselves the subject of political and ideological differences. The 1990 Ministerial Declaration of the Second World Climate Conference illustrates the tensions which exist as to the proper balance to be achieved in the use of two types of regulation, stating that:

Appropriate economic instruments may offer the potential for achieving environmental improvements in a cost-effective manner. The adoption of any form of economic or regulatory measures would require careful and substantive analyses. We *recommend* that relevant policies make use of economic instruments appropriate to each country's socio-economic conditions in conjunction with a balanced mix of regulatory approaches.

The Rio Declaration also reflects support for a balanced approach. Principle 10 indicates that states should enact effective environmental legislation, and that 'environmental standards, management objectives and priorities should reflect the environmental and developmental context to which they apply'. Principle 16, the use of economic instruments, suggests only that national authorities should 'endeavour to promote' their use. It is therefore likely that the international use of command-and-control regulation will remain the primary approach, as reflected in recent instruments such as the Climate Change and

Biodiversity Conventions, and supplemented (where a consensus exists) with economic instruments.

DIRECT REGULATION

Under direct regulation ('command-and-control') the state instructs environmental protection or pollution control bodies to adopt and apply standards which are generally applicable in a uniform manner to their addressees. Once they have been 'commanded', the standardsare enforced (or controlled) by public authorities (or, in some jurisdictions, by private persons as well). The environmental standards fall into four categories: environmental quality standards; product standards; emission standards; and technology or process standards.

Environmental quality standards

Environmental quality standards prescribe the levels of pollution, nuisance or environmental interference which are permitted and which must not be exceeded in a given environment or particular environmental media. International treaties and other acts frequently use this approach to environmental regulation. The earliest environmental treaties relating to the protection of flora and fauna provide for the designation of areas which are protected from environmental interference. Under the 1940 Western Hemisphere Convention, for example, 'strict wilderness reserves' are to be kept virtually inviolate and the quality of their flora and fauna are to be kept, as far as practicable, pristine.National parks, on the other hand, may be subjected to some environmental interference, although commercial activity is not allowed. International environmental law establishes a range of environmental quality standards which vary from the absolute prohibition of particular activities in order to maintain environmental and natural resources free from any change, to the more limited acceptance that certain changes in the quality of a given environment are inevitable and may be tolerated as a matter of law. Examples of international acts intended to maintain the environment or parts of it absolutely free from further interference by particular substances or activities include: the prohibitions on the dumping of certain hazardous substances at sea; the moratorium on dumping of all radioactive waste at sea; the moratorium on the killing or taking of whales for commercial purposes; and the prohibitions on mining and related activities in the Antarctic, interference with flora and fauna in certain protected areas, the production and consumption of certain ozone-depleting substances, the production and consumption of certain chemicals, incineration at sea, and the import of hazardous waste into Africa and other parts of the developing world.

Other environmental quality standards recognise that certain levels of environmental interference are the inevitable consequence of human activity. Rather than prohibit the activity and attempt to establish absolute protection of the environment at its existing level, these standards aim to establish a level beyond which pollution, nuisance or environmental interference is not permitted. Early examples of this approach include the limited protection given to certain areas under wildlife treaties. More recently, the same approach sets targets for acceptable levels of environmental interference by setting 'critical loads' which can be translated into individual country targets. Other examples include: 30 per cent cuts in atmospheric emissions of sulphur dioxide for all EC states; differentiated cuts of sulphur dioxide emissions of up to 70 per cent by EC member states; the general objective of stabilising levels of greenhouse gas concentrations in the atmosphere at 'a level that would prevent dangerous anthropogenic interference with the climate system'; and maximum admissible levels of concentrations in the marine environment.A different approach to achieving the same objective is reflected in the 1993 Lugano

Convention which imposes strict liability for an operator carrying out certain hazardous activities, but allows a defence where the operator can prove that damage was caused 'by pollution at tolerable levels under local relevant circumstances'. Implicit in this approach is the recognition that environmental quality standards will have been maintained until a threshold of intolerability has been reached. The Convention does not provide guidance as to when such a threshold will be crossed.

Product standards

Product standards establish levels for pollutants or nuisances which must not be exceeded in the manufacture or emissions of a product, or specify the properties or characteristics of design of a product, or are concerned with the ways in which a product is used. This approach was only infrequently applied, as it required a degree of specificity which would have been unusual for an international treaty. Recently, however, there has been an increased tendency to target specific industrial activities even at the international level. Examples of product standards in international agreements include: the permitted use of certain ozone-depleting substances in manufacture; the use of parts of endangered species in manufacturing; and the construction of new oil tankers with 'double hulls'. Product standards also include specifications relating to testing, packaging, marking, labelling and distribution. *Emission standards*

Emission standards set levels for pollutants or nuisances which are not to be exceeded in emissions from installations or activities. Examples of their international use include atmospheric emissions from aircraft, automobilesand large industrial utilities. *Process standards*

Process standards can be developed and applied to fixed installations and to mobile installations and activities. Two types are frequently used: 'installation design standards', which determine the requirements to be met in the design and construction of installations to protect the environment; and 'operating standards', which determine the requirements to be met in the course of activities and the operation of installations. Examples of process standards in international agreements include: processes for the treatment of municipal waste andthe incineration ofhazardouswaste; methodsandmeans ofcon-ducting fisheries activities (such as driftnet fishing) and the development of biotechnology. 'Process standards' involve the application of particular types of technology, technique and practice. Many international environmental agreements require their use, although the permissibility of applying national standards to processes carried out beyond a state's jurisdiction is subject to limits under WTO law. Examples of obligations imposed upon states include the requirement that they ensure the use of: 'best available techniques';or 'best environmental practice'; or 'best available technology'; or 'best available technology not entailing excessive cost'; or 'clean production meth-ods'; or environmentally sound management; or best available technology which is economically feasible.

The techniques for implementing these four types of standard at the national level demand a central role for public authorities. It is they who must set the standards (increasingly by implementing international standards), and implement them through authorising, permitting, licensing and receiving information from potential users. Public authorities are also required under many international environmental agreements, to enforce international standards at the national level through appropriate administrative, judicial and other means. Environmental impact assessment and the broad dissemination of information are other techniques which are increasingly used to ensure the implementation of environmental quality, process and product standards.

ECONOMIC INSTRUMENTS

OECD, *Economic Instruments for Environmental Protection* (1989); 'Report of the Working GroupofExperts fromtheMember Stateson the UseofEconomicandFis-cal Instruments in EC Environmental Policy (1990)', 14 *Boston College International and Comparative Law Review* 447 (1991); R. Hahn and R. Stavins, 'Incentive-Based Environmental Regulation: A New Era from an Old Idea?', 18 *Ecology Law Quarterly* 1 (1991); OECD, *Guidelines for the Application of Economic Instruments in Environmental Policy* (1991); E. Rehbinder, 'Environmental Regulation Through Fiscal and Economic Incentives in a Federalist System', 20 *Ecology Law Quarterly* 57 (1993); R. Wolfrum (ed.), *Enforcing Environmental Standards: Economic Mechanisms as Viable Means* (1996); P. Galizzi, 'Economic Instruments as Tools for the Protection of the International Environment', 6 *European Environmental Law Review* 155 (1997); K. Bosselmann and B. Richardson, *Environmental Justice and Market Mechanisms* (1999); R. Stewart and P. Sands, 'The Legal and Institutional Framework for a Plurilateral Greenhouse Gas Emissions Trading System', in UNCTAD, *Greenhouse Gas Market Perspectives, Trade and Investment Implications of Climate Change* (2001), 82; R. Stewart, 'The Importance of Law and Economics for European Environmental Law', 2 *Yearbook of European Environmental Law* 856 (2002).

The use of economic policy instruments to protect the environment has been under discussion for several years as the international community addresses the fact that many environmental regulations have not resulted in environmentally cleaner behaviour, technologies or products. It is believed that current mechanisms have failed to provide adequate economic incentives to limit activities which are environmentally damaging and have failed to achieve their environmental objectives. The use of economic instruments is premised on a belief that the market can be used to provide incentives to guide human behaviour:

If environmental resources are properly valued, the costs of using the environment will be taken fully into account in private economic decision-making. This implies that environmental resources are used in 'sustainable' quantities, provided that their prices are based on their scarcity and place an appropriate value on non-renewable resources. Economic instruments are meant to correct current market prices by internalising environmental costs which are treated by the market mechanisms as external.

Economic instruments 'affect throughthe marketmechanism costs and benefits of alternative actions open to economic agents, with the effect of influencing behaviour in a way which is favourable for the environment'.

The use of economic instruments at the international level to supplement, or supplant, regulatory approaches to environmental protection is supported, at least in principle, by a growing number of states. The practical application is nevertheless limited. In so far as economic instruments are defined by reference to their attempts to use the market to internalise environmental costs, the polluter-pays principle first developed by the OECD and the EC in the early 1970s can be seen as a precursor to more recent discussions and pro-posals. Explicit references in international acts to 'economic instruments' is a relatively recent phenomenon. In April 1990, the Presidency of the EC Environment Council concluded that EC Ministers 'acknowledged the value of supplementing existing regulatory instruments . . . b y the use of economic and fiscal instruments'. The following month, the UNECE Bergen Ministerial Declaration stated that to support sustainable development it would be necessary 'to make more extensive use of economic instruments in conjunction with . . . regulatory approaches'. By November 1990, the Ministerial Declaration of the Second World Climate Conference had found support for similar language at the global level.

Support for the use of economic instruments can also be found in other regional and global declarations such as the Rio Declaration. Agenda 21 refers frequently to the need to develop economic instruments. Support for the use of economic instruments is also reflected in soft law instruments and treaties. Examples include the 1992 Climate Change Convention, which requires developed country parties to co-ordinate relevant economic instruments, and the 1992 Biodiversity Convention, which although it does not specifically mention economic instruments, calls on parties to 'adopt economically and socially sound measures that act as incentives for the conservation and sustainable use of components of biological diversity'.

What are the different types of economic instruments available? The 1991 OECD Council Recommendation on the Use of Economic Instruments in Environmental Policy provided the clearest guidance yet adopted at the international level on the types of instrument the use of which is being envisaged in future years. It recommends that member countries make greater use of economic instruments, improve the allocation and efficient use of natural and environmental resources, and make efforts to reach further agreement at an international level on the use of economic instruments. The different types of economic instruments envisaged are set out in the Guidelines and Considerations for the Use of Economic Instruments in Environmental Policy contained in the Annex to the Recommendation. They include charges and taxes, marketable permits, deposit-refund systems and financial assistance. Other types of economic instrument not dealt with in the Recommendation include enforcement incentives, administrative charges, liability and compensation for damage, trade measures and consumer information incentives, as well as non-compliance fees and performance bonds. The permissibility of subsidies for environmentally beneficial activities is also premised upon an economic approach to environmental regulation.

Charges and taxes

The rationale behind charges and taxes is that they create an incentive for polluters to limit activities which can be harmful to the environment, such as emissions, the generation of waste, and the excessive use of natural resources. The difference between a charge and a tax reflects the different way in which the revenues are allocated: tax revenues are added to the general public budget, while charge revenues are used specifically to finance environmental measures. Charges can also have different purposes. Emission charges, which are levied on all dischargers, can be levied on discharges of effluents and gases and can be calculated on the basis of the quality and/or quantity of the pollution load. User charges are paid for services rendered by authorities, such as the collection and removal of municipal waste water and solid and hazardous wastes, and are only paid by persons who receive, or are associated with, the services.

Although widely used at the national level, charges and taxes have not yet been the subject of international legal measures. In May 1992, the first international environmental tax was proposed by the EC, to contribute to the implementation of its commitment to stabilise carbon dioxide emissions by the year 2000 at 1990 levels. The EC Commission proposal was to harmonise the introduction in the EC member states of a tax on certain fossil fuel products (coal, lignite, peat, natural gas, mineral oils, ethyl and methyl alcohol, electricity and heat), levying the tax on the basis of carbon dioxide emissions and energy content. The introduction of the tax was, however, conditional upon the introduction by the other OECD members of similar taxes or of measures having a financial impact equivalent to the draft Directive, and was to take account of issues of international competitiveness. The Directive was not adopted.

Joint implementation and tradeable permits

The suggestion that international law might encourage the use of tradeable permits is drawn from developments in the United States under the 1990 amendments to the Clean Air Act. According to this approach, regions or utilities are granted a limited number of pollution rights; if they manage to use less than the amount allocated to them, they may sell their excess to another region or utility. Although the idea has generated some interest, the first international scheme was only adopted in 2002, by the EC. Early environmental agreements allowed parties jointly to implement programmes and measures without specifying any criteria or conditions according to which this is to be achieved, and since they did not establish specific pollution limits there was no intention for inter-state trading.

The first elements of possible trading can be found in certain fisheries agreements (under which 'trade' in quotas may take place) and in Article 2(7) of the 1987 Montreal Protocol, which allows member states of a regional economic integration organisation (which currently might only include the EC) to agree to 'jointly fulfil their obligations respecting consumption' of certain ozone-depleting substances provided that their total combined calculated level of consumption does not exceed the levels required by the Montreal Protocol.

The 1992 Climate Change Convention allows developed country parties and other parties included in Annex 1 to implement policies and measures required under Articles 4(2)(a) and (b) 'jointly with other parties', subject to decisions taken by the conference of the parties at its first session 'regarding criteria for joint implementation'.

The language is unclear on a number of points. Is it envisaged that parties with specific targets and timetables under Article 4(2)(a) and (b) should be able to implement their commitments with parties which have no such targets? And may joint implementation under the Convention proceed in the absence of criteria established by the conference of the parties? Interpretation of these provisions on the basis of an effort to ensure the long-term effectiveness of the Convention suggests that the answer to both questions should be no.

A positive answer to the first question would, in effect, allow developed country parties to bypass their targets by supporting efforts in countries with no targets. While this may, over the short term, be cost-effective for developed countries, it may not, over the longer term, meet the commitment to be guided by principles of equity or to meet the ultimate objective of the Convention, as set out in Article 2. These questions have been overtaken by the 1997 Kyoto Protocol, which provides more detailed provisions on joint implementation. The Kyoto Protocol also provides for the emergence of a system of tradeable permits (emission reduction units), the details of which will be elaborated by the conference of the parties at its first meeting.

In March 2003, the EC Council adopted a common position on a Directive establishing a scheme for greenhouse gas emission allowance trading within the EC, which is intended 'to promote reductions of greenhouse gas emissions in a cost-effective and economically efficient manner' and which it would be desirable to link with project-based mechanisms under the Kyoto Protocol, including joint implementation and the Clean Development Mechanism.When it enters into force in December 2003, the Directive will establish the first international trading arrangement.

The Directive demonstrates the potential complexities – and degree of intrusion – which will underlie the operation of such arrangements. Its operation is premised on the allocation of allowancesto operators of installations involving designated activities and resulting in emissions of certain greenhouse gases. It requires each member state to ensure that with effect from 1 January 2005 all designated activities resulting in the emission of the designated gases must be authorised by a permit granted by a competent authority, which will be subject to certain conditions. Each member state must develop a national allocation plan stating the total quantity of allowances it will allocate for a three-year period from 1 January 2005 and for a five-year period beginning 1 January 2008 (and subsequent five-year periods), consistent with its obligations to limit its emissions pursuant to the 1997 Kyoto Protocol and implementing EC law, and in accordance with the criteria set forth in Article 9.

Allowances for the first period (three years) will be allocated free of charge, and 90 per cent of allowances for the first five-year period are to be allocated free of charge, and will be valid for emissions during the period in which they are issued. The allowances will be transferable between persons within the EU, and between persons within the EU and third countries listed in Annex B to the Kyoto Protocol which have ratified the Protocol and which have entered into agreements with the EU on the mutual recognition of allowances. Provision is made for a certain number of allowances to be surrendered (and cancelled) each year by the operator of each installation (to cover emissions during the previous year), and for the cancellation of allowances which are no longer valid. The EC Commission will adopt guidelines on the monitoring and reporting of emissions, and member states will be required to ensure that emissions are duly monitored and that reports submitted by operators are verified.

Member states will lay down rules on penalties for infringements of implementing provisions, which must be effective, proportionate and dissuasive, as well as payment of an excess emissions penalty where an operator does not surrender sufficient allowances by 30 April each year to cover its emissions during the previous year. Each member state is required to designate a competent authority, and to establish a registry to ensure the accurate accounting of the issue, holding, transfer and cancellation of allowances, and the Commission will designate a central authority to maintain an independent transaction log in relation to allowances, and to conduct automated checks. The Commission may make a proposal to amend the list of activities and gases by 31 December 2004, and must report on the application of the Directive by 30 June 2006.

Deposit-refund systems

Deposit-refund systems require a deposit to be paid on potentially polluting products, such as batteries. bottles and other packaging. The return of the product or its residuals is intended to avoid pollution and is compensated by a refund of the deposit. The system is frequently used at the national level but has not yet been used at the international level. In the *Danish Bottles* case, a Danish deposit-and-return system was challenged by the EC Commission and other member states as incompatible with the rules on the free movement of goods. The ECJ upheld the deposit-and-return system as having lawful objectives of environmental protection despite its limitation on the application of the EC rules on free movement of goods (Article 30). *Subsidies*

Governments often seek to justify the grant of subsidies which might otherwise be unlawful on the grounds that they bring environmental benefits. They can nevertheless distort competition and run against the inherent purpose of the polluter-pays principle and may, on those grounds, fall foul of international competition and trade rules. International practice (in the EC and under the WTO) on the environmental aspects of subsidies is considered in chapter 19 below.

Enforcement incentives

Enforcement incentives, such as non-compliance fees and performance bonds, are closely linked to fiscal regulation. Non-compliance fees penalise polluters who exceed prescribed environmental standards, and performance bonds are payments to authorities which are returned when the polluter performs in accordance with its licence. Enforcement incentives have not been the subject of international legal measures, although recent developments suggest that they may be emerging. In November 1992, the parties to the Montreal Protocol adopted an indicative list of measures that might be taken by a meeting of the parties in respect of non-compliance with the Protocol which included, *inter alia,* suspending specific rights and privileges under the Protocol such as those relating to the receipt of funds under the financial mechanism. The approach has been followed in other multilateral environmental agreements.

Liability and compensation for damage

One of the objectives of the rules of international law establishing civil and state liability for environmental and related damage is the establishment of economic incentives for complying with international environmental obligations. As will be seen in chapter 18, however, the limited state of development of the rules of state liability, and the low financial limits on liability established by most of the international civil liability conventions do not properly fulfil the incentive functions.

Trade measures

Regulations and prohibitions on international trade were among the first economic instruments to be used at the international level in aid of environmental protection objectives, and they are considered in detail in chapter 19 below. They are designed to influence behaviour (i.e. not killing endangered species or not producing or consuming certain harmful substances) by limiting the availability of markets for certain products or by making the availability of markets dependent upon participation in an international regulatory arrangement. Despite their evident attractiveness to government environmental departments as an efficient and effective means to achieve environmental objectives, trade measures remain controversial, and are subject to a trade regime under the WTO which raises questions as to the circumstances in which they may be relied upon.

Investment incentives

More recently, increased attention is being given to identifying incentives for directing investment in clean technologies towards developing countries and countries with economies in transition. The most elaborate arrangement is the Clean Development Mechanism established under the Kyoto Protocol, which will provide credits to states whose companies invest in certain greenhouse gas reduction activities abroad. Other arrangements aim to provide financial resources to developing countries to invest in certain clean technologies pursuant to the ozone and other international agreements. *Environmental agreements*

Alongside legislative and economic instruments, there has also been a growing use of 'environmental agreements', i.e. voluntary agreements betweenindustrial undertakings which supplement regulatory requirements. A leading example is the agreement between associations of European, Japanese and Korean car manufacturers on the reduction of carbon dioxide emissions from passenger cars, which has been acknowledged by EC Commission recommendations.In 1996, the EC Commission published a Communication on Environmental Agreements, which identified potential benefits as including a pro-active approach by industry, cost-effectiveness and tailor-made solutions, and the faster achievement of environmental objectives. In 1999, the OECD published a survey of environmental agreements, identifying more than 300 in the EU alone. In 2002, the EC Commission published a further Communication, identifying substantive and procedural criteria for the use of environmental agreements at the EU level, in the context of self-regulation (where economic and other actors establish on a voluntary basis in order to regulate and organise their activities) and co-regulation (where the legislator establishes the essential elements of the regulation and the economic and other actors then agree on the means for giving effect to it). *Consumer information incentives*

Consumer information incentives, which set out the environmental performance of companies, such as eco-labelling and eco-auditing, are designed to capitalise on the perception that many consumers take environmental considerations into account when buying products and services. In 1991, the EC adopted the first international eco-labelling scheme, and the compatibility of national eco-labelling schemes with WTO rules and other international trade agreements is under consideration at the WTO and has been the subject of an early GATT case. Integrated pollution control

The continuous increase in pollution levels and environmental degradation provides evidence of the fundamental failure of traditional law-making to change human behaviour and patterns of production and consumption. The traditional approach to environmental regulation has been to address particular activities, substances or environmental media (air, water, soil and biota), and to focus pollution control and prevention efforts on each environmental medium. In reality, different substances and activities can move among, and have effects upon, a range of environmental media as they travel along a 'pathway' from a particular source to a particular receptor, and in that process may accumulate in the environment. The regulation and establishment of controls over releases of a substance to one environmental medium can lead to that substance being shifted to another environmental medium. This is recognised by a number of international environmental agreements which include provisions requiring parties not to transfer pollution or environmental damage elsewhere in the implementation of their treaty obligations.

In the early 1990s, some states recognised that efforts to address each environmental medium separately may not be an efficient or effective way to protect the environment. Beginning at the national level, some began to rely upon 'integrated pollution prevention (or control)', which was defined in 1991 by the OECD Council as: taking into account the effects of activities and substances on the environment as a whole and the whole commercial and environmental life-cycles of substances when assessing the risks they pose and when developing and implementing controls to limit their release.

This broader holistic approach to environmental regulation and protection is now reflected in a number of international instruments, including the attempts by the EC to take a 'cradle-to-grave' approach to eco-labelling and to address 'waste streams' in its developing waste prevention policy. In 1992, the Oslo and Paris Commissions endorsed this approach by addressing particular industrial sectors and activities. In 1996, the EU adopted the first international rules on integrated pollution control.

The EU rules are premised on the approach recommended in the 1991 OECD Council Recommendation, which called on OECD member countries to support integrated pollution prevention and control by addressing impediments to an integrated approach, removing those impediments, and adopting appropriate new laws and regulations, taking account of the Guidance on Integrated Pollution Prevention and Control set out in the Appendix to the Recommendation. The Guidance set out, for the first time in an international instrument, a detailed approach to implementing integrated pollution prevention and control and preventing or minimising the risk of harm to the environmenttakenasa whole;itrecognisesthe integrated natureof theenviron-ment by taking account of the substances or activities on all the environmental media (air, water, soil), the living organisms (including people) that these media support, and the stock of cultural and aesthetic assets. The Guidance identified five important elements of an integrated approach: the 'cradle-to-grave' concept; the anticipation of effects in all environmental media of substances and activities; the minimisation of waste quantity and harmfulness; the use of a common means to estimate and compare environmental problems (such as risk assessment); and the complementary use of effects-oriented measures (environmental quality objectives) and source-oriented measures (emission limits).

The OECD Recommendation also recognised that certain policies were 'essential to an effective integrated approach', including sustainable development, the use of no- or low-waste technology and recycling strategies, cleaner technologies and safer substances, precautionary action, public information, the integration of environmental considerations into private and public decision-making, and consistent and effective compliance and enforcement policies.Under the Recommendation, an integrated approach would shift the focus of decision-making, to a combination of the substances, the sources (including processes, products and economic sectors) and the geographical regions; it would provide for the use of a range of legislative forms such as mineral rights, development aid and taxes. The Recommendation recognised that an integrated approach would require changes in institutional arrangements, management instruments and technical methods. New institutional arrangements would require the establishment of co-ordinating mechanisms within and among government bodies and international co-operative arrangements within and among different levels of government within countries. Proposals relating to management instruments included the following: issuing single permits which cover all releases and processes; linking environmental instruments with land-use planning and natural resource management; undertaking environmental impact assessments for policy proposals and projects; establishing integrated inspection and enforcement authorities; using economic instruments; encouraging and/or subsidising cleaner technologies; and covering whole life cycle issues in the development of industry management plans.An integrated approach to technical methods would encompass such things as life cycle analysis (from design through manufacture to disposal), analysis of multiple pathways of exposure, the use of inventories of releases and inputs, and more effective monitoring of the condition of environmental media, the biota they support, and the condition of cultural and aesthetic assets. The necessity for such changes remains equally apparent with regard to international institutions, in respect of both their internal practices and their external relations.

CONCLUSIONS

From the discussion in this chapter of the different sources of international legal obligation, it will be evident that the principles and rules of international environmental law are set forth or are reflected in thousands of acts adopted at the national, bilateral, sub-regional, regional and global levels. There is no international legal text which sets out the principles and rules which are of general application, and it is unlikely that one will be adopted in the foreseeable future, despite the efforts of the IUCN Commission on Environmental Law in the 1990s. The lack of a central legislative authority, or of a coherent set of international legislative arrangements, has resulted in a law-making process and a body of rules which are *ad hoc*, piecemeal and fragmented. The limitations of existing arrangements are well known. Although existing international arrangements have apparently not limited the international community's environmental law-making over the past decade, there remains a real need to establish a coherent framework for the co-ordination of existing rules and the development of new rules. The UNCED process could have contributed to such a framework, by addressing three priority needs: to establish improved mechanisms for identifying critical issues and priorities for law-making; to ensure that all relevant actors are able to participate fully and effectively in the international law-making process (in particular developing countries), including the negotiation, implementation, review and governance of international environmental agreements or instruments; and to rationalise the international law-making process by improving co-ordination between international organisations and their secretariats, in particular those established by environmental agreements. In the ten years since UNCED, however, it has become apparent that there is an absence of the political will which would be required to overhaul existing international structures.

It will also be clear from this chapter that the limitations and inadequacies of existing techniques for applying standards established by international principles and rules (principally by so-called 'command-and-control' methods) are, and should continue to be, the subject of critical international scrutiny. Developments since UNCED confirm that environmental protection will not be achieved merely by the adoption of a vast body of regulatory obligations. These regulations need fine-tuning, and they may need to be supplemented by introducing and applying a broad range of equitable and effective economic instruments which can provide incentives to improve compliance without exacerbating social injustice and which take account of the need to ensure that the poorer members of the international community are not disproportionately affected. So far, however, there has been little practical experience at the international level with the use of economic instruments, with the exception of trade instruments and the emerging efforts of the EC, and more work of a theoretical nature needs to be done to explore the implications and practical consequences of the various proposed arrangements. The limited experience of efforts to devise a system of 'joint implementation' under the 1992 Climate Change Convention suggests that legal and institutional issues of considerable complexity arise when economic theories are to be translated into practical, acceptable and effective international legal obligations and arrangements. That experience suggests that, although it mayyet bepremature toembark onabroad effort at adopting and applying economic instruments, international law may be about to embark on new efforts which selectively support such arrangements. In this regard, developments under the 1997 Kyoto Protocol will be of singular importance, even if – for the time being at least – traditional regulatory approaches will continue to be the primary approach. Efforts to devise new economic approaches will no doubt continue, supplemented by the obviously necessary move away from single-sector environmental regulation towards a more integrated approach to pollution prevention and control which seeks to address all environmental media on a comprehensive basis, and all products on a cradle-to-grave basis. Each of these new initiatives poses challenges to the international legal order.

COMPLIANCE: IMPLEMENTATION, ENFORCEMENT, DISPUTE SETTLEMENT

Ensuring compliance by members of the international community with their international environmental obligations continues to be a matter of increasing concern. This is evident not only from the attention which the issue received during UNCED, as well as in the negotiation and implementation of recent environmental agreements, but also in the growing number of environmental disputes which have been brought to international judicial bodies. The relevance of environmental concerns to international peace and security was affirmed by the UN Security Council in January 1992 when its members declared that 'non-military sources of instability in the . . . ecological fields have become threats to international peace and security'. The response to those concerns has includedthedevelopmentofexisting mechanisms forimplementation,enforce-ment and dispute settlement (such as the 1993 decision of the ICJ to establish a

Chamber for Environmental Matters), as well as new approaches such as the non-compliance mechanisms established under a number of environmental agreements, and the role given to the UN Compensation Commission over environmental claims, and the specialised rules for arbitrating environmental disputes which were promulgated by the Permanent Court of Arbitration in 2001.

Of the reasons proffered for renewed efforts, at least three are especially relevant. First, it is apparent that states are taking on ever more international environmental commitments which are increasingly stringent and which must be complied with. Secondly, the growing demands on access to finite natural resources provides fertile conditions for conflicts over the use of natural resources. And, thirdly, as international environmental obligations increasingly intersect with economic interests, states which do not comply with their environmental obligations are perceived to gain economic advantage from non-compliance. Non-compliance is therefore seen to be important because it limits the effectiveness of legal commitments, undermines the international legal process, and can lead to conflict and instability in the international order. Plainly, non-compliance occurs for different reasons, and it is widely recognised that the underlying causes require further attention so that existing and new international legal obligations are crafted to ensure their effective implementation. At UNCED, attention was focused on mechanisms to *prevent* disputes and to resolve them peacefully when they arise. Subsequent efforts have reflected a desire to address enforcement and dispute settlement in a non-contentious and non-adversarial manner.

Non-compliance can include a failure to give effect to substantive norms (e.g. to limit atmospheric emission of sulphur dioxide or greenhouse gases as required by treaty or to allow transboundary emissions of hazardous substances or gases in violation of any rules of customary law); or to fulfil procedural requirements (e.g. to carry out an environmental impact assessment or to consult with a neighbouring state on the construction of a new plant); or to fulfil an institutional obligation (e.g. to submit an annual report to an international organisation). Non-compliance raises three distinct but related issues relating to implementation, enforcement, and conflict resolution (traditionally referred to by international lawyers as 'dispute settlement'). These are:

1. What formal or informal steps must be taken to implement a state's international legal obligations?
2. What legal or natural person may enforce international environmental obligations of other states?
3. What techniques, procedures and institutions exist under international law to resolve conflicts or settle disputes over alleged non-compliance with international environmental obligations?

Over the years, a range of techniques have been adopted and used to improve compliance with environmental obligations, drawing upon other developments in international law. Today, techniques and practices specific to environmental matters are being developed. Despite the emergence of the concept of 'environmental security', the legal issues relating to the environment concerning implementation, enforcement and conflict resolution are not dissimilar to those of one hundred years ago. Since the *Fur Seals Arbitration* of 1893, numerous environmental disputes have been submitted to international dispute resolution arrangements, and the rate of submission appears to have increased significantly within the past decade.

These disputes have addressed a broad range of issues, including: transboundary air pollution; the diversion of the flow of international rivers; conservation of fisheries resources; protection of the marine environment; import restrictions adopted to enforce domestic conservation standards; the relationship between environmental lawsandfor-eign investment protection treaties; access to environmental information;environmental impact assessment; and responsibility for rehabilitation of mined lands. Recent cases illustrate the availability of a growing range of fora for the resolution of disputes over environment and natural resources.

In the context of the dispute over the Gabcikovo-Nagymaros barrages, Hungary and Slovakia had explored a range of enforcement and dispute settlement options including unilateral reference to the ICJ, arbitration, conciliation by the EC Commission, and the emergency procedures of the Conference on Security and Co-operation in Europe (CSCE) before they agreed to settle the dispute at the ICJ. The dispute between Ireland and the United Kingdom concerning the MOX plant at Sellafield has been litigated at ITLOS and two separate arbitration tribunals (OSPAR and UNCLOS), and other fora (including the ECJ, the ECHR and the ICJ) were also available. Historically, the available mechanisms were under-utilised, leaving it unclear whether they would be able to deal with the growing range of environmental issues which may require resolution. In the past decade, however, there has been an increasing willingness on behalf of states to invoke these traditional procedures, which have demonstrated an ability to contribute to the resolution of contentious disputes and, in the process, to the development of the rules of international environmental law.

IMPLEMENTATION

States implement their international environmental obligations in three distinct phases. First, by adopting national implementing measures; secondly, by ensuring that national measures are complied with by those subject to their jurisdiction and control; and, thirdly, by fulfilling obligations to the relevant international organisations, such as reporting the measures taken to give effect to international obligations. *National law*

Once a state has formally accepted an international environmental obligation, usually following the entry into force of a treaty which it has ratified or the act of an international organisation by which it is bound, it will usually need to develop, adopt or modify relevant national legislation, or give effect to national policies, programmes or strategies by administrative or other measures.

Some treaties expressly require parties to take measures to ensure the implementation of obligations, or to take appropriate measures within their competence to ensure compliance with the convention and any measures in effect pursuant to it. Numerous agreements require parties to designate a competent national authority or focal point for international liaison purposes to ensure domestic implementation. The 1982 UNCLOS provides a typical example, its provisions being drawn from different precedents in the field of marine pollution. It includes provisions on implementation of pollution requirements from different sources, and provides specifically for the enforcement by states of their laws and regulations adopted in accordance with the Convention and the implementation of applicable international rules and standards. It also requires states to ensure that recourse is available under their legal system for prompt and adequate compensation for damage caused by marine pollution by persons under their jurisdiction.

Treaty obligations which have not been implemented domestically will usually be difficult to enforce in national courts. EC law provides a notable exception, since it can create rights and obligations enforceable before national courts without being implemented provided that they fulfil certain conditions, such as being clear and unconditional. The failure by EC members to adopt measures implementing EC environmental law has been the subject of enforcement measures taken at the ECJ. In dealing with these cases the ECJ has rejected different arguments by states seeking to justify domestic non-implementation.

National compliance

Once an obligation has been domestically implemented, the party must ensure that it is complied with by those within its jurisdiction and control. Numerous treaties expressly require parties to ensure such compliance, or to apply sanctions for failing to implement measures. Others specifically provide for the application of criminal penalties or for the 'punishment' of violations. Ensuring national compliance is a matter for the public authorities of each state, although there is much evidence to suggest that domestic compliance with environmental obligations is inadequate and that compliance with international obligations needs to be enhanced. National judges meeting shortly before the World Summit on Sustainable Development adopted the Johannesburg 'Principles on the Role of Law and Sustainable Development', which affirmed their adherence to the 1992 Rio Declaration which laid down the basic principles of sustainable development, affirmed that members of the judiciary, as well as those contributing to the judicial process at the national, regional and global levels, are 'crucial partners for promoting compliance with, and the implementation and enforcement of, international and national environmental law', and recognised that 'the rapid evolution of multilateral environmental agreements, national constitutions and statutes concerning the protection of the environment increasingly require the courts to interpret and apply new legal instruments in keeping with the principles of sustainable development'.

Recognising that public authorities in many countries may not be able to ensure compliance, because of a lack of resources or commitment, and that individuals, groups and business can play a role in ensuring compliance, increasing numbers of states are encouraging private enforcement of national environmental obligations. These are sometimes referred to as 'citizen suits', allowing citizens (and businesses) to enforce national environmental obligations in the public interest. The importance of national remedies to challenge acts which damage the environment or violate environmental obligations has been recognised and is being addressed internationally. Principle 10 of the Rio Declaration states that '[e]ffective access to judicial and administrative proceedings, including redress and remedy, shall be provided'. The EC Commission has recognised that individuals and public interest 'groups should have practicable access to the courts in order to ensure that their legitimate interests are protected and that prescribed environmental measures are effectively enforced and illegal practices stopped', although the ECJ has not been willing to move away from its traditional and restrictive approach to recognising the rights of individuals and other non-state actors to challenge EC legislative and administrative acts. The 1993 Lugano Convention was the first international agreement to elaborate rules governing access to national courts to allow enforcement of environmental obligations in the public interest: Article 18 requires standing to be granted to environmental organisations to allow them to bring certain enforcement proceedings before national courts.

The 1998 Aarhus Convention goes a great deal further, giving concrete effect to the requirements of Principle 10 of the Rio Declaration on access to justice. Its Article 9(2) establishes an obligation on parties to ensure that members of the public which have a 'sufficient interest' or who claim an 'impairment of a right' shall have access 'to a review procedure before a court of law and/or another independent and impartial body established by law, to challenge the substantive and procedural legality of any decision, act or omission' which is subject to the Convention's Article 6.

The Convention provides that 'sufficient interest' and 'impairment of a right' are to be determined in accordance with national law and 'consistently with the objectiveof giving thepublic concernedwide accessto justice', and expressly provides that non-governmental organisations fulfilling certain conditions are deemed to have a 'sufficient interest' and rights capable of being impaired. The Convention also provides that members of the public should be able to challenge acts and omission by private persons and public authorities which contravene nationalprovisions relating to the environment, and that all the procedures available should provide adequate and effective remedies (including injunctive relief) and be fair, equitable, timely and 'not prohibitively expensive'.

The question of which state may or must ensure implementation is a difficult one where the environmental obligation relates to a shared natural resource or the global commons. This can lead to conflicts between states over which has jurisdiction over a particular activity or violation. Some treaties allocate enforcement obligations to particular states, and in respect of marine pollution the 1982 UNCLOS is notable for the detailed provisions on national enforcement responsibilities of flag states, port states or coastal states, depending on where a pollution incident occurred. No equivalent treaty rules apply for other matters, such as atmospheric pollution. However, under the 1979 Moon Treaty, the state of registration retains jurisdiction and control over personnel and equipment and is responsible for ensuring that 'national activities are carried out in conformity with the provisions' of the treaty. And under the 1988 CRAMRA each party would have been required to ensure that recourse was available in its national courts for adjudicating liability claims under Article 8 of the Convention (and consistently with Article 7), including the adjudication of claims against any operator it had sponsored.

The UNCLOS rules are detailed and may provide a model for enforcement jurisdiction in other matters. Generally the flag state will be responsible for ensuring that vessels flying its flag or of its registry comply with applicable international pollution rules and standards, and with laws and regulations adopted in accordance with UNCLOS, and for the effective enforcement of such measures 'irrespective of where a violation occurs'. Port states also have important enforcement functions. They may investigate and institute proceedings in respect of a vessel voluntarily within its port or at an offshore terminal for harmful discharges from that vessel outside the internal waters, territorial sea or exclusive economic zone (EEZ) in violation of international rules and standards. And they must take measures to prevent vessels from sailing where they have ascertained that the vessel is in violation of applicable international rules and standards relating to seaworthiness which may threaten the marine environment. A coastal state may institute proceedings against vessels within its port for violations of its laws and regulations adopted in accordance with UNCLOS or applicable international rules and standards for environmental violations occurring in its territorial sea or EEZ. Where there are grounds for believing that there is a 'substantial discharge causing or threatening significant pollution of the marine environment', the coastal state also has the right to investigate and institute proceedings against vessels navigating in its territorial sea, to obtain information from vessels navigating in its EEZ, and to undertake inspections of vessels in its EEZ. The coastal state may also institute proceedings – with sanctions including detention – against vessels in its territorial sea or EEZ if there is 'clear, objective evidence' that violation of applicable international rules and standards has occurred which results 'in a discharge causing major damage or threat of major damage to the coastline or related interests of the coastal state, or to any resources of its territorial sea or exclusive economic zone. UNCLOS does not prejudice the rights of states under international law to take and enforce measures to protect their coastlines or related interests from pollution or a threat of pollution. Such pollution may result from a maritime casualty, including collision or stranding, which may reasonably be expected to have major harmful consequences.

With regard to the sea-bed and ocean floor and its subsoil, beyond the limits of national jurisdiction (known as the 'Area') and which constitutes the 'common heritage of mankind', state parties must ensure that their activities, or the activities of their nationals or those effectively controlled by them or their nationals, are carried out in conformity with Part XI of UNCLOS. State parties will also be subject to rules adopted by the International Sea-bed Authority concerning pollution and other hazards to the marine environment. and the protection and conservation of natural resources.

The allocation of detailed enforcement powers to ensure compliance is not well developed in respect of many other environmental media involving shared resources. In the absence of specific treaty provisions, the applicable principles arise from general rules of international law concerning enforcement jurisdiction. Given the failure of many states, particularly developing states, to implement their international obligations by reason of lack of financial and other resources, an important development is the linkage now established between the extent to which developing countries meet their treaty obligations, and the provision to them of financial resources. The 1990 amendments to the 1987 Montreal Protocol established a mechanism to 'meet all agreed incremental costs' of developing country parties 'to enable their compliance with the control measures of the Protocol'. The 1992 Climate Change Convention goes further by requiring developed country parties 'to meet the agreed full costs incurred by developing country parties in complying with their [reporting requirements and] agreed full incremental costs' needed by developing country parties for implementing their substantive obligations under the Convention.Similar provisions exist in other agreements, including the 1992 Biodiversity Convention, the 1994 Desertification Convention and the 2001 POPs Convention.

Reporting

The third element of national compliance arises from the requirement that states must usually report national implementing measures. Most environmental agreements expressly require parties to report certain information to the international organisation designated by the agreement. The information to be reported typically includes: statistical information on production, imports and exports; information on emissions or discharges; information on the grant of permits or authorisations including criteria; information on implementation measures which have been adopted; details of decisions taken by national authorities; scientific information; and information on breaches or violations by persons under the jurisdiction or control of the party. Most EC Directives and Regulations also require the EC member states to provide regular information on measures taken to implement their obligations.

These reports may be required annually or bi-annually, or according to some other timeframe. They allow the international organisation and the other parties to assess the extent to which parties are implementing their obligations. It is clear, however, that many states fail to fulfil the basic reporting obligation, which suggests that more substantive obligations may also remain unimplemented. One report considered six environmental treaties requiring periodic reports, and found wide variations in compliance in the early 1990s. Some treaties revealed a strong record: all six parties to the International Whaling Convention required to submit information on their 1989 whale harvests did so, and sixteen of the seventeen parties to the 1988 NO_x Protocol submitted their 1990 report on their emissions in 1987 or another year. By October 1990, fifty-two of the then sixty-five parties to the 1987 Montreal Protocol had responded to the requirement to report information on their consumption of controlled substances in 1986, of which twenty-nine (representing 85 per cent of world consumption) submitted complete data.At the other end of the scale, however, only nineteen of the sixty-four parties to the 1972 London Convention reported on the number and types of dumping permits they issued in 1987, and only thirteen of the fifty-seven parties to MARPOL 73/78 (representing only about 27 per cent of the world's gross shipping tonnage) submitted reports summarising violations and penalties they had imposed in 1989. Finally, just twenty-five of the 104 parties to the 1973 CITES submitted reports summarising their 1989 import and export certificates for listed endangered species. These figures suggest the limited ability of many countries, particularly developing countries, to meet their reporting requirements. There is no evidence that the situation is improving, although steps are being taken to address the problem. Under the Biodiversity and Climate Change Conventions, financial resources are required to be made available to meet the incremental costs for developing countries of fulfilling their reporting requirements, and this has gone some way towards improving compliance.

INTERNATIONAL ENFORCEMENT

Once evidence is available that a state, or a party to a treaty, has failed to implement an international environmental obligation, the question arises as to which persons having international legal personality may enforce that obligation internationally. In this context, 'enforcement' is understood as the right to take measures to ensure the fulfilment of international legal obligations or to obtain a ruling by an appropriate international court, tribunal or other body, including an international organisation, that obligations are not being fulfilled. International enforcement may occur at the instigation of one or more states, or an international organisation, or by non-state actors. In practice, international enforcement usually involves a combination of the three, each acting in different capacities. The extent to which any of these actors may invoke enforcement measures depends on the nature and legal basis of the alleged violation, the subject matter involved, and the international legal obligations at issue. This aspect of enforcement is essentially about the standing required to bring international claims.

Enforcement by states

As the principal subjects of international law, states have the primary role in enforcing rulesof international environmental law.To beinaposition toenforce a rule of international environmental law, a state must have standing, and to have standing it must be able to show that it is, in the words of the International Law Commission (ILC), an 'injured state'.

Article 42 of the ILC's 2001 Articles on State Responsibility provides:

A State is entitled as an injured State to invoke the responsibility of another State if the obligation breached is owed to:

(a) that State individually; or

(b) a group of States including that State, or the international community as a whole, and the breach of the obligation:

  (i) Specially affects that State; or

  (ii) Is of such a character as radically to change the position of all the other States to which the obligation is owed with respect to the further performance of the obligation.

The rights concerning the first category include those arising from: a bilateral treaty; a multilateral treaty where particular performance is incumbent under the treaty as between one party and another; a unilateral commitment made by one state to another; or a rule of general international law which may give rise to individual obligations as between two states (for example, rules concerning riparian states and the non-navigational uses of international watercourses).Rights arising under the second category are considered by the ILC to include a case of pollution of the high seas in breach of Article 194 of UNCLOS which may particularly impact on one or several states whose beaches may be polluted by toxic residues or whose coastal fisheries may be closed and hence considered to be specially affected, or a nuclear free zone treaty or any other treaty 'where each parties' performance is effectively conditioned upon and requires the performance of each of the others'.

The ILC Articles also envisage that a state other than an 'injured state' is entitled to invoke the responsibility of another state if:

(a) The obligation breached is owed to a group of states including that state, and is established for the protection of a collective interest of the group; or

(b) The obligation breached is owed to the international community as whole.

In cases involving environmental damage, at least three situations are to be distinguished. The first is where a state permits activities which cause damage to its own environment; the second is where a state permits activities which cause damage to the environment of another state; and the third is where a state permits or causes damage to the environment in an area beyond national jurisdiction.

5

Damage to the Environment of Another State

INTRODUCTION

In situations involving damage to its environment, or consequential damage to its people or their property or other economic loss, a state will not find it difficult to claim that it is an 'injured state' and that it may bring an international claim. In the *Trail Smelter* case, the United States invoked its right not to be subjected to the consequences of transboundary air pollution from sulphur emissions in Canada and to bring a claim against Canada for having violated its rights.

As a riparian state and a party to an international agreement with France, in the *Lac Lanoux Arbitration* Spain relied upon *prima facie* rights to challenge France over proposed works which it alleged would violate its right to use the waters of the River Carol under certain conditions. Similar considerations apply in respect of the *Gabcikovo-Nagymaros* dispute submitted by Hungary and Slovakia to the ICJ for a determination of rights on the basis of a bilateral treaty between those two states and 'principles of general international law'.

Australia, in the *Nuclear Tests* case, argued that French nuclear tests deposited radioactive fallout on Australian territory which violated its sovereignty and impaired its independent right to determine the acts which should take place within its territory. And Ireland, in the *MOX* case, claimed that it was injured by transboundary movements of radioactive substances introduced into the Irish Sea by the United Kingdom in violation of its international commitments.

DAMAGE TO A STATE'S OWN ENVIRONMENT

A numberof international environmental agreements commit parties to protect environmental resources located exclusively within their territory, for example the conservation of non-migratory species or habitats or watercourseslocated within their territories. In these circumstances, other parties to the agreement could claim to be an injured state such as to allow them – at least in theory – to bring an international claim. In practice, this has not happened: it is only where the interference with the environmental resource crosses a national boundary that one or more states have felt compelled to act. Exceptionally, in the EU context the EC Commission will institute proceedings for non-compliance with EC environmental rules even in the absence of transboundary consequences.

DAMAGE TO THE ENVIRONMENT IN AREAS BEYOND NATIONAL JURISDICTION

Not all cases will be as straightforward as the *Trail Smelter* case, however. In the *Nuclear Tests* cases, brought by Australia and New Zealand against France calling on the latter to halt its atmospheric nuclear testing in the South Pacific region, the claim raised a more complicated legal question than the allegation of a violation of sovereignty by the deposit of radioactive fallout in its territory: did Australia and New Zealand have the right to bring a claim to the ICJ on the basis of a violation of an obligation owed *erga omnes* to all members of the international community to be free from nuclear tests generally or in violation of the freedom of the high seas? Similar issues had been raised in the *Fur Seals* case. Both cases raised the issue of whether a state had standing to bring an environmental claim to preventdamage to an area beyond national jurisdiction, even if it had not itself suffered any material damage. This raises the possibility of bringing an action on the basis of obligations which are owed *erga omnes*, either on the basis of a treaty or on the basis of customary law. As a general matter, where one party to a treaty or agreement believes that another party is in violation of its obligations under that treaty or agreement, it will have the right, under the treaty or agreement, to seek to enforce the obligations of the party alleged to be in violation, even if it has not suffered material damage. In most cases involving a violation of a treaty obligation, however, the applicant state is likely to have been induced into bringing a claim because it has suffered some form of material damage and not because it wishes to bring a claim to protect the interests of the international community. Such an example was Mexico's claim against the United States under the GATT over the US import ban on yellow-fin tuna caught by Mexican vessels on the high seas in violation of United States fisheries laws.

For breaches of treaty obligations, the right of a state to enforce obligations will usually be settled by the terms of the treaty. Various human rights treaties permit any party to enforce the obligations of any other party by bringing a claim before the relevant treaty organs. The EC Treaty allows a member state which considers that another member state has failed to fulfil an EC obligation, including an environmental obligation, to bring the matter before the ECJ.Although this right has been relied upon on numerous occasions to threaten court proceedings, it appears to have resulted in a decision by the ECJ on just one occasion, when France successfully brought proceedings against the United Kingdom for unlawfully having enforced domestic legislation setting a minimum mesh size for prawn fisheries. Under EC law, there is also no need to show that the claimant state has suffered damage: the mere violation of EC law is sufficient to allow standing. Thus a failure by a member state to carry out an environmental impact assessment as required under Directive 85/337 would allow any other member state to bring an action to the ECJ in accordance with Article 227 (formerly Article 170) of the EC Treaty cven if the environmental consequences might not be noticed beyond the country required to carry out the assessment. Under EC law, each member state has an actionable legal interest in the proper fulfilment by every other member state of its environmental obligations. Given that the environment is, in many instances, a shared natural resource in the protection of which each member of the international community has an interest, compelling policy arguments can be raised to apply the rationale underlying the EC approach to the international legal protection of the environment generally.

The 1995 Straddling Stocks Agreement has introduced innovative and far-reaching provisions in its Part VI (on compliance and enforcement). Article 19 requires flag states to ensure compliance with sub-regional and regional conservation and management measures for straddling fish stocks and highly migratory fish stocks. Article 20 establishes arrangements for international co-operation in enforcement.

These include the requirement that, where a vessel is alleged to have been engaged in unauthorised fishing in an area under the jurisdiction of a coastal state, the flag state must, at the request of the coastal state concerned, 'immediately and fully' investigate the matter. Moreover, state parties which are members of a regional or sub-regional fisheries management organisation or participants in regional or sub-regional management arrangements may take action to deter vessels which have engaged in activities which undermine or violate the conservation measures established by the organisation or arrangement from fishing on the high seas until appropriate action is taken by the flag state.

Article 21 addresses sub-regional and regional co-operation in enforcement. It provides that a state party which is a member of a regional or sub-regional fisheries management organisation or a participant in a regional or sub-regional management arrangement may board and inspect fishing vessels flying the flag of another party to the 1995 Agreement (whether or not that party is a member of the organisation or a participant in the arrangement) in any high seas area covered by an organisation or arrangement, for the purpose of ensuring compliance with conservation and management measures. Article 21 goes on to provide detailed rules on the enforcement obligations of the flag state and the rights of the state party to the 1995 Agreement, particularly with regard to 'serious violations', including the requirement that actions taken other than by flag states must be proportionate to the seriousness of the violation.

The situation in general international law is less well developed, although there is a move in the direction taken by the EC under some recent environmental treaties and in international practice. Thus, New Zealand's 1995 application to the ICJ challenging France's resumption of underground nuclear tests was premised on the view that it would be unlawful for France to conduct such tests before it had carried out an environmental impact assessment as required (it was argued) by international law. A failure by a party to the 1987 Montreal Protocol to fulfil its obligations under that treaty entitles any other party to the Protocol to enforce the obligation by invoking the non-compliance or dispute settlement mechanisms under the Protocol, without having to show that it had suffered material damage as a result of the alleged failure. The 1989 Basel Convention similarly provides that any party 'which has reason to believe that another party is acting or has acted in breach of its obligations' under the Convention may inform the Secretariat and the party against whom the allegations are made. Most other environmental treaties are less explicit, establishing dispute settlement mechanisms which will settle the question of enforcement rights in accordance with the provisions available under that treaty or related instruments. Some treaties specifically preclude their application to the global commons. The 1991 Espoo Convention, for example, precludes parties from requesting an environmental impact assessment or other measures in respect of harm to the global commons.

Whether a state has, in the absence of a specific treaty right such as those under the Montreal Protocol, a general legal interest in the protection of the environment in areas beyond its national jurisdiction such as to allow it to exercise rights of legal protection on behalf of the international community as a whole (sometimes referred to as *actio popularis*) is a question which remains difficult toanswer intheabsenceof statepractice.This may happenin asituation where the activities of a state were alleged to be causing environmental damage to the global commons, such as the high seas, the seabed beyond national jurisdiction, outer space or perhaps the Antarctic, or to living resources found in or passing through those areas. In such cases, the question is which states, if any, have the right to enforce such international legal obligations as may exist to avoid causing environmental damage to an area of the global commons?

The matter has been considered in passing by the ICJ on two occasions, and by some of the ICJ judges in a third case. In the *South West Africa (Preliminary Objections)* case, the ICJ stated that, 'although a right of this kind [*actio popularis*] may be known to certain municipal systems of law, it is not known to international law as it stands at present; nor is the Court able to regard it as imported by the "general principles of law" referred to in Article 38, paragraph 1(c), of its Statute'. However, a majority of judges in the *Barcelona Traction* case implicitly recognised the possibility of what might be considered to be an *actio popularis* under international law where an obligation exists *erga omnes*. The ICJ held that: an essential distinction should be drawn between the obligations of a state towards the international community as a whole, and those arising vis-a'-vis another state in the field of diplomatic protection. By their very nature the former are the concern of all states. In view of the importance of the rights involved, all states can be held to have a legal interest in their protection; they are obligations *erga omnes*.

In the *Nuclear Tests* cases, four judges in their joint Dissenting Opinion (Judges Ortyeama, Dillard, Jimenezde Arechega and SirHumphrey Waldock) identified the conditions in which the *actio popularis* might be argued:

If the materials adduced by Australia were to convince the Court of the existence of a general rule of international law, prohibiting atmospheric nuclear tests, the Court would at the same time have to determine what is the precise character and content of that rule and, in particular, whether it confers a right on every state individually to prosecute a claim to secure respect for the rule. In short, the question of 'legal interest' cannot be separated from the substantive legal issue of the existence and scope of the alleged rule of customary international law. Although we recognise that the existence of a so-called *actio popularis* is a matter of controversy, the observations of this Court in the *Barcelona Traction, Light and Power Company, Limited* Case suffice to show that the question is one that may be considered as capable of rational legal argument and a proper subject of litigation before this Court.

Despite the fact that the notion of *actio popularis* and rights and obligations *erga omnes* may be treated as distinct but related concepts, this Dissenting Opinion suggests that the two are closely linked. There has been little judicial consideration of what rights and obligations exist *erga omnes,* although the lists cited usually include obligations arising from the outlawing of acts of aggression and of genocide and relating to the protection of fundamental human rights.Some support has been expressed by commentators for the view that obligations owed *erga omnes* might extend to environmental damage in areas beyond national jurisdiction, and support for this view might also be found in the ILC's previous classification of a 'massive pollution' of the atmosphere or of the seas as an international crime. It has also been suggested that obligations *erga omnes* could be created by the actions of a limited number of states.

There thus appears to be some support favouring the right of a state to bring an action in its capacity as a member of the international community to prevent significant damage from occurring to the environment in areas beyond its national jurisdiction. Although most discussions focus on damage occurring in the global commons, there may be equally compelling policy reasons for allowing the *actio popularis* concept to apply also in respect of damage occurring to the environment within another state's jurisdiction. To the extent, then, that a rational legal argument can be made in favour of the *actio popularis,* in respect of which international environmental obligations could it be relied upon? At this stage, it is most likely to be successfully invoked in a case involving very significant damage to the environment, perhaps even at the level of 'massive pollution' or harm. Likely candidates would probably include those environmental obligations that have been associated with the 'common concern' or 'common heritage' principles. They might therefore include the protection of the global environment from significant harm (Principle 21 of the Stockholm Declaration and Principle 2 of the Rio Declaration) and rights established by treaty which relate to, *inter alia,* protection of the high seas, the climate system, the ozone layer, biodiversity (including fisheries), plant genetic resources and, to a lesser extent, wetlands and cultural property, as well as in respect of environmental matters which are associated with human rights obligations.

On a more cautious note, it should be remembered that not all international organisations or their non-compliance bodies are likely to favour the *actio popularis* concept. The GATT Dispute Settlement Panel in the *Yellow-Fin Tuna* case specifically rejected the claim by the United States that it was entitled to take measures to protect dolphins on the high seas, although in that case the Panel applied GATT law and not public international law, and no evidence was presented by the United States that the dolphins were protected or endangered under international law. The decision of the WTO Appellate Body in the *Shrimp/Turtle* case, recognising that the United States had a legitimate interest in migratory sea-turtles which were internationally endangered, marks a shift towards recognition of the *actio popularis* concept, although in that case it is important to recall that the species of sea turtle in question (if not the turtles actually harmed) were known to be located from time to time in United States waters. International law is in this respect still finding its centre of gravity, and states have not generally sought to assert a legal right to act on behalf of the whole international community in the protection of environmental issues on the basis of customary law or national law. Prior to the *Shrimp/Turtle* case, where they have sought to assert a legal right to act on behalf of the whole international community, as in the early *Fur Seals Arbitration* and the *Yellow-Fin Tuna* case, they have been rebuffed on the ground that they were seeking to apply *national* laws extra-territorially. In both of the latter cases, the result might have been different if the complainant states had relied upon, and could prove the existence of, a rule of customary international law, as Australia and New Zealand sought to do in 1973 in the *Nuclear Tests* cases.

In many respects, the discussion of *actio popularis* at the international level is similar to that which is taking place at the national level. In international affairs, the function of a state might be compared to that of an attorney general in national law. These national discussions suggest a further limitation on the likelihood of actions being brought by public authorities to enforce the environmental rights of the community as a whole. The views of one scholar on the clear limitations of an attorney general's ability to enforce rules to protect the environment on behalf of the community as a whole are equally applicable to international matters:

> Their statutory powers are limited and sometimes unclear. As political creatures, they must exercise the discretion they have with an eye towards advancing and reconciling a broad variety of important social goals, from preserving morality to increasing their jurisdiction's tax base. The present state of our environment, and the history of cautious application and development of environmental protection laws long on the books, testifies that the burdens of an attorney general's broad responsibility have apparently not left much manpower for the protection of nature.

The reluctance of states to enforce obligations towards the protection of the environment is, regrettably, supported by many examples. One leading example is the failure of any state to seek to enforce compliance by the former USSR with its international legal obligations arising out of the consequences of the accident at the Chernobyl nuclear power plant in 1986. This and other examples suggest that it is unlikely that the same states would seek to enforce obligations owed to the global commons, the violation of which may only lead to indirect or nominal harm to the state. This suggests the need for an increased enforcement role for international organisations, or other members of the international community, particularly where the mere attempt to enforce obligations may establish a precedent which could subsequently apply to the enforcing state.

Enforcement by international organisations

Whilst international organisations play an important legislative role in the development of international environmental law, their enforcement function is limited. International organisations are international legal persons which may seek to protect their own rights and enforce the obligations that others have towards them.

Sovereign interests have, however, led states to be unwilling to transfer too much enforcement power to international organisations and their secretariats, although there are some indications that this reluctance is being overcome.

Early examples of limited enforcement roles granted to international organisations include: the right of the River Danube Mixed Commission to 'work out agreed measures' for the regulation of fishing in the Danube; the right of certain international fisheries institutions to 'recommend' international enforcement measures or systems; and the right of the International Commission for the Protection of the Rhine Against Pollution to regularly compare the draft national programmes of the parties to ensure that 'their aims and means coincide'. Marginally more ambitious is the obligation of the CITES Secretariat, when it is satisfied that information it has received indicates that certain endangered species are being affected adversely by trade in specimens, to communicate that information to the relevant party or parties, which may then lead to the matter being reviewed by the next conference of the parties, which may make whatever recommendations it deems appropriate.

Developments for the protection of the marine environment and the Antarctic environment foresee an enhanced enforcement role for international organisations. The approach of the 1992 Oil Fund Convention is particularly ambitious, since it establishes and endows the Fund with legal personality in the laws of each party and gives it rights and obligations, including being a party in legal and enforcement proceedings before the national courts of that party. The 1982 UNCLOS also introduces innovative arrangements by endowing some of its institutions with a range of enforcement powers. Thus, the Council of the International Sea-Bed Authority can: 'supervise and co-ordinate the implementation' of Part XI of UNCLOS and 'invite the attention of the Assembly to cases of non-compliance'; institute proceedings on behalf of the Authority before the Sea-Bed Disputes Chamber in case of non-compliance; issue emergency orders 'to prevent serious harm to the marine environment arising out of activities in the Area'; and direct and supervise inspectors to ensure compliance. A Legal and Technical Commission, one of the Council's organs, will be entitled to make recommendations to the Council on the institution of proceedings and the measures to be taken following any decision by the Sea-Bed Disputes Chamber.

The Antarctic Mineral Resources Commission, which would have been established under the 1988 CRAMRA, could draw to the attention of all parties any activity which affected the implementation of CRAMRA or compliance by any party, as well as any activities by a non-party which affected implemen-tation. The Commission could also designate observers, and 'ensure the effective application' of the provisions in the Convention concerning notification, reporting of mineral prospecting,and keeping underreview the conductof Antarctic mineral resource activities with a view to safeguarding the protection of the Antarctic environment in the interest of all mankind.

The 1988 CRAMRA will not come into force since being 'replaced' by the 1991 Antarctic Environment Protocol, the main environmental institution for which there is a Committee for Environmental Protection. The Committee's enforcement role under the 1991 Protocol is more limited than that envisaged for the Commission under CRAMRA: its Committee will provide advice and adopt recommendations on matters such as the effectiveness of measures taken, the application and implementation of environmental impact assessment procedures, and the state of the Antarctic environment. The advice and recommendations are to be drawn upon fully by the Antarctic Treaty Consultative Meetings in adopting measures under the 1959 Antarctic Treaty for implementation of the Protocol. The Committee is not, however, granted any formal enforcement powers.

The 1992 OSPAR Convention also goes some way towards establishing a limited role for the Commission it creates to ensure compliance. Under Article 23, entitled 'Compliance', the Commission has two functions. First, it must 'assess' compliance with the Convention by parties, and make any decisions and recommendations on the basis of the reports submitted by the parties.Secondly, when appropriate, the Commission may: decide upon and call for steps to bring about full compliance with the Convention, and decisions adopted thereunder, and promote the implementation of recommendations, including measures to assist a contracting party to carry out its obligations. Although these provisions do not allow the Commission to take measures such as court proceedings in national courts, or arbitration proceedings, they go beyond the provisions of many other international environmental agreements. Other arrangements endow particular organisations with enforcement or quasi-enforcement functions. In relation to weapons agreements, the UN Security Council may 'take action in accordance with the [UN] Charter' if the consultation and co-operation procedure established under the relevant treaties does not remove doubts concerning fulfilment of obligations under certain nuclear weapons treaties. More generally, many of the institutions established by environmental treaties are required, as their primary task, to keep under review the relevant treaty and to promote its effective implemen-tation. This general function could be interpreted, over time and under the right conditions, to allow institutions to play an enforcement role.

No discussion of international enforcement powers would be complete without mention of the EC Commission, which must, under Article 211 (formerly Article 155) of the EC Treaty, ensure that the provisions of the EC Treaty and the measures taken by the institutions (i.e. secondary legislation) are applied. Article 226 (formerly Article 169) of the EC Treaty provides that:

> If the Commission considers that a member state has failed to fulfil an obligation under this Treaty, it shall delivera reasoned opinion onthe matter after giving the state concerned the opportunity to submit its observations.
>
> If the member state concerned does not comply with the opinion within the period laid down by the Commission, the Commission may bring the matter before the European Court of Justice (ECJ).

It has done so on many occasions.

Before the Commission can bring a member state before the ECJ it must first present its case and evidence to the member state and request observations. The member state then has an opportunity to make observations, following which the Commission will deliver a 'reasoned opinion'. Tnis allows a full airing of the differences between the Commission and the member state and often allows the matter to be resolved before the case is actually brought to the ECJ. In environmental matters, the Commission has frequently and controversially used its powers under Article 226 (formerly Article 169). In 1982, the Commission commenced sixteen infringement proceedings against member states under the former Article 169; by 1990, that number had risen to 217 infringement proceedings. In 2001, the Commission brought seventy-one cases to the ECJ against member states under Articles 226 and 228, and delivered 197 reasoned opinions. At any one time, the Commission is likely to have several dozen matters pending under Article 226, and has to date brought more than two hundred cases to the ECJ alleging violations of EC environmental laws.

The Commission can also apply to the ECJ for interim measures under Article 243 (formerly Article 186) of the EC Treaty – a form of interlocutory relief well established in EC jurisprudence and quite often employed, for example, in competition and anti-trust cases. The Commission must show that it has a good arguable case, that the need for relief is urgent and that irreparable damage to the EC interest will be done if the order is not granted. The member state can defend itself by establishing that it will suffer irreparable harm if the order is made. The Commission does not have to give a cross-undertaking in damages in the event that it ultimately loses the case. In Case 57/89, *EC Commission* v. *Germany*, the ECJ considered the circumstances in which it would be prepared to prescribe necessary interim measures in environmental cases. The case concerned the construction in Germany of a reservoir and related site, and the Commission sought a declaration that the construction violated Article 4(1) of the 1979 Wild Birds Directive, and the adoption of interim measures to suspend the work until the ECJ had given its decision on the main application. The ECJ held that for a measure of this type to be ordered the application must state the circumstances giving rise to the urgency and the factual and legal grounds establishing a *prima facie* case for the interim measures. The ECJ rejected the application on the grounds that the Commission had failed to prove urgency: the application had been submitted after the project was well under way and the interim measures had not been sought until a large part of the work had already been partially completed, and it could not be shown that 'it [was] precisely the next stage in the construction work which will cause serious harm to the protection of birds'.

Enforcement by non-state actors

According to traditional rules of public international law, non-state actors are not international legal persons except within the limited confines of international human rights law and its associated fields. It is still difficult to find many textbooks on international law which make any reference to the role of environmental and other non-state actors in the international environmental legal process, although it is widely recognised that they have become in many areas, and particularly in the field of international environmental law, *de facto* international actors who are, in limited circumstances, endowed with *de jure* rights. In practice, non-state actors play a central role in the development and application of international environmental law. Environmental organisations have been involved in the international implementation and enforcement process although their primary role continues to be at the national level, through political means or by recourse to administrative or judicial procedures for enforcing national measures adopted by a state in implementing its international treaty and other obligations.

ENFORCEMENT IN THE NATIONAL COURTS

'Judicial Application of International Environmental Law', 7 RECIEL 1–67 (1998) (special issue); M. Anderson and P. Galizzi, *International Environmental Law in National Courts* (2001).

UNCED endorsed a stronger role for the non-governmental sector in enforcing national environmental laws and obligations before national courts and tribunals, as reflected in Agenda 21 and the Rio Declaration, and now applied in the 1998 Aarhus Convention. This occurred in the context of earlier treaties and agreements which recognised and encouraged their role, particularly where individuals were the victims of pollution or environmental damage in a transboundary context. These earlier efforts sought either to establish principles governing equal access to national courts by victims of transfrontier pollution, or to establish the jurisdiction of courts in the event of transboundary incidents. The 1974 OECD Council Recommendation on Principles Concerning Transfrontier Pollution prepared the ground for the adoption of more detailed principles to ensure the legal protection of persons who suffer trans-frontier pollution damage. The 1976 OECD Council Recommendation on Equal Right of Access in Relation to Transfrontier Pollution identified the constituent elements of a system of equal right of access. According to the Recommendation, these were a set of rights recognised by a country in favour of persons who are affected or likely to be affected in their personal or proprietary interests by transfrontier pollution originating in that country. They include rights relating to access to information and participation in hearings and enquiries, and 'recourse to and standing in administrative and judicial procedures' to prevent pollution, have it abated, or obtain compensation for the damage caused. These general rights were further elaborated the following year by a more detailed OECD Council Recommendation for the Implementation of a Regime of Equal Right of Access and Non-Discrimination in Relation to Transfrontier Pollution.

The non-binding OECD instruments are supplemented by a range of treaty obligations which address equal access or the jurisdiction of courts over trans-boundary disputes. The 1974 Nordic Environmental Protection Convention allows any person who is affected or may be affected by a nuisance caused by 'environmentally harmful activities' in another contracting state to bring before the appropriate court or administrative authority of that state the question of the permissibility of such activities, including the questions of compensation and measures to prevent damage.

The 1974 Nordic Convention also provides for the appointment of a supervisory authority in each state 'to be entrusted with the task of safeguarding general environmental interests in so far as regards nuisances arising out of environmentally harmful activities in another contracting state', including the right to institute proceedings before or be heard by the courts or administrative authority of another contracting state. The supervisory authority of the state in which damage occurs is also required to facilitate on-site inspections to determine such damage.

An enforcement role for individuals is envisaged by several treaties establishing international rules on civil liability. In relation to the jurisdiction of national courts, these fall into two categories: those treaties requiring victims to bring proceedings before the courts of the state in which the transboundary pollution originated, and those allowing victims to choose either the court of the state in which the pollution originated or the courts of the state in which the damage was suffered.

The nuclear liability conventions adopted in the 1960s fall into the former category. They require victims of nuclear damage to make their claims before courts which may be several thousands of miles away from the area where the damage occurred, thus imposing an onerous burden. Moreover, they do not expressly allow for claims for environmental damage, although negotiations are currently underway to extend the definition of damage to include environmental damage. The oil pollution conventions adopted a decade or so later also provide support for the enforcement role of individuals, and are more accessible to individuals since they allow victims to claim before the courts of any contracting state in which an incident has caused pollution damage.

The second category of conventions ensuring a role for non-state enforcement establish private international law rules allocating jurisdiction to national courts over a range of civil and commercial matters, including disputes arising out of the law of tort. These generally allow victims a choice of courts. Although they were not prepared with environmental pollution and disputes in mind, they can apply to transboundary environmental disputes. The 1968 Brussels Convention on Jurisdiction and Enforcement of Judgments in Civil and Commercial Matters (1968 Brussels Convention), to which EC member states alone may become parties, has a number of purposes, including the free circulation of judgments throughout the EC, and has established jurisdiction rules for civil and commercial matters. Under Article 5(3) of the Convention (and now Regulation 44/2001), jurisdiction in matters 'relating to tort, delict or quasi-delict' is conferred on the courts of the place 'where the harmful event occurred'. In *Handelskwekerij*

GJ Bier v. *Mines de Potasses d'Alsace,* the ECJ was asked to interpret 'where the harmful event occurred' in a case in which the defendant was alleged to have discharged over 10,000 tonnes of chloride every twenty-four hours into the Rhine River in France but the damage was suffered by horticultural businesses in the Netherlands.

The Dutch plaintiffs wished to bring proceedings in the Netherlands rather than in France. On an Article 177 preliminary reference request from the Appeal Court of The Hague, the ECJ held that Article 5(3) should be interpreted 'in such a way as to acknowledge that the plaintiff has an option to commence proceedings either at the place where the damage occurred or the place of the event giving rise to it'. This allows victims of transboundary pollution in EC member states to choose the jurisdiction in which they wish to bring environmental cases which could be classified as tortious, delictual or quasi-delictual in nature. In 1988, the Brussels Convention was supplemented by the Lugano Convention on Jurisdiction and Enforcement of Judgments in Civil and Commercial Matters, which applies similar rules to relations between EC and EFTA countries.

INTERNATIONAL ENFORCEMENT

At the international level, opportunities for non-state actors to play an enforcement role are limited. Under some regional human rights treaties, individual victims, including non-governmental organisations, may bring complaints directly to an international body. Thus, the European Convention on Human Rights allows any person, non-governmental organisation or group of individuals claiming to be the victim of a violation of the rights in the Convention by one of the parties to bring a case to the European Court of Human Rights.Similar provisions exist in the Optional Protocol to the 1966 International Covenant on Civil and Political Rights for communications by individuals to the Human Rights Committee, alleging breaches of the Covenant.

The InternationalCovenant onEconomic,Social andCultural Rights,however,does not grant individuals and non-governmental organisations such rights. The UN Commission on Human Rights cannot receive individual complaints concerning human rights violations, although its subsidiary Sub-Commission on the Prevention of Discrimination and Protection of Minorities can receive complaints about a consistent pattern of gross and reliably attested violations of human rights, and then refer them to the Commission on Human Rights.

Non-governmental organisations and individuals have played an active role in supporting the enforcement role of the EC Commission, usually by submitting complaints to that institution concerning the non-implementation by member states of their environmental obligations. In 1991, for example, more than four hundred complaints were received by the EC Commission concerning non-compliance with environmental obligations, leading to a number of formal investigations by the Commission.

It is in their capacity as watchdogs that environmental organisations play an important role in the development, application and enforcement of international environmental law. Environmental organisations have long been active in monitoring and seeking to enforce compliance by states of international environmental laws and standards.

In this context, development, application and enforcement are so closely intertwined that it may be misleading to attempt to separate the tasks. In practice, environmental organisations seek to influence government positions at the national and international levels, to participate in international decision-making and law-making, and to enforce rules of international environmental law (at both the national and international levels).Examples of the way in which these actors have sought to promote or give effect to international obligations include – at the international level – their role in bringing about requests from the WHO and the UN General Assembly for an advisory opinion on the legality of the use of nuclear weapons from the ICJ,and informal assistance to states in the preparation (and even presentation) of a case.

At the national level, environmental organisations are increasingly active in bringing legal proceedings to enforce international environmental obligation. In recent years, they have also gained a degree of access to some international proceedings from which they were previously excluded, in the sense that they may be able to file *amicus curiae* submissions.

INTERNATIONAL CONFLICT RESOLUTION (SETTLEMENT OF DISPUTES)

A range of international procedures and mechanisms are available to assist in the pacific settlement of environmental disputes. Article 33 of the UN Charter identifies the traditional mechanisms, including negotiation, enquiry, mediation, conciliation, arbitration, judicial settlement, resort to regional agencies or arrangements, or other peaceful means of the parties' own choice.

These techniques can be divided into two broad categories: diplomatic means according to which the parties retain control over the dispute insofar as they may accept or reject a proposed settlement (negotiation, consultation, mediation, conciliation); and legal means which result in legally binding decisions for the parties to the dispute (arbitration and judicial settlement).

Recourse to regional arrangements and international organisations as mediators and conciliators provides something of a middle way: the legal consequences of any decision taken by the institution will depend on the treaty establishing the institution.

Many of the earliest environmental treaties did not provide for any dispute settlement mechanisms whether of a diplomatic or legal nature, or of a voluntary or mandatory character.

Initially, the trend was towards the use of informal and non-binding mechanisms, such as negotiation and consultation, supplemented by the use of more formal mechanisms, such as conciliation, arbitration and judicial settlement. More recently, there has been a move towards thedevelopmentof new techniquesto establishnon-contentious mech-anisms. Recent treaties provide parties with a range of options for settling disputes and encouraging implementation.

The 1992 Climate Change Convention envisages no fewer than threemechanisms to assist in dispute resolutionor non-implementation: a Subsidiary Body for Implementation, to provide assistance in implementation; a multilateral consultative process to address questions regarding implementation in a non-confrontational way; and the settlement of remaining disputes in more traditional ways by negotiation, submission to arbitration or the ICJ, or international conciliation.

Diplomatic means of dispute settlement Negotiation and consultation

The technique of negotiation has been used to resolve a number of environmental disputes. In the *Fisheries Jurisdiction* case, the ICJ set forth the basic objectives underlying negotiation as an appropriate method for the resolution of a dispute. The ICJ held that the objective of negotiation should be: the delimitation of the rights and interests of the parties, the preferential rights of the coastal state on the one hand and the rights of the applicant on the other, to balance and regulate equitably questions such as those of catch-limitation, share allocations and 'related restrictions concerning areas closed to fishing, number and type of vessels allowed and forms of control of the agreed provisions'.

The ICJ also set out conditions establishing that future negotiations should be conducted: on the basis that each must in good faith pay reasonable regard to the legal rights of the other . . . thus bringing about an equitable apportionment of the fishing resources based on the facts of the particular situation, and having regard to the interests of other states which have established fishing rights in the area. It is not a matter of finding simply an equitable solution, but an equitable solution derived from the applicable law.

Environmental treaties refer, more or less as a matter of standard practice, to the need to ensure that parties resort to negotiation and other diplomatic channels to resolve their disputes before making use of other more formal methods. Since negotiations of this type invariably take place behind closed doors, it is difficult to identify specific examples involving the successful resolution of claims and disputes by negotiation. One case involved the settlement between Canada and the USSR concerning damage caused by the disintegration over Canada of Cosmos 954, a nuclear-powered satellite launched by the USSR. The negotiated settlement was agreed in the context of the USSR's consideration of the question of damage 'in strict accordance with the provisions' of the 1972 Space Liability Convention to which both countries were parties.

Consultation between states is also encouraged by environmental treaties as a technique to avert and resolve disputes and potential disputes between states. In the *Lac Lanoux* case, the arbitral tribunal held that France had a duty to consult with Spain over certain projects likely to affect its interests, and that, in this context, the reality of the obligations thus undertaken is incontestable and sanctions can be applied in the event, for example, of an unjustified breaking off of the discussions, abnormal delays, disregard of the agreed procedures, systematic refusals to take into consideration adverse proposals or interests, and, more generally, in cases of violation of the rules of good faith.

Specific examples of environmental treaties requiring consultation in certain situations include: development plans which may affect the natural resources of another state; measures to prevent the pollution of coastlines from oil pollution incidents on the high seas; the authorisation of ocean dumping in emergency situations; pollution by certain substances from land-based sources; the permissibility of environmentally harmful activities; and generally problems in applying a treaty or the need for and nature of remedial measures for breaches of obligation. The 1979 LRTAP Convention requires early consultations to be held between parties 'actually affected by or exposed to a significant risk of long-range transboundary air pollution' and the parties in which a significant contribution to such pollution originates.

6

Mediation, Conciliation, and International Society

INTRODUCTION

Where negotiations and consultations fail, a number of environmental treaties endorse mediation and conciliation (or the establishment of a committee of experts) to resolve disputes, all of which involve the intervention of a third person. In the case of mediation, the third person is involved as an active participant in the interchange of proposals between the parties to a dispute, and may even offer informal proposals.

There are few reported examples of mediation being relied upon to resolve environmental disputes. Of recent note, however, is the outcome of a mediation conducted under the auspices of the OAS, relating to a long-standing territorial dispute between Guatemala and Belize.

In September 2002, the two facilitators appointed by the OAS put forward proposals, approved by the two states and Honduras, for a resolution of the dispute, including the establishment of an ecological park and a tri-state sub-regional fisheries commission. In the case of conciliation, the third person assumes a more formal role and often investigates the details underlying the dispute and makes formal proposals for the resolution of the dispute. Examples of conciliation include the role of the International Joint Commission established by Canada and the United States in the 1909 Boundary Waters Treaty, which fulfils a combination of quasi-judicial, investigative recommendatory and co-ordinatingfunctions.

The now defunct European Commission on Human Rights also performed conciliation functions: once a petition had been referred to it, it was required to ascertain the facts, to place itself at the disposal of the parties concerned with a view to securing a friendly settlement of the matter on the basis of respect for human rights as defined in the Convention, and, where no such friendly settlement was reached, to draw up a report on the facts and state its opinion as to whether the facts found disclosed a breach of obligations under the Convention.

The Dispute Settlement Panels established under the GATT performed a similar function of conciliation. Under Article XXIII(2) of the GATT, the Panels assisted the parties to a dispute to reach a solution and, failing that, made an objective assessment of the matter before them, including an objective assessment of the facts of the case and the applicability of and conformity with the GATT. If requested by the contracting parties, the Panels made such other findings, including recommendations, as would assist them in making recommendations or in giving rulings.

The 1997 Watercourses Convention provides that where negotiation fails to lead to a successful outcome the parties may jointly seek the good offices of, or request mediation or conciliation by, a third party, or make use, as appropriate, of any joint watercourse institutions that may have been established by them. Where a dispute has not been settled within six months of a request for negotiations, any of the parties to the dispute may submit the dispute to impartial fact-finding in accordance with the Convention, unless the parties otherwise agree, and the fact-finding commission is to submit its report to the parties concerned setting forth its findings (with reasons) and such recommendations as it deems appropriate for an equitable resolution of the dispute, which the parties concerned must consider in good faith.

Under the 1985 Vienna Convention, the 1992 Biodiversity Convention and the 2001 Treaty on Plant Genetic Resources, conciliation will be used if the parties to the dispute have not accepted compulsory dispute settlement procedures by arbitration or the ICJ.

The political organs of international institutions and regional agencies also play an importantrole in the settlement of disputes. Such organs may be granted an express mandate to consider disputes between two or more parties to the treaty. Alternatively, they may attempt to resolve disputes between parties in theabsenceof aspecificmandateto doso.Examplesofthe latterincludethe1985 decision of the conference of the parties to CITES concerning the application of the Convention to endangered species acquired prior to the entry into force of the Convention, and the 1991 decision of the Executive Committee of the 1971 Oil Pollution Fund Convention to exclude claims by Italy against the Fund for non-quantifiable damage to the marine environment.

Another example of this approach includes the 1974 Nordic Environmental Protection Convention, which provides for the establishment of a Commission upon the demand of any party to give an opinion on the permissibility of environmentally harmful activities which entail considerable nuisance in another party.

The 1985 South Pacific Nuclear Free Zone Treaty establishes a control system which includes a complaints procedure involving the possible convening of a Consultative Committee to consider complaints and evidence of breach of obligations, with certain inspection powers, and the right to report fully to members of the South Pacific Forum and to give its decision as to whether a breach of obligation has occurred.

Under the 1991 Espoo Convention, if the parties cannot agree on whether a proposed activity is likely to result in a 'significant adverse transboundary impact', any party involved in the disagreement may submit that question to an Inquiry Commission. The Inquiry Commission, comprising three members, will advise and prepare an opinion based on 'accepted scientific principles' on the likelihood of significant adverse transboundary impact, and may take all appropriate measures to carry out its functions.

Finally, the procedure established under the Conference on Security and Co-operation in Europe provides an alternative means of achieving conciliation.

NON-COMPLIANCE PROCEDURES

One of the most significant developments in the field of international environmental law has been the emergence of non-compliance procedures under various multilateral environmental agreements, occupying a function between conciliation and traditional dispute settlement. Since the early 1990s, a significant number of treaties have established subsidiary bodies to deal with compliance and disputes over non-compliance. The first was the non-compliance procedure established under the 1987 Montreal Protocol, including the Implementation Committee established by the second meeting of the parties to the Protocol.

Under the non-compliance procedure, any party which has reservations about another party's implementation of its obligations under the Protocol may submit its concerns in writing to the secretariat, with corroborating information.

The secretariat will then determine, with the assistance of the party alleged to be in violation, whether it is unable to comply with its obligations under the Protocol, and will transmit the original submission, its reply and other information to the Implementation Committee.The Implementation Committee has a membership often parties (originally five) elected by the meeting of the parties on the basis of equitable geographical distribution for a two-year period.

Its functions are to receive, consider and report on submissions made by any party regarding another party's implementation of its obligations under the Protocol, and any information or observations forwarded by the secretariat in connection with the preparation of reports based on information submitted by the parties pursuant to their obligations under the Protocol. The Committee may, at the invitation of the party concerned, undertake information gathering in the territory of that party, and will also maintain an exchange of information with the Executive Committee of the Multilateral Fund related to the provisions of financial and technical co-operation to developing country parties.

The Committee is to try to secure 'an amicable resolution of the matter on the basis of respect for the provisions of the Protocol' and report to the meeting of the parties, which may decide upon and call for steps to bring about full compliance with the Protocol. The fourth meeting of the parties also adopted an indicative list of measures that might be taken by a meeting of the parties in respect of non-compliance, which comprise:

- appropriate assistance;
- issuing cautions; and
- suspension (in accordance with the applicable rules of international law concerning the suspension of the operation of a treaty) of specific rights and privileges under the Protocol.

The Committee's report must not contain confidential information and is to be made available to any person upon request. Significantly, resort to the non-compliance procedure does not prejudice the dispute settlement provisions available under Article 11 of the 1985 Vienna Convention, which include negotiation, good offices, mediation, arbitration, submission to the ICJ and the establishment of a conciliation commission.

Following the developments under the Montreal Protocol, non-compliance procedures have been established (or are in the process of being established) under other multilateral environmental agreements, including the 1989 Basel Convention, the 1991 VOC and 1994 Sulphur Protocols to the LRTAP Convention, the 1996 Protocol to the London Convention, the 1998 Chemicals Convention, the 2000 Biosafety Protocol, and the 2001 POPs Convention. The two most significant arrangements, however, are reflected in the mechanisms established under the 1997 Kyoto Protocol and the 1998 Aarhus Convention.

Article 18 of the Kyoto Protocol calls on the conference of the parties serving as the meeting of the parties to the Kyoto Protocol to approve, at its first session, 'appropriate and effective procedures and mechanisms to address cases of non-compliance', with the caveat that any procedures and mechanisms entailing binding consequences 'shall be adopted by means of an amendment to [the] Protocol'. In 2001, at the seventh conference of the parties, the parties adopted a decision on the compliance regime for the

Kyoto Protocol, which is among the most comprehensive and rigorous established thus far. The compliance regime consists of a Compliance Committee made up of two branches: a Fa-cilitative Branch and an Enforcement Branch. The Facilitative Branch aims to provide advice and assistance to parties to promote compliance; the Enforcement Branch has the power to apply consequences to parties not meeting their commitments. Both branches are to be composed of ten members, including one representative from each of the five official UN regions, one from the small island developing states, and two each from Annex I and non-Annex I parties. Decisions of the Facilitative Branch may be taken by a three-quarters majority, but decisions of the Enforcement Branch require, in addition, a double majority of both Annex I and non-Annex I parties.

The Committee also meets in a plenary composed of members of both branches, and a Bureau supports its THE LEGAL AND INSTITUTIONAL FRAMEWORK work. Certain commitments fall under the remit of one or the other branch. The requirement, for example, of the flexibility mechanisms to be 'supplemental' to domestic action is under the purview of the Facilitative Branch, as is the commitment of Annex I parties to strive to minimise adverse impacts on developing countries.

The Facilitative Branch also provides 'early-warning' of cases where a party is in danger of not complying with its emission targets. In response to problems, the Facilitative Branch can make recommendations and also mobilise financial and technical resources to help parties comply.

The Enforcement Branch, for its part, is responsible for determining whether an Annex I party is not complying with its emission targets or reporting requirements, or has lost its eligibility to participate in the mechanisms. It can also decide whether to adjust a party's inventory or correct the compilation and accounting database, in the event of a dispute between a party and the expert review team.

The remedies it may decide on are to be aimed at the 'restoration of compliance to ensure environmental integrity'. In the case of compliance with emission targets, Annex I parties are granted 100 days after the expert review of their final annual emissions inventory has finished to remedy any shortfall in compliance. If, at the end of this period, a party's emissions are still greater than its assigned amount, it must make up the difference in the second commitment period, plus a penalty of 30 per cent. It will also be barred from 'selling' under emissions trading and, within three months, it must develop a compliance action plan detailing the action it will take to ensure that its target is met in the next commitment period.

Any party not complying with reporting requirements must develop a similar plan, and parties that are found not to meet the criteria for participating in the mechanisms will have their eligibility withdrawn. In all cases, the Enforcement Branch will make a public declaration that the party is in non-compliance and will also make public the consequences to be applied. A potential compliance problem can be raised either by an expert review team, or by a party about its own compliance, or by a party raising concerns about another party. After a preliminary examination, the matter will be considered in the relevant branch of the Compliance Committee. The Compliance Committee will base its deliberations on reports from expert review teams, the subsidiary bodies, parties and other official sources. Competent intergovernmental and non-governmental organisations may submit relevant factual and technical information to the relevant branch.

In October 2002, the parties to the Aarhus Convention established a Compliance Committee to review compliance by the parties with their obligations under the Convention. The Committee consists of eight members, elected from candidates nominated by parties and signatories and - innovatively -non-governmental organisations. The functions of the Committee are to consider any submission, referral or communication made to it, to prepare a report on compliance with or implementation of the provisions of the Convention, and to monitor, assess and facilitate the implementation of and compliance with reporting requirements. In consultation with the party concerned, the Committee may provide advice and facilitate assistance to individual parties regarding the implementation of the Convention. Subject to agreement with the party concerned the Committee may also:

- make recommendations to the party concerned;
- request the party concerned to submit a strategy to the Committee regarding the achievement of compliance with the Convention and to report on the implementation of this strategy; and
- in cases of communications from the public, make recommendations to the party concerned on specific measures to address the matter raised by the member of the public.

The meeting of the parties may, upon consideration of a report and any recommendations of the Committee, decide upon appropriate measures to bring about full compliance with the Convention, including declarations of non-compliance, issuing cautions, suspending special rights and privileges under the Convention, and taking such other non-confrontational, non-judicial and consultative measures as maybe appropriate. The Committee may receive submissions from parties and referrals from the secretariat. Breaking new ground, the Committee may also receive communications from the public. Communications from the public are to be addressed in writing to the Committee through the secretariat and supported by corroborating information. In language which will be familiar to human rights lawyers, the Committee is to consider any such communication unless it determines that the communication is anonymous, or an abuse of the right to make such communications, or manifestly unreasonable, or incompatible with the provisions of the decision establishing the Committee or with the Convention. Although there is no rule requiring exhaustion of local remedies, the Committee 'should at all relevant stages take into account any available domestic remedy unless the application of the remedy is unreasonably prolonged or obviously does not provide an effective and sufficient means of redress'. The Committee must bring any communications so submitted to the attention of the party alleged to be in non-compliance, and the party must within five months after any communication is brought to its attention by the Committee submit to the Committee a written statement clarifying the matter and describing any response that it may have made. The Committee may hold hearings.

INSPECTION PROCEDURES OF MULTILATERAL DEVELOPMENT BANKS

In September 1993, the World Bank became the first multilateral development bank to create an Inspection Panel to receive and review requests for inspection from a party which claimed to be affected by a World Bank project, including claims in respect of environmental harm. This innovation was followed by similar arrangements established at the Inter-American Development Bank (an Independent Investigation Mechanism, established in 1994) and the Asian Development Bank (1995). These new mechanisms provide substantive and independent review of the activities of these banks and have enhanced access to international remedies for non-state actors.

The World Bank Inspection Panel became operational in late 1994. An affected party (or, in limited cases, its representatives) may request an inspection if it can demonstrate that its rights or interests have been or are likely to be directly affected by an action or omission of the Bank as a result of a failure of the Bank to follow its operational policies and procedures with respect to the design, appraisal and/or implementation of a project financed by the Bank . . . provided in all cases that such failure has had, or threatens to have, a material adverse effect.

The Panel, which consists of three members, may make a recommendation to the Executive Directors as to whether a matter complained of should be investigated, having been provided by evidence from the management of the Bank as to its compliance with the Bank's policies and procedures.

If the Executive Directors decide to investigate the matter, one or more members of the Panel (the Inspector(s)) will conduct an inspection and report to the Panel, which will then submit its report to the Executive Directors on whether the Bank has complied with its relevant policies and procedures. This new review body represents an important development in international law, creating for the first time within a multilateral development bank an administrative procedure to permit review of the institution's compliance with its internal law at the instigation of third parties other than employees.

The well-developed practice of administrative tribunals addressing employment and contractual matters for Bank staff is, in effect, extended into the fields of environmental and social review. By October 2002, the Panel had received twenty-seven requests, the largest number concerning compliance with the operational directive on environmental assessment (OD 4.01).

Requests have also addressed the environmental policy for dam and reservoir projects (OD 4.00), environmental aspects of Bank work (OMS 2.36), indigenous peoples (OD 4.20), water resource and management (OP 4.07), wildlands (OPN 11.02) and natural habitats (OP/BP 4.04).

NAFTA COMMISSION ON ENVIRONMENTAL CO-OPERATION

Citizen access to an independent fact-finding mechanism is available under the NAFTA: the secretariat of NAFTA's Commission on Environmental Cooperation may receive and consider submissions from any non-governmental organisation or person asserting that a party is 'failing to effectively enforce its environmental law', and may request a response from the party concerned if it determines that the submission so merits. The Secretariat may be instructed by the Council, by a two-thirds vote, to prepare a 'factual record' which may be made public by the Council. Since 1996, the secretariat has received submissions in respect of thirty-six matters, of which twelve are currently active. The secretariat has published factual records in respect of three matters: *Cozumel* (24 October 1997); *BC Hydro* (11 June 2000); and *Metales y Derivados* (11 February 2002). *Legal means of dispute settlement*

Mediation and conciliation do not produce legally binding decisions. If the parties to a dispute seek such a result, they must opt for arbitration or recourse to an international court.

ARBITRATION

International arbitration has been described as having 'for its object the settlement of disputes between states by judges of their own choice and on the basis of respect for the law. Recourse to arbitration implies an engagement to submit in good faith to the award.' In recent years, states negotiating environmental treaties have favoured the inclusion of specific provisions for the establishment of an arbitration tribunal, with the power to adopt binding and final decisions. Early examples providing for the establishment of a body to take binding decisions include the 'special commission' to be established at the request of any of the parties to disputes relating to high seas fishing and conservation, and the detailed provisions on the establishment of an arbitration tribunal in the Annex to the 1969 Oil Pollution Intervention Convention. Other environmental treaties include provisions, including annexes or protocols, for the submission of disputes to arbitration at the instigation of one party to a dispute or both produced in several cases but as yet no arbitral panel has been established to hear a complaint. Records of the submissions made, factual reports and responses of NAFTA parties are made available by the Commission for Environmental Co-operation on its website, www.cec.org/citizen/index.cfm?varlan=english. parties. Other treaties refer simply to the possibility of submitting disputes to arbitration without providing details on the establishment of such a body or its working arrangements.

Certain environmental treaties provide for the submission of disputes to arbitration by mutual consent of the relevant par-ties or allow a party to declare, at the time of signature or ratification, that it is not bound by parts of the dispute settlement provisions, including submission to arbitration, or provide for a party to declare, at the time of signature or ratification, or at any time thereafter, its acceptance of compulsory recourse to arbitration and/or the ICJ.

The *Pacific Fur Seals Arbitration* (1893), the *Trail Smelter* case (1935/41)and the *Lac Lanoux* case (1957) reflect the historical importance played by arbitration in the development of international environmental law, in interstate cases. More recently, there is growing evidence to support the view that states view arbitration as an attractive means of resolving international disputes. Within the past few years, the 1982 UNCLOS Annex VII arbitration procedure has been invoked on two occasions: in 1998 by Australia and New Zealand against Japan, in relation to a dispute concerning the conservation of southern bluefin tuna; and in 2001 by Ireland against the United Kingdom, in the dispute concerning the authorisation of the MOX plant. Additionally, France and the Netherlands have submitted a dispute to arbitration in relation to a dispute under the 1976 Rhine Chloride Convention and its 1991 Protocol, and Ireland initiated arbitration proceedings against the United Kingdom in relation to freedom of information under Article 9 of the 1992 OSPAR Convention. Against that background, the Permanent Court of Arbitration (which has served as the registry in most of these disputes) has sponsored the adoption of arbitration rules specifically designed to address needs arising from the arbitration of disputes relating to the environment and natural on the Protection of the Rhine Against Pollution by Chlorides, Art. 13 and Annex B; 1979 Berne Convention, Art. 18; 1988 CRAMRA, Arts. 55 to 59 and Annex; 1992 OSPAR Convention, Art. 32(2); 1994 Danube Convention, Art. 24; 1995 SADC Water Protocol, Art. 7; 1996 LDC Protocol, Art. 16; 1998 Rhine Convention, Art. 16; 2000 SADC Revised Water Protocol, Art. 7. resources. The growing role of arbitration is also reflected in the case law of arbitral tribunals in investor/state disputes involving allegations of interference with foreign investments occasioned by municipal concerns to protect the environment.

INTERNATIONAL COURTS

The settlement of international disputes may also be referred to an international court, which is a permanent tribunal competent to deliver a legally binding decision. In the environmental field, a number of international courts have assumed particular importance, namely, the ICJ, the ITLOS, the WTO Appellate Body (and panels), the ECJ, and the courts created by regional human rights treaties. In addition, several non-governmental efforts aim to establish 'international courts' to address international environmental issues. While not creating binding arrangements, these provide a useful way to bring environmental issues to the attention of the public. Notwithstanding certain calls for its creation, there is as yet no international environmental court, and none is likely to emerge in the foreseeable future.

INTERNATIONAL COURT OF JUSTICE

The ICJ, sometimes referred to as the World Court or the Hague Court, is the UN's principal judicial organ. It was established as a successor (although not formally the legal successor) to the Permanent Court of International Justice (PCIJ) in 1945. Jurisdiction of the ICJ over a dispute depends on whether the Court has been invoked in a contentious case between two or more states, or asked to give an advisory opinion on a question of law at the request of states or certain international organisations.

In July 1993, the ICJ established a seven-member Chamber for Environmental Matters. This decision followed previous consideration by the ICJ on the possible formation of such a chamber, and was taken in view of the developments in the field of environmental law which have taken place in the last few years and the need to be prepared to the fullest possible extent to deal with any environmental case falling within its jurisdiction.

Contentious cases The contentious jurisdiction of the ICJ can arise in at least two ways. First, under Article 36(1) of its Statute, the ICJ has jurisdiction by agreement between the parties to the dispute, either by a special agreementwhereby two or more states agree to refer a particular dispute and defined matter to the ICJ, or by a compromissory clause in a multilateral or bilateral treaty. The treaty could be a general treaty for the peaceful settlement of disputes, a treaty dealing with the general relations between the states, or a treaty regulating a specific topic, such as environmental protection. Many environmental treaties provide for possible recourse to the ICJ to settle disputes. Occasionally, they recognise its compulsory jurisdiction, but more usually the reference of a dispute to the ICJ requires the consent, in each case, of all parties to the dispute. Recent practice in environmental treaties allows parties at the time of signature, ratification or accession, or at any time thereafter, to accept compulsory dispute settlement by recourse to arbitration or to the ICJ. Few parties accept this option. A second way in which contentious cases come before the ICJ is under Article 36(2) of its Statute (the 'Optional Clause'), under which parties to the Statute may declare that they recognise its compulsory jurisdiction, in relation to other states accepting the same obligation, in all legal disputes concerning the interpretation of a treaty; any question of international law; the existence of any fact which, if established, would constitute a breach of an international obligation; and the nature or extent of the reparation to be made for the breach of an international obligation. Acceptance of the jurisdiction of the ICJ under Article 36(2) may be made unconditionally, or on condition of reciprocity, or for a limited period of time. Additionally, the practice of the ICJ has been to accept reservations or conditions to declarations made under the Optional Clause, as happened in the *Fisheries Jurisdiction* case (*Spain* v. *Canada*).

Unlike its predecessor, the PCIJ, the ICJ has now been presented with opportunities to address international environmental disputes – raising matters concerning environment and conservation – and has given judgments which establish – or imply – important general principles. Relevant cases before the PCIJ include the *Diversion of the Waters of the River Meuse* and the *Te r r i -torial Jurisdiction of the International Commission of the River Oder*. Early cases before the ICJ which have influenced the development of international environmental law include the *Corfu Channel* case, where the ICJ affirmed 'every state's obligation not to allow knowingly its territory to be used for acts contrary to the rights of other states'; the *Fisheries Jurisdiction* case, where the ICJ set forth basic principles governing consultations and other arrangements concerning the conservation of shared natural resources; and the *Nuclear Tests* cases. The ICJ has since had a number of cases before it which it considers as having important implications for international law 'on matters relating to the environment': the *Certain Phosphate Lands in Nauru* case, concerning the obligation, if any, of trustee states for, *inter alia*, the physical destruction of the island as a unit of self-determination accompanied by a failure to rehabilitate the land, as well as the nature and extent of obligations relating to permanent sovereignty over natural resources and entitlement to the costs of rehabilitation; the *Gabcikovo-Nagymaros Project (Hungary/ Slovakia)* case, addressing, *inter alia*, the use of international watercourses and international environmental law in relation to an agreement for the construction of two barrages which would result in the diversion of the Danube river; the *Request for an Examination of the Situation*, brought by New Zealand in relation to the resumption of underground nuclear tests by France; and the *Fisheries Jurisdiction* case, where Spain challenged the enforcement of fisheries conservation measures taken by Canada in areas beyond its exclusive economic zone.

Advisory opinions The UN Charter allows the General Assembly or the Security Council to request the ICJ to give an advisory opinion on any legal question, and allows other organs of the UN and specialised agencies authorised by the General Assembly to request advisory opinions of the ICJ on legal questions arising within the scope of their activities. Advisory opinions are not binding in law upon the requesting body, although in practice they are accepted and acted upon by that body. Although no legal question on an environmental issue has been the subject of a request for an advisory opinion, this route could provide a useful and non-contentious way of obtaining independent international legal advice on environmental matters. In July 1996, the ICJ gave an advisory opinion on the legality of the use of nuclear weapons in the context of their effects on human health and the environment, arguably the most significant of the ICJ's pronouncements on international environmental law.

Interim measures of protection If it considers that the circumstances so require, the ICJ has the power to indicate interim measures of protection to preserve the rights of the parties to a dispute. The irreparability of serious environmental damage could make interim measures particularly important in cases concerning environmental protection. During the preliminary phase of the *Nuclear Tests* cases, the ICJ indicated interim measures of protection, asking the parties to ensure that no action should be taken which might aggravate or extend the dispute or prejudice the rights of another party, and calling on France to 'avoid nuclear tests causing the deposit of radio-active fall-out on Australian territory'. Interim measures of protection were also indicated in the *Fisheries Jurisdiction* cases, but were refused by the ICJ in the *Passage Through the Great Belt* case. They were also refused by the ICJ in ten cases brought by the Federal Republic of Yugoslavia to bring a halt to a bombing campaign. It was argued, *inter alia,* that attacks on oil refineries and chemical plants were having 'serious environmental effects on cities, towns and villages in the Federal Republic of Yugoslavia'.

UNCLOS AND ITLOS

Part XV of the 1982 UNCLOS addresses compulsory dispute settlement, allowing states at the time of signature, ratification or accession or at any time thereafter to designate any of the following dispute settlement procedures: the International Tribunal for the Law of the Sea (established in accordance with Annex VI to UNCLOS); the ICJ; an arbitral tribunal (constituted in accordance with Annex VII to UNCLOS); and a special arbitral tribunal (constituted in accordance with Annex VIII to UNCLOS). A state which does not designate one of these means is deemed to have designated arbitration in accordance with Annex VII, and where two or more states have designated different means the dispute will go to arbitration (unless the parties agree otherwise).

The compulsory dispute settlement procedure is limited to certain disputes under the Convention. The exercise by a coastal state of its sovereign rights or jurisdiction under UNCLOS is only subject to the compulsory procedures when it is alleged that a coastal state has violated certain UNCLOS provisions, including internationally lawful uses of the exclusive economic zone (EEZ) or specified international rules and standards for the protection and preservation of the marine environment which are applicable to that state and which are established under UNCLOS or by a competent international organisation or diplomatic conference. Fisheries disputes will be subject to the compulsory procedure, except for disputes over the sovereign right of a coastal state regarding the living resources of the EEZ (including the discretionary powers for determining allowable catch, harvesting capacity, the allocation of surpluses and the terms and conditions of its conservation and management laws and regulations). Such disputes may be submitted to the conciliation procedure if it is alleged that the coastal state has manifestly failed to comply with its obligations to maintain the living resources in the EEZ. Parties may also optionally declare that the compulsory procedures do not apply to disputes concerning boundary delimitations, military activities, and those in respect of which the Security Council is exercising its functions.

Disputes relating to the exploration and exploitation of the international seabed and ocean floor (known as the 'Area') and its resources are subject to special, and rather complex,dispute settlementprocedures, which will generally involve disputes going to a Seabed Disputes Chamber of the International Tribunal for the Law of the Sea. The Seabed Disputes Chamber will have jurisdiction over a wide range of disputes, including environmental disputes involving those engaged in activities in the Area (states parties, the Authority, state enterprises, legal or natural persons, and prospective contractors).

The jurisdiction of ITLOS may also be invoked in certain circumstances where the parties to UNCLOS have not designated its use. Article 290(5) of the Convention provides that ITLOS may prescribe provisional measures pending the constitution of an arbitral tribunal to which a dispute is submitted. This provision has been invoked on two occasions: in 1998, Australia and New Zealand requested – and obtained – provisional measures from ITLOS in respect of fishing for southern bluefin tuna by Japanese vessels; and in 2001 ITLOS prescribed a provisional measure requiring Ireland and the United Kingdom to co-operate pending the constitution of the Annex VI arbitral tribunal.Additionally, ITLOS has jurisdiction pursuant to Article 292 of UNCLOS to order the 'prompt' release of vessels apprehended by a coastal state.

ITLOS has given judgment on the merits in four cases, all of which involved vessels alleged to have been engaged in illegal fishing activities. In addressing these cases, ITLOS has sought to avoid expressing views on the underlying merits of the case, although in the most recent case – involving the Volga (*Russia v. Australia*) – its judgment expressed understanding as to 'international concerns about illegal, unregulated and unreported fishing' and appreciation as to the objectives 'behind the measures taken by states, including the states parties to CCAMLR, to deal with the problem'.

DISPUTE SETTLEMENT BODY OF THE WORLD TRADE ORGANIZATION

The 1994 WTO Agreement introduced as an Annex the 'Understanding on Rules and Procedures Governing the Settlement of Disputes' (DSU). The DSU is intended to prevent and resolve disputes arising under the WTO Agreement and related instruments. It replaces the arrangements which had emerged in the context of the GATT, principally a system of panels with the power to make non-binding recommendations. Under the prior system, the adoption of panel recommendations could be blocked by any single contracting party. One of the principal innovations of the new WTO system is that panel decisions (as well as those of the Appellate Body) will be adopted and become legally binding unless these is a consensus to the contrary. The new WTO system therefore constitutes a system of compulsory third party adjudication with binding effects for its members. In this sense, it has potentially the most far-reaching and important jurisdiction of any of the global bodies. Its first eight years of operation suggest that it could significantly influence the development of international environmental law.

The DSU establishes a dispute settlement system consisting of three bodies – the Dispute Settlement Body (DSB), *ad hoc* panels and the Appellate Body – all based in Geneva. The DSB is a political body, comprising representatives of all WTO members. It administers the dispute settlement process. The WTO system establishes a detailed 'road map' for intergovernmental dispute settlement, characterised by its speed and relative procedural clarity. In the event of a dispute between members of the WTO over their respective trade-related obligations, one party may request the other to enter into consultations and notify the DSB of this request. If the consultations fail, each party may propose that other traditional dispute settlement procedures (good offices, conciliation or mediation) be employed, with the possible assistance of the WTO Director General. If this fails to settle the dispute, the DSB may be asked to establish an *ad hoc* panel. Once established, a panel will conduct hearings and issue a non-binding report on the merits of the case. The recommendations of a panel become binding only after they have been adopted by the DSB (adoption is automatic, unless there is a consensus against it in the DSB). Unlike the old GATT system, the panel report may be appealed on legal grounds to a permanent seven-member Appellate Body. The appeal is heard before a three-judge division of the Appellate Body, which may uphold, modify or reverse the legal findings of the panel. The report of the Appellate Body is then adopted by the DSB and given binding force, unless the DSB unanimously decides otherwise. The WTO dispute settlement system is governed principally by Articles III and IV of the WTO Agreement and the DSU. Working Procedures have been adopted for panel and Appellate Body proceedings, as have Rules of Conduct. The substantive law to be applied by the panels and the

Appellate Body is to be found in the 1994 WTO Agreement, and in the various multilateral and plurilateral side-agreements to the GATT (including the Multilateral Agreement on Trade in Services, the General Agreement on Trade in Services and the Agreement on Trade-Related Aspects of Intellectual Property Rights). In its first decision, the Appellate Body stated that these trade rules were 'not to be read in clinical isolation from public international law'. It has subsequently referred to – and applied – principles and rules of international environmental law in the *Beef Hormones* case (precautionary principle), the *Shrimp/Turtle* case (including sustainable developments, fisheries conventions, the 1973 CITES, the 1992 Biodiversity Convention and the 1982 UNCLOS), and the *Asbestos* case.

EUROPEAN COURT OF JUSTICE

N. Brown and F. Jacobs, *The Court of Justice of the European Communities* (1989); H. G. Schermers and D. Waelbroeck, *Judicial Protection in the European Communities* (1992); K. P. E. Lasok, *The European Court of Justice – Practice and Procedure* (1994 2nd edn);

D. Anderson, *References to the European Court* (1995); N. March Hunnings, *The European Courts* (1996).

The ECJ is the judicial institution of the EC and is required to ensure that in the interpretation and application of the EC Treaty 'the law is observed'. Environmental cases reach the ECJ in a number of ways. The most frequent route is under Article 226 (formerly Article 169) of the EC Treaty, and since 1980 the EC Commission has brought more than two hundred cases to the ECJ alleging the failure of a member state to comply with its environmental obligations, most of which have been successful. Its judgments have determined that member states may not plead circumstances existing in their internal legal system to justify a failure to comply with an environmental obligation; that administrative practices which may be altered at the whim of the administration do not constitute the proper fulfilment of an environmental obligation under a Directive; that the legal obligations imposed on a member state by an environmental Directive are limited to those dangerous substances specifically listed in the Directive and not to other unlisted dangerous substances as well; and that member states should achieve an 'environmental result' when implementing the Drinking Water Directive. The ECJ has also addressed the legality of national environmental measures and trade obligations and the failure to execute its judgment in an environmental case. The ECJ also has the power to impose fines for non-compliance with its judgments, which it did for the first time (in an environmental case) in 2000. Under Article 227 (formerly Article 170) of the EC Treaty, a member state which believes another member state has breached its obligations has a similar right to bring a matter before the ECJ.

Under Article 230 (formerly Article 173) of the EC Treaty, the ECJ may review the legality of certain acts of the EC Council, Commission, Parliament and European Central Bank on the grounds of lack of competence, infringement of an essential procedural requirement, infringement of the EC Treaty or any rule relating to its application, or misuse of powers. Actions may be brought by a member state or by a Community institution, other than the institution complained against, or by any legal or natural person provided that the act concerned is a decision addressed to that person or is of direct or individual concern to it. Under this head, the ECJ has considered the legality of the treaty basis of EC environmental legislation, and received applications from environmental groups alleging violations by the EC Commission of its legal obligations under the EC Treaty. The ECJ also has jurisdiction under THE LEGAL AND INSTITUTIONAL FRAMEWORK

Article 232 (formerly Article 175) under conditions similar to those governing Article 230, to challenge the failure of the Community institutions (in particular the Council or Commission) to act in pursuance of its environmental obligations under the EC Treaty. To date no environmental case appears to have been brought under this provision.

Finally, the ECJ has also considered environmental questions on the basis of its jurisdiction under Article 234 (formerly Article 177), the 'preliminary reference procedure'. Under this provision, the national courts of the EC member states may refer to the ECJ questions concerning the interpretation of the EC Treaty and the validity and interpretation of acts of the EC institutions, provided that a decision on the question is necessary to enable the national court to give a ruling on the question. Preliminary references from national courts to the ECJ are used when a dispute before the national courts raises a complex question of EC law or where the dispute turns on the EC law point and no appeal lies against the decision of the national court. The Article 234 procedure has been used on many occasions in relation to environmental matters, for example the disposal of waste from a nuclear power plant, the compatibility with EC law of the ban by an Italian municipality on the sale and distribution of plastic bags and other non-biodegradable packaging material, and the circumstances in which a member state may take account of economic, social and cultural requirements or regional and local characteristics when selecting and defining the boundaries of sites to be proposed to the Commission as eligible for identification as sites of Community importance, for the purposes of the 1992 Habitats Directive.

Court of First Instance of the European Union In 1988, the EC Council, acting under an amendment to the EC Treaty introduced by the 1986 Single European Act, established the Court of First Instance (CFI) with limited jurisdiction (over staff and competition cases and cases arising under the 1957 ECSC Treaty) and a right of appeal on points of law to the ECJ. In 1993, following the amendments to the EC Treaty made by the 1992 Treaty on European Union, the competence of the CFI was extended and it may now hear environmental cases brought under, *inter alia*, Articles 230 and 232 of the EC Treaty, although it cannot hear and determine preliminary references requested under Article 234 (formerly Article 177). Appellate review on points of law is to the ECJ.

HUMAN RIGHTS COURTS

The human rights courts established under regional human rights conven-tions may also have jurisdiction over environmental matters, although so far only the European Court of Human Rights appears to have addressed such issues in a sustained manner. From 1950 to 1998, the European Convention's machinery consisted of two organs, a Commission and a Court. Following the entry into force in November 1998 of the Eleventh Protocol to the Convention, the Commission was abolished and most of its functions transferred to the Court. As a result, claimants (whether state parties or individuals) now submit applications directly to the Court. The Court provides for traditional inter-state dispute resolution, as well as the rights of recourse by victims of violations. By Article 33, any state party may bring to the Court a case against any other state party which is alleged to have breached the provisions of the Convention or its Protocols. In fact, very few inter-state cases have been brought. Individuals, NGOs and groups of individuals, who claim to have been victims of a human rights violation may also bring a case against the state party which has committed the alleged violation. In the past few years, the Court has given far-reaching judgments in relation to Article 8 (privacy) and Article 1 of the First Protocol (property rights).

UNCED

Whereas the 1972 Stockholm Conference did not really address the compliance issue, the subject was clearly an important one for

UNCED. UN General Assembly Resolution 44/228 determined that UNCED should 'assess the capacity of the United Nations system to assist in the prevention and settlement of disputes in the environmental sphere and to recommend measures in this field, while respecting existing bilateral and international agreements that provide for the settlement of such disputes'. This task was only partly fulfilled. Principles 10 and 26 of the Rio Declaration call on states to provide, at the national level, 'effective access to judicial and administrative proceedings, including redress and remedy', and internationally to 'resolve all their environmental disputes peacefully and by appropriate means and in accordance with the Charter of the United Nations'. Agenda 21 recognises the limitations of existing arrangements, including the inadequate implementation by parties of their obligations, the need to involve international institutions and environmental organisations in the implementation process, and the gaps in dispute settlement mechanisms. Chapter 39 of Agenda 21 ('International legal instruments and mechanisms') addresses some of the needs. The international community is called upon to ensure 'the full and prompt implementation of legally binding instruments',and parties to international agreements are instructed to 'consider procedures and mechanisms to promote and review their effective, full and prompt implementation', including the establishment of 'efficient and practical reporting systems on the effective, full and prompt implementation of international legal instruments' and consideration of the ways in which international bodies might contribute towards the further development of such mechanisms.

The enhanced role of international institutions is endorsed. UNEP is called upon to promote the implementation of international environmental law; UNDP will play a lead role in support of the implementation of Agenda 21 and capacity-building at the country, regional, inter-regional and global levels; and the UN Commission on Sustainable Development is required to consider information regarding the implementation of environmental conventions made available by the relevant conferences of the parties. On dispute settlement, the international community is called upon to consider broadening and strengthening the capacity of mechanisms in the UN system to identify, avoid and settle international disputes in the field of sustainable development, taking into account existing bilateral and multilateral agreements for the settlement of such disputes. Specifically, this includes: mechanisms and procedures for the exchange of data and information, notification and consultation regarding situations that might lead to disputes with other states in the field of sustainable development and for effective peaceful means of dispute settlement in accordance with the Charter of the United Nations including, where appropriate, recourse to the International Court of Justice, and their inclusion in treaties relating to sustainable development.

CONCLUSIONS

As this chapter shows, the increased attention being given to compliance has generated new measures in the environmental field which supplement those measures available under general international law. The decision by the ICJ to establish an Chamber for Environmental Matters marked a further recognition that the effectiveness of the growing body of principles and rules required the availability of appropriate dispute settlement mechanisms. The limitations inherent in international arrangements for ensuring compliance with international environmental obligations should be apparent. Developments in international law alone will not be sufficient to overcome the political, economic and social reasons lying behind non-compliance.

Nevertheless, the law, processes and institutions can make a difference, and recent developments suggest that changes in the importance attached by the international community to compliance reflect the changing structure of the traditional international legal order. Important developments within the past decade include the broadening and strengthening of non-compliance mechanisms under various multilateral environmental agreements, the Permanent Court of Arbitration's new rules on arbitration of environmental disputes, the 'environmental justice' provisions of the 1998 Aarhus Convention, and a significant body of environmental jurisprudence at the ICJ, ITLOS and the WTO Appellate Body. Addressing compliance will require a comprehensive effort to develop rules and institutional arrangements at three levels: implementation, enforcement, and dispute settlement. First, with regard to implementation, the provision of technical, financial and other assistance to states, particularly developing states, points to the growing 'internationalisation' of the domestic implementation and legal process, and an awareness that international environmental law will not achieve its objectives if it does not also take account of the need, and techniques available, for improving domestic implementation of international environmental obligations.

Secondly, with regard to enforcement, states have been unwilling, for a variety of reasons, to bring international claims to enforce environmental rights and obligations. Within the past decade, however, it appears that this reluctance is being replaced by an increasing willingness by states to have resort to international adjudicatory mechanisms to enforce international environmental obligations, and important decisions have been handed down by the ICJ, ITLOS and the WTO Appellate Body. Nevertheless, the role of states can be reinforced by the supplementary role of international organisations and, to a lesser extent, non-state actors in the international enforcement process. Broadening the category of persons formally entitled to identify violations and to take measures to remedy them is a process which is underway and which should be further encouraged if states and other members of the international community are to be subjected to the sorts of pressure that will lead them to improve compliance with their obligations.

Thirdly, as the disputes before various international courts have shown, the availability of a broad and growing range of mechanisms for dispute settlement, including the compulsory jurisdiction of certain regional and sectoral courts and other international bodies, suggests an important and growing role for independent international adjudication. Finally, Principle 10 of the Rio Declaration and the adoption of the 1998 Aarhus Convention reflect the recognition that ensuring effective access to national judicial and administrative proceedings, including redress and remedies, is appropriately a matter for regulation by the international community.

7

Sovereignty and Extra-Territoriality

INTRODUCTION

The sovereign rightto exploitnatural resources includes theright to be free from external interference over their exploitation. This aspect of Principle 21/Princi-ple 2 is brought into question in disputes over the extra-territorial application of environmental laws of one state to activities taking place in areas beyond its national jurisdiction, either within the jurisdiction of another state or in activities beyond national jurisdiction. In 1893, the arbitral tribunal in the *Fur Seals Arbitration* rejected a claim by the US to be entitled to protect fur seals in areas beyond the three-mile limit of the territorial sea and the right to interfere in the internal affairs of other states to secure the enjoyment of their share in the 'common property of mankind'.

Nearly one hundred years later, the US banned the import of yellow-fin tuna caught by Mexican vessels, in Mexico's exclusive economic zone and on the high seas, with purse-seine nets the compliance of which with US environmental protection standards could not be proved. This 'extra-jurisdictional' application of US environmental standards was rejected by a GATT panel as being contrary to the GATT, holding that a country 'can effectively control the production or consumption of an exhaustible natural resource only to the extent that the production or consumption is under its jurisdiction' and that to allow the 'extra-jurisdictional' application of its environmental law would allow the US to 'unilaterally determine the conservation policies' of Mexico. More recently, however, the WTO's Appellate Body has taken a broader approach, and recognised the existence of a 'sufficient nexus' between migratory and endangered populations of sea-turtles located in Asian waters and the United States to allow the latter to claim an interest in their con-servation. The traditional and absolute prohibition on extra-territorial (or extra-jurisdictional) application of national environmental laws recognised by the earlier decisions is consistent with the principle of absolute sovereignty over natural resources. Those decisions do not rest easily, however, with a more modern conception of an ecologically interdependent world in which limits are placed on the exercise of sovereignty or sovereign rights, an approach with which the Appellate Body seemed sympathetic.

In the absence of generally accepted international standards of environmental protection and conservation, states with strict national environmental standards may seek to extend their application to activities carried out in areas beyond their territory, particularly where they believe that such activities cause significant environmental damage to shared resources (such as migratory species, transboundary watercourses, or air quality and the climate system) or affect vital economic interests. For 'shared natural resources' such as the high seas and atmosphere it will often be difficult, if not impossible, to draw a clear line between natural resources over which a state does and does not have sovereignty or exercise sovereign rights. In such circumstances, it is unlikely that the principle of territorial sovereignty, or permanent sovereignty over natural resources, can provide much assistance in allocating rights and responsibilities of states over environmental policy.

The permissibility of the extra-territorial application of national laws remains an open question in international law. The PCIJ has stated that 'the first and foremost restriction imposed by international law upon a state is that – failing the existence of a permissive rule to the contrary – it may not exercise its power in any form in the territory of another state outside its territory except by virtue of a permissive rule derived from international custom or from a convention'. However, in the same case the PCIJ went on to state that 'international law as it stands at present' does not contain 'a general prohibition to states to extend the application of their laws and the jurisdiction of their courts to persons, property and acts outside their territory' and that the territoriality of criminal law was 'not an absolute principle of international law and by no means coincides with territorial sovereignty'.

Subsequent state practice, as well as decisions of international tribunals, has not determined precisely the circumstances in which a state may take measures over activities outside its territory in relation to the conservation of shared resources. In the *Fisheries Jurisdiction* case, Spain challenged the application and enforcement by Canada of its fisheries conservation legislation in areas beyond its exclusive economic zone, but the ICJ declined jurisdiction, and the case did not reach the merits phase.

The right of states to exercise jurisdiction, either by legislation or adjudication, over activities in other states, or in areas beyond national jurisdiction, which are harmful to the environment at the global, regional or local level, could be justified on several grounds. First, corporations carrying on activities abroad might be subject to the environmental laws of their state of registration or incorporation, by application of the 'nationality' principle of jurisdiction.

International law does not, according to Oppenheim, prevent a state from exercising jurisdiction within its own territory over its nationals (including corporations) whoresidein aforeignstate,although thepower toen-force such laws depends upon the nationals being in the territorial jurisdiction or having assets therein against which judgment can be enforced. The application of the 'nationality' principle is likely to cause difficulty, however, since the foreigner abroad might be subject to the concurrent jurisdiction of the home state of registration or incorporation and the host state in which it carries out its activities, with the home state having more stringent rules of environmental protection. This will lead to jurisdictional disputes where some states use lower standards of environmental protection perhaps to gain economic advantage and attract foreign investment, and other states apply the nationality principle and require their companies to apply national environmental protection rules wherever they carry out their activities. In such circumstances, it has been suggested that the home state must not require compliance with its laws at the expense of its duty to respect the territorial sovereignty of the host state. When faced with such a conflict a court would be likely to balance the public policy of the home state, the interests of the host state, and the damage to international comity if it gave precedence to the laws of the home state, and only accord priority to those laws 'where the balance of interest clearly lies in that direction'. The factors applied by a court will also need to be applied by reference to the environment which is being affected or damaged. It would be difficult to justify a home state's taking measures where only the environment of the host state was being damaged. But if the damage was being caused to the environment of the home state or to areas beyond national jurisdiction (global commons) then the home state might have a stronger basis for asserting jurisdiction extra-territorially.

This latter situation creates a second possible basis for allowing the extraterritorial application of national laws: where activities carried out in one state have, or are likely to have, 'effects' in another state, recourse might be had to the 'objective' application of the territorial principle, otherwise known as the 'effects' doctrine. However, the application of the 'effects' principle is said to have 'doubtful consistency' with international law: the justification for assertions of jurisdiction on the basis of an alleged 'effects' principle of jurisdiction has not been generally accepted, and the matter is still one of controversy.

The extra-territorial application of national environmental laws has been particularly controversial in relation to trade issues. Principle 12 of the Rio Declaration declares that unilateral actions addressing environmental challenges 'outside the jurisdiction of the importing country should be avoided' and that 'environmental measures should, as far as possible, be based on an international consensus'. The Rio Declaration and Agenda 21 do not, however, prohibit *per se* all unilateral environmental measures, an approach which now appears to have been endorsed by the WTO Appellate

Body, subject to certain conditions being satisfied. The same approach has been taken in the WSSD Plan of Implementation. The challenge for the international community in coming years will be to determine the circumstances in which, in the absence of international consensus on agreed environmental standards, a state will be permitted, under the general rules of international law and specific WTO rules, to adopt unilateral environmental measures and apply them extra-territorially. *Responsibility not to cause environmental damage*

The second element of Principle 21/Principle 2 reflects the view of states that they are subject to environmental limits in the exercise of their rights under the principle of permanent sovereignty over natural resources. In the form presented by Principle 21/Principle 2, the responsibility not to cause damage to theenvironmentof otherstates orof areasbeyond national jurisdictionhasbeen accepted as an obligation by all states; without prejudice to its applications on a case-by-case basis, following the ICJ's 1996 Advisory Opinion on *The Legality of the Threat or Use of Nuclear Weapons* there can be no question but that Principle 21 reflects a rule of customary international law, placing international legal constraints on the rights of states in respect of activities carried out within their territory or under their jurisdiction.

Saying that Principle 21/Principle 2 reflect customary international law is not, however, decisive, and will be of only partial assistance in support of an international claim. In the context of activity which causes pollution and environmental degradation, Principle 21/Principle 2 indicate the need to address other questions: what is environmental damage? What environmental damage is prohibited (any damage, or just damage which is serious or significant)? What is the standard of care applicable to the obligation (absolute, strict or fault)? What are the consequences of a violation (including appropriate reparation)? And what is the extent of any liability (including measure of damages)? These and related questions are considered in chapter 18 below.

The responsibility of states not to cause environmental damage in areas outside their jurisdiction pre-dates the Stockholm Conference, and is related to the obligation of all states 'to protect within the territory the rights of other states, in particular their right to integrity and inviolability in peace and war'. This obligation was subsequently relied upon, and elaborated, by the arbitral tribunal in the much-cited *Trail Smelter* case, which stated that:

Under the principles of international law . . . no state has the right to use or permit the use of territory in such a manner as to cause injury by fumes in or to the territory of another of the properties or persons therein, when the case is of serious consequence and the injury is established by clear and convincing evidence.

Most writers accepted this formulation as a rule of customary international law and it was cited, with apparent approval, by Judge de Castro in his dissent in the *Nuclear Tests* case. In that case, Australia had asked the ICJ to adjudge and declare that the carrying out of further atmospheric nuclear tests was inconsistent with applicable rules of international law and would be unlawful 'in so far as it involves the modification of the physical conditions of and over Australian territory [and] pollution of the atmosphere and of the resources of the seas'. The Rapporteur to the ILA Committee on Legal Aspects of the Environment concluded from an examination that state practice was founded upon the rule in the *Trail Smelter* case.

In fact, consistent state practice is not readily discernible. As will be seen in chapter 18, there are relatively few claims which have been brought by states relying upon the rule reflected in Principle 21/Principle 2, and one is left to rely upon state practice as evidenced in particular by participation in and support for treaties and other international acts, as well as their statements as to what they consider to be the extent of their obligations. Following the Chernobyl accident in 1986, a discussion under the auspices of the IAEA threw some light on the views of states, although the record on this discussion alone cannot be considered as representing a comprehensive view. The general rule relied upon in the *Trail Smelter* case derives from an extension of the principle ofgood-neighbourliness. Althoughthe UN Charter doesnotexpressly address environmental issues, Article 74 of the Charter reflects the agreement of the UN members that 'their policy in their metropolitan areas must be based on the general principle of good neighbourliness' and must take account of 'the interests and well-being of the rest of the world, in social, economic and commercial matters'. The principle of good-neighbourliness underlies the *dicta* of the ICJ that the principle of sovereignty embodies 'the obligation of every state not to allow its territory to be used for acts contrary to the rights of other states'. In the *Lac Lanoux Arbitration*, involving the proposed diversion of an international river by an upstream state, the arbitral tribunal affirmed that a state has an obligation not to exercise its rights to the extent of ignoring the rights of another:

France [the upstream state] is entitled to exercise her rights; she cannot ignore the Spanish interests. Spain [the downstream state] is entitled to demand that her rights be respected and that her interests be taken into consideration.

The thread was further developed in 1961 when the UN General Assembly declared, specifically in relation to radioactive fallout, that:

The fundamental principles of international law impose a responsibility on all states concerning actions which might have harmful biological consequences for the existing and future generations of peoples of other states, by increasing the levels of radioactive fallout.

By1972,shortlybeforethe Stockholm Conference,theGeneral Assemblywas able to direct that the Conference must 'respect fully the exercise of permanent sovereignty over natural resources, as well as the right of each country to exploit its own resources in accordance with its own priorities and needs and in such a manner as to avoid producing harmful effects on other countries'.

The development of the second element of Principle 21/ Principle 2 can also be traced to earlier environmental treaties. The 1951 International Plant Protection Convention expressed the need to prevent the spread of plant pests and diseases across national boundaries. The 1963 Nuclear Test Ban Treaty prohibits nuclear tests if the explosion would cause radioactive debris 'to be present outside the territorial limits of the state under whose jurisdiction or control such explosion is conducted'; and the 1968 African Conservation Convention requires consultation and co-operation between parties where development plans are 'likely to affect the natural resources of any other state'.Under the 1972 World Heritage Convention, the parties agreed that they would not take deliberate measures which could directly or indirectly damage heritage which is 'situated on the territory' of other parties.

Principle 21 thus developed earlier state practice. It has been affirmed in many General Assembly resolutions and acts of other international organisations. Shortly after the Stockholm Conference, Principle 21, with Principle 22, was expressly stated by UN General Assembly Resolution 2996 to lay down the 'basic rules' governing the international responsibility of states in regard to the environment. It was also the basis of Article 30 of the Charter of Economic Rights and Duties of States, which provides that:

> All states have the responsibility to ensure that activities within their jurisdiction or control do not cause damage to the environment of other states or of areas beyond the limits of national jurisdiction.

It is endorsed by the 1975 Final Act of the Helsinki Conference on Security and Co-operation in Europe, Principle 3 of the 1978 UNEP Draft Principles, which requires states to ensure that 'activities within their jurisdiction or control do not cause damage to the natural systems located within other states or in areas beyond the limits of national jurisdiction', and the 1982 World Charter for Nature, which declares the need to 'safeguard and conserve nature in areas beyond national jurisdiction'. Perhaps more compelling is the reference to Principle 21 in treaties. It has long been referred to, or wholly incorporated,in the preamble to several treaties, and was fully reproduced in the operational part of a treaty, for the first time, as Article 3 of the 1992 Biodiversity Convention without express limitation to matters within the scope of the Convention.Principle 2 of the Rio Declaration is incorporated into the Preamble to the 1992 Climate Change Convention.

Similar language to the second element of Principle 21 also appears in treaties. The 1978 Amazonian Treaty fudges the issue of the legal status of Principle 21, declaring that 'the exclusive use and utilisation of natural resources within their respective territories is a right inherent in the sovereignty of each state and that the exercise of this right shall not be subject to any restrictions other than those arising from International Law'. The 1981 Lima Convention goes a little further by requiring activities to be conducted so that 'they do not cause damage by pollution to others or to their environment, and that pollution arising from incidents or activities under their jurisdiction or control does not, as far as possible, spread beyond the areas where [they] exercise sovereignty and jurisdiction'. The 1982 UNCLOS transforms the 'responsibility' into a 'duty', although it is unclear what was intended by the change. Under Article 193 of UNCLOS, states have the sovereign right to exploit their natural resources pursuant to their environmental policies and in accordance with their duty to protect and preserve the marine environment. UNCLOS shifts the emphasis from a negative obligation to prevent harm to a positive commitment to preserve and protect the environment. To that end, however, Article 194(2) does provide that states: shall take all measures necessary to ensure that activities under their jurisdiction or control are so conducted as not to cause damage by pollution to other states and their environment, and that pollution arising from incidents or activities under their jurisdiction or control does not spread beyond the areas where they exercise sovereign rights in accordance with [the] Convention.

The 1985 ASEAN Convention goes further, by recognising the second element of Principle 21 as a 'generally accepted principle of international law'.

Against this background, the time was plainly ripe for confirmation of the customary status of the obligation not to cause transboundary environmental harm. France's 1995 announcement of its resumption of underground nuclear tests provided the unlikely catalyst. In its Order rejecting New Zealand's request, the ICJ stated, somewhat cryptically, that its Order was 'without prejudice to obligations of States torespect and protect the natural environment, obligations to which both New Zealand and France have in the present instance reaffirmed their commitment'. A review of the pleadings indicates that New Zealand's affirmation that Principle 21/Principle 2 reflected a 'well established proposition of customary international law' was not opposed by France. It was also endorsed by Judge Weeramantry in his dissenting opinion.

Withintwomonthsofthe ICJ'sOrder,oralarguments opened attheICJinthe *Legality of the Threat or Use of Nuclear Weapons* Advisory Opinion proceedings. Several states argued that Principle 21/ Principle 2 reflected customary law, and none challenged that view (although some argued that they did not consider the principles to be of relevance to the case). In its Advisory Opinion, the ICJ stated that:

> The existence of the general obligation of States to ensure that activities within their jurisdiction and control respect the environment of other States or of areas beyond national control is now part of the corpus of international law relating to the environment.

It is interesting that the ICJ did not merely restate the language of Principle 21 and Principle 2, and it is unclear whether the ICJ intended to effect substantive changes by its reformulation. That does not, however, appear to have been the intention, since (arguably) the formulation adopted by the ICJ may be broader than that of Principle 21/Principle 2.

GENERAL PRINCIPLES AND RULES

This chapter describes the general principles and rules of international environmental law as reflected in treaties, binding acts of international organisations, state practice, and soft law commitments. These principles are general in the sense that they are potentially applicable to all members of the international community across the range of activities which they carry out or authorise and in respect of the protection of all aspects of the environment. From the large body of international agreements and other acts, it is possible to discern general rules and principles which have broad, if not necessarily universal, support and are frequently endorsed in practice. These are:

1. the obligation reflected in Principle 21 of the Stockholm Declaration and Principle 2 of the Rio Declaration, namely, that states have sovereignty over their natural resources

and the responsibility not to cause transboundary environmental damage;

2. the principle of preventive action;
3. the principle of co-operation;
4. the principle of sustainable development;
5. the precautionary principle;
6. the polluter-pays principle; and
7. the principle of common but differentiated responsibility.

In the absence of judicial authority and in view of the conflicting interpretations under state practice, it is frequently difficult to establish the parameters or the precise international legal status of each general principle or rule. The application of each principle in relation to a particular activity or incident, and its consequences, must be considered on the facts and circumstances of each case, having regard to several factors including: the source of the principle; its textual content and language; the particular activity at issue; the environmental and other consequences of the activity; and the circumstances in which it occurs (including the actors and the geographical region). Some general principles or rules reflect customary law, others may reflect emerging legal obligations, and yet others might have a less developed legal status. In each case, however, the principle or rule has broad support and is reflected in extensive state practice through repetitive use or reference in an international legal context.

Of these general principles and rules, Principle 21/Principle 2 and the cooperation principle are sufficiently well established to provide the basis for an international cause of action; that is to say, to reflect an international customary legal obligation the violation of which would give rise to a free-standing legal remedy. The same may now be said generally in respect of the precautionary principle in the European context, and perhaps also more globally in respect of particular activities or subject areas. The status and effect of the other principles is less clear, although they may bind as treaty obligations or, in particular contexts, as customary obligations. Whether they give rise to actionable obligations of a general nature is open to question. Finally, the principles and rules described in this chapter should be distinguished from the general principles described in chapter 4, as well as the substantive rules establishing environmental standards (i.e. air and water quality, conservation of biodiversity) and rules establishing techniques for implementing those standards (i.e. environmental impact assessment, participation in decision-making, access to information, economic instruments).

Principles and rules

References to principles and rules of general application have long been found in the preambular sections of treaties and other international acts, and in the jurisprudence of international courts and tribunals. More recently, however, principles of general or specific application have been incorporated into the operative part of some treaties. Article 3 of the 1992 Climate Change Convention lists 'Principles' intended to guide the parties '[i]n their actions to achieve the objective of the Convention and to implement its provisions'. Article 3 of the 1992 Biodiversity Convention introduces the text of Principle 21 of the Stockholm Declaration as the sole 'Principle'. The EC Treaty, as amended in 1986, 1992 and 1997, sets forth principles and rules of general application in Article 174(2) (formerly Article 130r). Other treaties follow a similar approach.

What consequences flow from the characterisation of a legal obligation as a legal principle or a legal rule? This question has hardly been addressed in detail by international courts and tribunals, and apparently not at all in the context of environmental principles. The Umpire in the *Gentini* case, in 1903 adopted the following distinction, which may provide some guidance about the legal effect of principles and their relationship to rules:

A 'rule' . . . 'is essentially practical and, moreover, binding . . . [T]here are rules of art as there are rules of government' while principle 'expresses a general truth, which guides our action, serves as a theoretical basis for the various acts of our life, and the application of which to reality produces a given consequence'.

In this sense, positive rules of law may be treated as the 'practical formulation of the principles', and the 'application of the principle to the infinitely varying circumstances of practical life aims at bringing about substantive justice in every case'. This view suggests that principles and rules point to particular decisions about legal obligations in particular circumstances, but they differ in the character of the direction they give. Rules are applicable in an all-or-nothing fashion . . . [A principle] states a reason that argues in one direction, but does not necessitate a particular decision. . . . All that is meant, when we say that a particular principle is a principle of our law, is that the principle is one which officials must take into account, if it is relevant, as a consideration inclining in one way or another.

This distinction finds some support in the practice of international courts and allows the conclusion that principles 'embody legal standards, but the standards they contain are more general than commitments and do not specify particular actions', unlike rules. The fact that legal principles, like rules, can have international legal consequences has focused attention on their content while being elaborated in recent treaties. The negotiations of the 1992 Climate Change Convention reflected differing views on the need to adopt a section on 'Principles' at all: generally, developing countries supported the inclusion of principles, whereas developed countries opposed them. The US and some other 'common law' delegations were concerned that the requirements included in Article 3 might be subject to the Convention's dispute settlement provisions or create specific commitments beyond those set out in Article 4 and elsewhere. Although the US failed in their efforts to have the whole of Article 3 deleted, or for the text to be amended to make clear that Article 3 could not be subject to the dispute settlement provisions, the US amendments were accepted to limit the application of principles to informing obligations under the Convention. A similar concern to limit the scope of application of a principle was reflected by the UK declaration made upon signature of the 1992 Biodiversity Convention, declaring the understanding that 'Article 3 of the Convention . . . sets out a guiding principle to be taken into account in the implementation of the Convention', implying that no legal consequences arose outside the Convention, and that within the Convention Article 3 did not give rise to a rule in the sense proposed by the Umpire in the *Gentini* case or by Professor Dworkin. It is far from clear, however, that the plain meaning of Article 3 supports the UK's understanding, particularly when the text is compared to Article 3 of the Climate Change Convention, and in particular the introductory 'chapeau' which seeks to limit the effect of the principles identified thereunder.

The international community has not adopted a binding international instrument of global application which purports to set out the general rights and obligations of the international community on environmental matters. No equivalent to the Universal Declaration of Human Rights, the International Covenant on Civil and Political Rights or the International Covenant on Economic, Social and Cultural Rights has yet been adopted, and none appears imminent. Any effort to identify general principles and rules of international environmental law must necessarily be based on a considered assessment of state practice, including the adoption and implementation of treaties and other international legal acts, as well as the growing number of decisions of international courts and tribunals. The efforts of governmental and nongovernmental lawyers in assessing the evidence which supports the existence of principles and rules has provided some guidance, and has influenced subsequent international law-making. The 1978 UNEP Draft Principles and the 1986 WCED Legal Principles have supplemented the 1972 Stockholm Declaration and influenced the 1992 Rio Declaration, which continues to reflect 'to the extent any international instrument can do so, the current consensus of values and priorities in environment and development'.

Since UNCED, further guidance may be obtained from the International Law Commission's Draft Articles on Prevention of Transboundary Harm from Hazardous Activities (2001), and the International Law Association's New Delhi Declaration of Principles of International Law Relating to Sustainable Development (2002).

Sovereignty over natural resources and the responsibility not to cause damage to the environment of other states or to areas beyond national jurisdiction responsibility to ensure that activities within their jurisdiction or control do not cause damage to the environment of other States or of areas beyond the limits of national jurisdiction.

Principle 21 remains the cornerstone of international environmental law; twenty years after its adoption, states negotiating the Rio Declaration were unable to improve significantly upon, develop, scale back or otherwise alter the language in adopting Principle 2. At UNCED, two words were added to recognise that states have the right to pursue 'their own environmental *and developmental* policies'.

Principle 21 and Principle 2 each comprise two elements which cannot be separated without fundamentally changing their sense and effect: the sovereign right of states to exploit their own natural resources; and the responsibility, or obligation, not to cause damage to the environment of other states or of areas beyond the limits of national jurisdiction. Taken together (state practice since 1972 has assiduously avoided their de-coupling), they establish the basic obligation underlying international environmental law and the source of its further elaboration in rules of greater specificity. That Principle 21 reflects customary law is now confirmed by the ICJ's 1996 Advisory Opinion on *The Legality of the Threat or Use of Nuclear Weapons*.

Sovereign rights over natural resources

The principle of state sovereignty allows states within limits established by international law to conduct or authorise such activities as they choose within their territories, including activities which may have adverse effects on their own environment. This fundamental principle underlies the first part of Principle 21/ Principle 2. The extension of the sovereignty principle into environmental affairs pre-dates the StockholmDeclaration and is rooted in theprinciple of permanent sovereignty over natural resources as formulated in various resolutions of the UN General Assembly regularly adopted after 1952. These resolutions were closely related to arrangements between states and foreign private companies for the exploitation of natural resources, particularly oil and minerals, in developing countries. They addressed the need to balance the rights of the sovereign state over its resources with the desire of foreign companies to ensure legal certainty in the stability of its investment. A landmark resolution was adopted by the UN General Assembly in 1962, when it resolved that the 'rights of peoples and nations to permanent sovereignty over their natural wealth and resources must be exercised in the interest of their national development of the well-being of the people of the state concerned'. The resolution reflects the right to permanent sovereignty over national resources as an international legal right, and has been accepted by some international tribunals as reflecting customary international law.

By the 1970s, limits to the application of the principle of state sovereignty over natural resources were emerging as the international community recognised a need to co-operate to protect the environment. In 1972, before the Stockholm Conference, the UN General Assembly declared that 'each country has the right to formulate, in accordance with its own particular situation and in full enjoyment of its national sovereignty, its own national policies on the human environment'. The relationship between permanent sovereignty over natural resources and responsibilities for the environment was formally recognised by Principle 21.

The importance placed by states on the principle of permanent sovereignty over natural resources is also reflected by its frequent invocation, in various forms, in international environmental agreements and during their negotiation. The 1933 London Convention affirmed that all animal trophies were 'the property of the Government of the territory concerned'. The 1971 Ramsar Convention emphasised that the inclusion of national wetland sites in its List of Wetlands did 'not prejudice the exclusive sovereign rights of . . . the party in whose territory the wetland is situated'. The 1983 International Tropical Timber Agreement recalled 'the sovereignty of producing members over their natural resources'. Recent treaties also refer to the sovereign rights of states over natural resources in their territory: the Preamble to the 1989 Basel Convention recognised that 'all states have the sovereign right to ban the entry or disposal of foreign hazardous wastes and other wastes in their territory'. The Preamble to the 1992 Climate Change Convention reaffirmed 'the principle of sovereignty of states in international co-operation to address climate change'. The 1992 Biodiversity Convention more specifically reaffirmed that states have 'sovereign rights . . . over their natural resources', and that 'the authority to determine access to genetic resources rests with the national governments and is subject to national legislation'.

PRINCIPLE OF PREVENTIVE ACTION

Closely related to the Principle 21 obligation is the obligation requiring the prevention of damage to the environment, and otherwise to reduce, limit or control activities which might cause or risk such damage. This obligation, sometimes referred to as the 'principle of preventive action' or the 'preventive principle', is distinguishable from Principle 21/Principle 2 in two ways. First, the latter arise from the application of respect for the principle of sovereignty, whereas the preventive principle seeks to minimise environmental damage as an objective in itself. This difference of underlying rationale relates to the second distinction: under the preventive principle, a state may be under an obligation to prevent damage to the environment within its own jurisdiction, including by means of appropriate regulatory, administrative and other measures.

The preventive principle requires action to be taken at an early stage and, if possible, before damage has actually occurred. The principle is reflected in state practice in regard to a broad range of environmental objectives. Broadly stated, it prohibits activity which causes or may cause damage to the environment in violation of the standards established under the rules of international law. It has been described as being of 'overriding importance in every effective environmental policy, since it allows action to be taken to protect the environment at an earlier stage. It is no longer primarily a question of repairing damage after it has occurred.' The preventive principle is supported by an extensive body of domestic environmental protection legislation which establishes authorisation procedures, as well as the adoption of international and national commitments on environmental standards, access to environmental information, and the need to carry out environmental impact assessments in relation to the conduct of certain proposed activities. The preventive principle may, therefore, take a number of forms, including the use of penalties and the application of liability rules.

The preventive approach has been endorsed, directly or indirectly, by the 1972 Stockholm Declaration, the 1978 UNEP Draft Principles and the 1982 World Charter for Nature. Principle 11 of the 1992 Rio Declaration requires states to enact 'effective environmental legislation'. More significantly for its development as an international legal principle is the fact that the principle has been relied upon or endorsed in a large number of treaties dealing with particular environmental media or activities. The preventive principle has also been specifically incorporated into treaties of more general application, including those in the field of international economic law, such as the EC Treaty, the 1989 Lome´ Convention and the 2001 Treaty establishing the East African Community. The preventive principle is implicitly supported in relation to transboundary resources by the awards in the *Trail Smelter* case and the *Lac Lanoux Arbitration*.

It was supported in the pleadings of Australia in the *Nuclear Tests* case and in the claim by Nauru that Australia had breached its legal obligation to administer the territory of Nauru in such a way as to not bring about changes in the territory which would cause irreparable damage to, or substantially prejudice, Nauru's legal interests in respect of that territory. The principle of prevention may also be discerned in Hungary's Original Application to the ICJ in the case concerning the Gabcikovo-Nagymaros Project. The preventive approach is endorsed by the large number of international environmental treaties, aiming to prevent *inter alia:*

- the extinction of species of flora and fauna;
- the spread of occupational disease, including radioactive contamination of workers;
- the introduction and spread of pests and diseases;
- pollution of the seas by oil, radioactive waste, hazardous waste and substances, from land-based sources, or from any source;
- river pollution;

- radioactive pollution of the atmosphere;
- hostile environmental modification;
- adverse effects of activities that prevent the migration of species;
- air pollution;
- modification of the ozone layer;
- degradation of the natural environment;
- all pollution;
- significant adverse environmental impacts;
- transboundary impacts generally;
- dangerous anthropogenic interference with the climate system;
- loss of fisheries and other biodiversity, including as a result of the release of genetically modified organisms; and
- damage to health and the environment from chemicals and persistent organic pollutants.

Taken together, this extensive body of international commitments provides compelling evidence of: the wide support for the principle of preventive action; the different environmental media for which general preventive measures are required; the types of activities which should be regulated; and the basis upon which states should carry out their commitment to enact effective national environmental legislation pursuant to the general requirement of Principle 11 of the Rio Declaration.

CO-OPERATION

The principle of 'good-neighbourliness' enunciated in Article 74 of the UN Charter in relation to social, economic and commercial matters has been translated into the development and application of rules promoting international environmental co-operation. This is traditionally considered by reference to the application of the maxim *sic utere tuo et alienum non laedas*. The principle is reflected in many treaties and other international acts, and is supported also by state practice, particularly in relation to hazardous activities and emergencies.Principle 24 of the Stockholm Declaration reflects a general political commitment to international co-operation in matters concerning the protection of the environment, and Principle 27 of the Rio Declaration states rather more succinctly that 'States and people shall co-operate in good faith and in a spirit of partnership in the fulfilment of the principles embodied in this Declaration and in the further development of international law in the field of sustainable development'. The importance attached to the principle of cooperation, and its practical significance, is reflected in many international instruments, such as the Preamble to the 1992 Industrial Accident Convention, which underlined (in support of the Convention's specific commitments) 'the principles of international law and custom, in particular the principles of good-neighbourliness, reciprocity, non-discrimination and good faith', and the procedural rules reflected in the 1997 Watercourses Convention.

The obligation to co-operate is affirmed in virtually all international environmental agreements of bilateral and regional application, and global instruments. It also underscores the ICJ's reminder of the need to establish suitable common regimes. The obligation may be in general terms, relating to the implementation of the treaty's objectives or relating to specific commitments under a treaty. The general obligation to co-operate has also been translated into more specific commitments through techniques designed to ensure information sharing and participation in decision-making. These specific commitments, which are considered in more detail in subsequent chapters, include: rules on environmental impact assessment (see chapter 16); rules ensuring that neighbouring states receive necessary information (requiring information exchange, consultation and notification) (see chapter 17); the provision of emergency information (see chapter 12); and transboundary enforcement of environmental standards (see chapter 5). The extent to which these commitments are interrelated is reflected in Principle 7 of the 1978 UNEP Draft Principles, which states that:

> Exchange of information, notification, consultation and other forms of cooperation regarding shared natural resources are carried out on the basis of the principle of good faith and in the spirit of good neighbourliness.

A similar commitment is expressed in Article 4 of the ILC's draft Articles on Prevention of Transboundary Harm (2001). State practice supporting good-neighbourliness and international co-operation is reflected in decisions and awards of international courts and tribunals discussed in subsequent chapters, including the *Lac Lanoux* case. The nature and extent of the obligation to co-operate is being invoked in international disputes. It was a central issue in the dispute between Hungary and Slovakia in the *Gabcikovo-Nagymaros Project* case, at least as originally formulated by Hungary (claiming that Czechoslovakia and then Slovakia had not co-operated in good faith in the implementation

of principles affecting transboundary resources, including the obligation to negotiate in good faith and in a spirit of co-operation, to prevent disputes, to provide timely notification of plans to carry out or permit activities which may entail a transboundary interference or a significant risk thereof and to engage in good faith consultations to arrive at an equitable resolution of the situation).The ICJ did not address in any detail what the obligation to co-operate entailed, beyond recalling what it had said earlier in the *North Sea Continental Shelf* cases, as well as the principle of good faith which obliged the parties to apply their 1977 treaty 'in a reasonable way and in such a manner that its purpose can be realized'.

The requirements of the obligation to co-operate are at the heart of the *MOX* case. In its application instituting arbitration proceedings under the 1982 UNCLOS, Ireland claimed that the United Kingdom had failed to co-operate as required by Articles 123 and 197 of UNCLOS, for example by failing to reply to communications and requests for information in a timely manner or at all, by withholding environmental information requested by Ireland, and by refusing to prepare a supplementary environmental statement. In its Provisional Measures Order, the ITLOS affirmed that: the duty to co-operate is a fundamental principle in the prevention of pollution of the marine environment under Part XII of the Convention and general international law and that rights arise therefrom which the Tribunal may consider appropriate to preserve under article 290 of the Convention.

The Tribunal ordered the parties to co-operate and, for that purpose, to enter into consultations forthwith to '(a) exchange further information with regard to possible consequences for the Irish Sea arising out of the commissioning of the MOX plant; (b) monitor risks or the effects of the operation of the MOX plant for the Irish Sea; (c) devise, as appropriate, measures to prevent pollution of the marine environment which might result from the operation of the MOX plant'.

SUSTAINABLE DEVELOPMENT

The general principle that states should ensure the development and use of their natural resources in a manner which is sustainable emerged in the run-up to UNCED. Although the ideas underlying the concept of sustainable development have a long history in international legal instruments, and the term itself began to appear in treaties in the 1980s, the general 'principle of sustainable development' appears to have been first referred to in a treaty in the Preamble to the 1992 EEA Agreement. The term now appears with great regularity in international instruments of an environmental, economic and social character and has been invoked by various international courts and tribunals, and is now established as an international legal concept.

The term 'sustainable development' is generally considered to have been coined by the 1987 Brundtland Report, which defined it as 'development that meets the needs of the present without compromising the ability of future generations to meet their own needs'. It contains within it two concepts:

1. the concept of 'needs', in particular the essential needs of the world's poor, to which overriding priority should be given; and
2. the idea of limitations imposed, by the state of technology and social organisation, on the environment's ability to meet present and future needs.

State practice, however, suggests that the idea of 'sustainability' has been a feature in international legal relations since at least 1893, when the United States asserted a right to ensure the legitimate and proper use of seals and to protect them, for the benefit of mankind, from wanton destruction. Since then, many treaties and other international instruments, as well as decisions of international courts, have supported, directly or indirectly, the concept of sustainable development and the principle that states have the responsibility to ensure the sustainable use of natural resources. Its application has been recognised in relation to all parts of the world.

Four recurring elements appear to comprise the legal elements of the concept of 'sustainable development', as reflected in international agreements:

1. the need to preserve natural resources for the benefit of future generations (the principle of intergenerational equity);
2. the aim of exploiting natural resources in a manner which is 'sustainable', or 'prudent', or 'rational', or 'wise' or 'appropriate' (the principle of sustainable use);
3. the 'equitable' use of natural resources, which implies that use by one state must take account of the needs of other states (the principle of equitable use, or intragenerational equity); and
4. the need to ensure that environmental considerations are integrated into economic and other development plans, programmes and projects, and that development needs are taken into account in applying environmental objectives (the principle of integration).

These four elements are closely related and often used in combination (and frequently interchangeably), which suggests that they do not yet have a well-established, or agreed, legal definition or status. The 1989 Lomé Convention indicated how some of the elements of the concept of sustainable development can be brought together in a single legal text. Article 33 of the Convention provides that:

In the framework of this Convention, the protection and the enhancement of the environment and natural resources, the halting of the deterioration of land and forests, the restoration of ecological balances, the preservation of natural resources and their rational exploitation are basic objectives that the [states parties] concerned shall strive to achieve with Community support with a view to bringing an immediate improvement in the living conditions of their populations and to safeguarding those of future generations.

Without referring directly to 'sustainable development', the text introduced into a legal framework the elements identified by the Brundtland Report.There can be little doubt that the concept of 'sustainable development' has entered the corpus of international customary law, requiring different streams of international law to be treated in an integrated manner. In the *Gabcikovo-Nagymaros* case, the ICJ invoked the concept in relation to the future regime to be established by the parties. The ICJ said:

Throughout the ages, mankind has, for economic and other reasons, constantly interfered with nature. In the past this was often done without consideration of the effects upon the environment. Owing to new scientific insights and to a growing awareness of the risks for mankind – for present and future generations – of pursuit of such interventions at an unconsidered and unabated pace, new norms and standards have been developed [and], set forth in a great number of instruments during the last two decades. Such new norms have to be taken into consideration, and such new standards given proper weight, not only when States contemplate new activities, but also when continuing with activities begun in the past. This need to reconcile economic development with protection of the environment is aptly expressed in the concept of sustainable development. For the purposes of the present case, this means that the Parties together should look afresh at the effects on the environment of the operation of the Gabcikovo power plant. In particular they must find a satisfactory solution for the volume of water to be released into the old bed of the Danube and into the side-arms on both sides of the river.

By invoking the concept of sustainable development, the ICJ indicates that the term has a legal function and both a procedural/ temporal aspect (obliging the parties to 'look afresh' at the environmental consequences of the operation of the plant) and a substantive aspect (the obligation of result to ensure that a 'satisfactory volume of water' be released from the by-pass canal into the main river and its original side arms). The ICJ does not provide further detail as to the practical consequences, although some assistance may be obtained from the Separate Opinion of Judge Weeramantry, who joined in the majority judgment and whose hand may have guided the drafting of paragraph 140 quoted above.

In the *Shrimp/Turtle* case, the WTO Appellate Body noted that the Preamble to the WTO Agreement explicitly acknowledges 'the objective of sustainable development', and characterises it as a concept which 'has been generally accepted as integrating economic and social development and environmental protection'. The concept appears to have informed the conclusion that sea turtles are an 'exhaustible natural resource' (within the meaning of Article XX(g) of the GATT) and that they have a sufficient nexus with the United States to justify the latter state's conservation measures, at least in principle. The Appellate Body also invokes 'sustainable development' in assessing whether those measures have been applied in a discriminatory fashion – as it concludes they have – and in this regard refers to 'sustainable development' in the preamble to the WTO Agreement as adding: color, texture and shading to our interpretation of the agreements annexed to the WTO Agreement, in this case the GATT 1994. We have already observed that Article XX(g) of the GATT 1994 is appropriately read with the perspective embodied in the above preamble.

Future generations

Theidea that as 'membersof thepresent generation,weholdthe earthin trust for future generations' is well known to international law, having been relied upon as early as 1893 by the United States in the *Pacific Fur Seals Arbitration*. It is also expressly or implicitly referred to in many of the early environmental treaties, including the 1946 International Whaling Convention, the 1968 African Conservation Convention and the 1972 World Heritage Convention. Other, more recent treaties have sought to preserve particular natural resources and other environmental assets for the benefit of present and future generations. These include wild flora and fauna; the marine environment;essential renewable natural resources; the environment generally; the resources of the earth;

natural heritage; natural resources; water re-sources; biological diversity; and the climate system.

International declarations often make reference to intergenerational equity as an important aspect of the concept of sustainable development. According to Principle 1 of the 1972 Stockholm Declaration, man bears 'a solemn responsibility to protect and improve the environment for present and future generations', and UN General Assembly Resolution 35/8, adopted in 1980, affirmed that the responsibility to present and future generations is a historic one for the 'preservation of nature'. The Rio Declaration associates intergener-ational equity with the right to development, providing in Principle 4 that the 'right to development must be fulfilled so as to equitably meet developmental and environmental needs of present and future generations'.

In its Advisory Opinion on *The Legality of the Threat or Use of Nuclear Weapons*, the ICJ recognized that 'the environment is not an abstraction but represents the living space, the quality of life and the very health of human beings, including generations unborn'. The purpose of the ICJ's reliance on the concept is not immediately apparent, and it is sometimes said that the undertakings in favour of future generations have limited practical legal consequences. They are considered by some to be closely associated with the civil and political aspects of the relationship between environmental protection and human rights protection. According to this view, the rights of future generations might be used to enhance the legal standing of members of the present generation to bring claims, in cases relying upon substantive rules of environmental treaties where doubt exists as to whether a particular treaty creates rights and obligations enforceable by individuals. *Sustainable use of natural resources*

A second approach, reflected in treaties adopting a 'sustainable' approach, is to focus on the adoption of standards governing the rate of use or exploitation of specific natural resources rather than on their preservation for future generations. Particularly for marine living resources, a standard approach has emerged requiring exploitation to be conducted at levels which are 'sustainable' or 'optimal'. The failure of the 1946 International Whaling Convention to prevent the depletion of many whale species can be measured by reference to its stated objective of achieving 'the optimum level of whale stocks' and confining whaling operations 'to those species best able to sustain exploitation in order to give an interval for recovery to certain species of whales now depleted in numbers'. Similar commitments to limit catches or productivity to 'maximum sustained' levels have been agreed for other marine species, such as tuna, North Pacific fish, Pacific fur seals, and living resources in the EEZ. Other treaties limit catches to 'optimum sustainable yields', or subject them to a required standard of 'optimum utilisation'; this applies, for example, in relation to Antarctic seals, high seas fisheries, and some highly migratory species.

Sustainable use is a concept also applicable to non-marine resources. The 1968 African Nature Convention provides that the utilisation of all natural resources 'must aim at satisfying the needs of man according to the carrying capacity of the environment', and the 1983 International Tropical Timber Agreement encouraged 'sustainable utilisation and conservation of tropical forests and their genetic resources'. The 1985 ASEAN Agreement was one of the first treaties to require parties to adopt a standard of 'sustainable utilisation of harvested natural resources . . . with a view to attaining the goal of sustainable development'. Further support for sustainable use or management as a legal term may be found in the 1987 Zambezi Action Plan Agreement, the 1992 Climate Change Convention, the 1992 Biodiversity Convention and its 2000 Biosafety Protocol, and the 1992 OSPAR Convention. The fact that so many species and natural resources are in fact not sustainably managed illustrates the difficulty in translating the concept of sustainable development into a practical conservation tool.

The term also now appears frequently in instruments relating to international economic law and policy. Under its Articles of Agreement, the European Bank for Reconstruction and Development must 'promote in the full range of its activities environmentally sound and sustainable development'. Under the 1989 Lome' Convention, the development of the sixty-six ACP countries as supported by the EC and its member states was to 'be based on a sustainable balance between its economic objectives, the rational management of the environment and the enhancement of natural and human resources'. The 1992 Maastricht Treaty, which made changes to the EC Treaty, introduced new objectives for the EC, including the promotion of 'sustainable and non-inflationary growth respecting the environment'. The Preamble to the 1994 WTO Agreement commits parties to 'the optimal use of the world's resources in accordance with the objective of sustainable development'.

Other acts of the international community have also relied upon the concept of 'sustainable development', or the spirit which underlies it, without specifying what, precisely, it means. Although the 1972 Stockholm Declaration did not endorse 'sustainable development', it did call for the non-exhaustion of renewable natural resources and the maintenance and improvement of 'the capacity of the earth to produce vital renewable resources'.

The 1982 World Charter for Nature stated that resources which are utilised are to be managed so as to 'achieve and maintain optimum sustainable productivity', and provided that living resources must not be utilised 'in excess of their natural capacity for regeneration'. The 1992 Rio Declaration goes further than most instruments by expressly defining the content of the concept of sustainable development, and actively calls for the 'further development of international law in the field of sustainable development', which suggests that international law in this field already existed.

Apart from the environmental component of 'sustainable development', the Rio Declaration links environmental issues to matters which might previously be more properly considered as belonging to the realm of economic and development law. These issues, increasingly considered for their environmental implications, include the eradication of poverty, the special responsibility of developed countries, the reduction and elimination of unsustainable patterns of production and consumption, the promotion of appropriate population policies, and a supportive and open international economic system.

Treaties and other international acts have also supported the development of the concept of 'sustainable use' through the use of terms which are closely related; international legal instruments have aimed for conservation measures and programmes which are 'rational', or 'wise', or 'sound', or 'appropriate', or a combination of the above. In some instruments, the preferred objective is the 'conservation' of natural resources, which has been subsequently defined by reference to one or more of the terms identified above. Moreover, the term 'conservation' itself includes elements similar to 'sustainable development'. The Legal Experts Group of the World Commission on Environment and Development defined 'conservation' in terms which recall the principle of sustainable development as: [the] management of human use of a natural resource or the environment in such a manner that it may yield the greatest sustainable benefit to present generations while maintaining its potential to meet the needs and aspirations of future generations. It embraces preservation, maintenance, sustainable utilisation, restoration and enhancement of a natural resource or the environment.

'Rational', 'wise', 'sound' and 'appropriate' use are usually used without definition and often interchangeably, and accordingly the meaning of each term will depend upon its application in each instrument. Although attempts at definition have been made, no generally accepted definitions exist, and it is unlikely that distinguishable legal definitions could be agreed. The use of various terms in a single instrument is illustrated by the 1982 UNCLOS: it requires conservation at 'maximum sustainable yield' for the living resources of the territorial and high seas, the 'optimum utilisation' of the living resources found in the EEZ, and the 'rational management' of the resources in the 'Area' in accordance with 'sound principles of conservation'.

'Rational' utilisation and management are the governing standard for migratory birds, fisheries, salmon, all natural resources, sealsand hydro resources. They are the required standard called for by Principles 13 and 14 of the Stockholm Declaration, and the 1980 CCAMLR defines 'conservation' objectives as including 'rational use', as does the 1982 Jeddah Regional Seas

Convention.

'Proper' utilisation and management has been adopted as a governing standard for fisheries and forests. 'Wise use' has been endorsed for flora and fauna, wetlands and natural resources generally. Other standards introduced by international agreements include: 'judicious exploitation'; 'sound environmental management'; 'appropriate environmental management';and 'ecologically sound and rational' use of natural resources.

The significance of these terms is that each recognises limits placed by international law on the rate of use or manner of exploitation of natural resources, including those which are shared or are in areas beyond national jurisdiction. These standards cannot have an absolute meaning. Rather, their interpretation is, or should be, implemented by states acting co-operatively, or by decisions of international organisations, or, ultimately, by international judicial bodies in the event that a dispute arises.

Equitable use of natural resources

Equity and equitable principles are terms which are frequently relied upon in international environmental texts. In the absence of detailed rules, equity can provide a conveniently flexible means of leaving the extent of rights and obligations to be decided at a subsequent date, which may explain its frequent usage at UNCED. In many respects, UNCED was about equity: how to allocate future responsibilities for environmental protection between states which are at different levels of economic development, which have contributed in different degrees to particular problems, and which have different environmental and developmental needs and priorities. This is reflected in each UNCED instrument, which reflects efforts to apply equity to particular issues. Principle 3 of the Rio Declaration invokes the 'right of development' as a means of 'equitably' meeting the developmental and environmental needs of future generations. Under the Climate Change Convention, all the parties undertake to be guided on 'the basis of equity' in their actions to achieve the objective of the Convention, and Annex 1 parties agree to take into account the need for 'equitable and appropriate contributions' by each of them to the global effort regarding the achievement of the objective of the Convention. The objectives of the 1992 Biodiversity Convention include the 'fair and equitable' sharing of the benefits arising out of the use of genetic resources.

The application of equity in international environmental affairs pre-dates UNCED, having been associated with the protection of the environment for the benefit of future generations (intergenerational equity); the principle of common but differentiated responsibility which takes into account the needs and capabilities of different countries and their historic contribution to particular problems; and the allocation of shared natural resources, shared fisheries stocks, or shared freshwater resources. Equity has also been relied upon in relation to the participation of states in environmental organisations,financial and other contributions to activities, and the equitable distribution of the benefits of development.

It is, however, in relation to the allocation of shared natural resources that equity is likely to play an important role in coming years, as underscored by the ICJ's ruling in the *Gabcikovo-Nagymaros* case that Czechoslovakia had violated international law by unilaterally assuming control of a shared resource and depriving Hungary of its right to an equitable and reasonable share of the natural resources of the Danube. The Preamble to the 1987 Montreal Protocol reflects the aim of controlling 'equitably total global emissions of substances that deplete the ozone layer', an aim usually translated into specific obligations through the process of intergovernmental negotiations (as reflected in the 1990 and 1992 Adjustments and Amendments to the 1987 Montreal Protocol). The 1992 Climate Change Convention requires the equitable allocation of emission rights, and the Biodiversity Convention requires the determination of what constitutes an equitable sharing of the benefits arising out of the use of genetic resources. In each of these cases, the factors to be taken into account in establishing specific rights and obligations must be determined in the circumstances of each instrument, including its provisions, the context of its negotiation and adoption, and subsequent practice by the organs it establishes and by parties.

Integration of environment and development

A fourth element of 'sustainable development' is the commitment to integrate environmental considerations into economic and other development, and to take into account the needs of economic and other social development in crafting, applying and interpreting environmental obligations. In many ways, this element is the most important and the most legalistic: its formal application requires the collection and dissemination of environmental information, and the conduct of environmental impact assessments. The integration approach may also serve as the basis for allowing, or requiring, 'green conditionality' in bilateral and multilateral development assistance, and the adoption of differentiated legal commitments on the basis of the historic responsibility of states (including the resulting economic benefits) and their capacity to respond to environmental requirements.

For many years, the international regulation of environmental issues has taken place in international fora, such as UNEP and the conferences of the parties to environmental treaties, which are not directly connected to international economic organisations, particularly the World Bank and the GATT. One consequence has been a divergence in approaches. This is a constitutional problem, which appears also in the organisation of national governments. The constituent instruments which originally created the UN and its specialised agencies, and in particular the GATT, the World Bank, the multilateral development banks, and regional economic integration organisations such as the European Community, did not address environmental protection requirements or the need to ensure that development was environmentally sustainable. Environmental concerns had historically been addressed on the margins of international economic concerns, and it is only since UNCED that the relationship between environmental protection and economic development has been more fully recognised by the international community. The UNCED process and the instruments reflect the need to integrate environment and development, and it is unlikely that the two objectives could now be easily separated.

Principle 4 of the Rio Declaration provides that: 'In order to achieve sustainable development, environmental protection shall constitute an integral part of the development process and canno be considered in isolation from it.' An integrated approach to environment and development has significant practical consequences, most notably that environmental considerations will increasingly be a feature of international economic policy and law (and that lawyers working in the area of environmental protection will need to familiarise themselves with economic law and concepts). This is borne out by the changes which have taken place since the late 1980s. Examples include: the various amendments to the EC Treaty to include and then develop specific language on the environment; the establishment of an Environment Department at the World Bank and the adoption of environmental assessment and related requirements; the convergence of trade with environment at the GATT and then the WTO; the elaboration of language on sustainable development in the Articles of Agreement of the EBRD and the WTO; and the development of environmental jurisprudence in competition, subsidy, foreign investment and intellectual property law.

The integration of environment and development began prior to the 1972 Stockholm Conference. Linkage between conservation and development was made at the first UN Conference on conservation and utilisation of resources in 1949. In 1971, the General Assembly expressed its conviction that 'development plans should be compatible with a sound ecology and that adequate environmental conditions can best be ensured by the promotion of development, both at the national and international levels'. Principle 13 of the Stockholm Declaration called on states to adopt 'an integrated and co-ordinated approach to their development planning so as to ensure that their development is compatible with the need to protect and improve the human environment'. The 1982 World Charter for Nature provided that the conservation of nature was to be taken into account in the planning and implementation of economic and social development activities and that due account was to be taken of the long-term capacity of natural systems in formulating plans for economic development.

Numerous regional treaties support an approach which integrates environment and development. Examples include: the

1974 Paris Convention, which calls for an 'integrated planning policy consistent with the requirement of environmental protection'; the 1978 Kuwait Convention, which supports an 'integrated management approach . . . which will allow the achievement of environmental and development goals in a harmonious manner'; the 1978 Amazonian Treaty, which affirms the need to 'maintain a balance between economic growth and conservation of the environment'; the 1985 ASEAN Convention, which seeks to ensure that 'conservation and management of natural resources are treated as an integral part of development planning at all stages and at all levels'; and the 1989 Fourth Lomé Convention, which provided that the development of ACP states 'shall be based on a sustainable balance between its economic objectives, the rational management of the environment and the enhancement of natural . . . resources', and requires the 'preparation and implementation of coherent modes of development that have due regard for ecological balances'. The global treaties at UNCED – and those adopted subsequently – include similar provisions.

The integration of environment and development has re-opened debate over the 'right to development', after efforts to establish a New International Economic Order in the mid-1970s met with opposition from some of the larger industrialised countries. Principle 3 of the Rio Declaration implicitly accepts the 'right to development', although the United States declared that it did not, by joining consensus on the Rio Declaration, change its long-standing opposition to the 'so-called "right to development"'; for the United States, development 'is not a right . . . [it] is a goal we all hold', and the US disassociated itself from any interpretation of Principle 3 that accepted a 'right to development'. Developing countries have, in this context, been careful to introduce language into treaties to safeguard their future development and limit the extent to which international environmental regulation might limit such development. Both UNCED treaties include language to the effect that the overriding priority needs of developing countries are the achievement of economic growth and the eradication of poverty, an objective given more concrete expression by making the effective implementation by developing countries of their commitments dependent upon the effective implementation by developed countries of their financial obligations. Despite the US language, Principle 3 of the Rio Declaration, with which Principle 4 must be read to be fully understood, is part of the bargain struck between developed and developing countries, which is also evident in the convoluted language of Article 3(4) of the Climate Change Convention. This provides that the parties 'have a right to and should, promote sustainable development', which reflects a compromise text between those states which sought an express recognition of a 'right to development' and those states which sought to dilute such a right by recognising only a 'right to promote sustainable development'.

PRECAUTIONARY PRINCIPLE

Whereas the preventive principle can be traced back to international environmental treaties and other international acts since at least the 1930s, the precautionary principle only began to appear in international legal instruments in the mid-1980s, although prior to then it had featured as a principle in domestic legal systems, most notably that of West Germany. The precautionary principle aims to provide guidance in the development and application of international environmental law where there is scientific uncertainty. It continues to generate disagreement as to its meaning and effect, as reflected in particular in the views of states and international judicial practice. On the one hand, some consider that it provides the basis for early international legal action to address highly threatening environmental issues such as ozone depletion and climate change. On the other hand, its opponents have decried the potential which the principle has for over-regulation and limiting human activity. The core of the principle, which is still evolving, is reflected in Principle 15 of the Rio Declaration, which provides that:

> Where there are threats of serious or irreversible damage, lack of full scientific certainty shall not be used as a reason for postponing cost-effective measures to prevent environmental degradation.

Principle 15 also provides that 'the precautionary approach shall be widely applied by states according to their capabilities'. The precautionary principle (or precautionary approach, as the US and some others prefer to call it) has been adopted in many international environmental treaties since 1989. Although its precise formulation is not identical in each instrument, the language of Principle 15 of the Rio Declaration now attracts broad support. The principle finds its roots in the more traditional environmental agreements which call on parties to such agreements, and the institutions they create, to act and to adopt decisions which are based upon 'scientific findings' or methods, or 'in the light of knowledge available at the time'. These standards suggest that action shall only be taken where there is scientific evidence that significant environmental damage is occurring, and that in the absence of such evidence no action would be required. Examples of a traditional approach include the 1974 Paris Convention, which allows parties to take additional measures 'if scientific evidence has established that a serious hazard may be created in the maritime area by that substance and if urgent action is necessary': this requires the party wishing to adopt measures to 'prove' a case for action based upon the existence of sufficient scientific evidence, which may be difficult to obtain.

The 1969 Intervention Convention was one of the earliest treaties to recognise the limitations of the traditional approach, concerning the environmental consequences of a failure to act. It allows proportionate measures to be taken to prevent, mitigate or eliminate grave and imminent danger to coastlines from threat of oil pollution, taking account of 'the extent and probability of imminent damage if those measures are not taken'. Developments in the mid-1980s to address ozone depletion reflected growing support for precautionary action. The first treaty which refers to the term is the 1985 Vienna Convention, which reflected the parties' recognition of the 'precautionary measures' taken at the national and international levels. By 1987, the parties to the Montreal

Protocol noted the 'precautionary measures' to control emission from certain CFCs which had already been taken at the national and regional (EEC) levels and stated their determination to 'protect the ozone layer by taking precautionary measures to control equitably total global emissions of substances that deplete it'. The precautionary approach has been relied upon in relation to measures to protect other environmental media, especially the marine environment. The Preamble to the 1984 Ministerial Declaration of the International Conference on the Protection of the North Sea reflected a consciousness that states 'must not wait for proof of harmful effects before taking action', since damage to the marine environment can be irreversible or remediable only at considerable expense and over a long period. This introduces the idea that precautionary action may be justified on economic grounds. The Ministerial Declaration of the Second North Sea Conference (1987) accepted that 'in order to protect the North Sea from possibly damaging effects of the most dangerous substances, a precautionary approach is necessary'. At the Third North Sea Conference (1990), Ministers pledged to continue to apply the precautionary principle.The 1990 Bergen Ministerial Declaration on Sustainable Development in the ECE Region was the first international instrument to treat the principle as one of general application and linked to sustainable development. The Declaration provides that:

In order to achieve sustainable development, policies must be based on the precautionary principle. Environmental measures must anticipate, prevent and attack the causes of environmental degradation. Where there are threats of serious or irreversible damage, lack of full scientific certainty should not be used as a reason for postponing measures to prevent environmental degradation.

Central to this text is the element of anticipation, reflecting a need for effective environmental measures to be based upon actions which take a longer-term approach and which might predict changes in the basis of our scientific knowledge. Moreover, for the precautionary principle to apply, the threat of environmental damage must be 'serious' or 'irreversible', although there is not yet any limitation on grounds of cost-effectiveness as to the measures which should not be postponed. While the amendments to the Montreal Protocol were being prepared, the UNEP Governing Council recognised that 'waiting for scientific proof regarding the impact of pollutants discharged into the marine environment could result in irreversible damage to the marine environment and in human suffering', and recommended that all governments adopt the 'principle of precautionary action' as the basis of their policy with regard to the prevention and elimination of marine pollution.

Since that time, numerous environmental treaties, including some which are of global applicationon environmental mattersofbroadconcern andapplicable to almost all human activities, have adopted the precautionary principle or its underlying rationale. Among the earliest was the 1991 Bamako Convention, which requires parties to strive to adopt and implement the preventive, precautionary approach to pollution which entails, *inter alia*, preventing the release into the environment of substances which may cause harm to humans or the environment without waiting for scientific proof regarding such harm. The parties shall co-operate with each other in taking the appropriate measures to implement the precautionary principle to pollution prevention through the application of clean production methods.

This formulation is one of the most far-reaching. It links the preventive and precautionary approaches, does not require damage to be 'serious' or 'irreversible', and lowers the threshold at which scientific evidence might require action. The parties to the 1992 Watercourses Convention agreed to be guided by the precautionary principle by virtue of which action to avoid the potential transboundary impact of the release of hazardous substances shall not be postponed on the ground that scientific research has not fully proved a causal link between those substances, on the one hand, and the potential transboundary impact, on the other hand.

This formulation limits the application of the principle to transboundary effects alone, although the level of environmental damage is raised above that required by the Bamako Convention to 'significant adverse effect'. The 1992 Biodiversity Convention does not specifically refer to the precautionary principle, although the Preamble notes that 'where there is a threat of significant reduction or loss of biological diversity, lack of full scientific certainty should not be used as a reason for postponing measures to avoid or minimise such a threat'. The level of environmental damage here is well below the 'serious' or 'irreversible' level required by the 1990 Bergen Declaration. The 2000 Biosafety

Protocol relies extensively on the precautionary approach. The objective of the Protocol is, however, stated to be 'in accordance' with Principle 15 of the Rio Declaration, and, to that end, the Protocol affirms that 'lack of scientific certainty due to insufficient relevant scientific information and knowledge regarding the extent of the potential adverse effects of a living modified organism on the conservation and sustainable use of biological diversity' shall not prevent a party from prohibiting imports. The reference to precaution in the 1992 Climate Change Convention was a controversial matter, and the text as finally adopted established limits on the application of the precautionary principle by requiring a threat of 'serious or irreversible damage' and by linking the commitment to an encouragement to take measures which are 'cost effective'.

Beyond these two conventions, many others now commit their parties to apply the precautionary principle or approach. The 1992 OSPAR Convention links prevention and precaution: preventive measures are to be taken when there are 'reasonable grounds for concern . . . even when there is no conclusive evidence of a causal relationship between the inputs and the effects'. The threshold here is quite low. The standard applied by the 1992 Baltic Sea Convention introduces yet another variation: preventive measures are to be taken 'when there is reason to assume' that harm might be caused 'even when there is no conclusive evidence of a causal relationship between inputs and their alleged effects'. The 1995 Straddling Stocks Agreement commits coastal states and states fishing on the high seas to apply the precautionary approach widely, and sets out in detail the modalities for its application. A growing number of other conventions – both regional and global – also give effect to a precautionary approach in relation to a range of different subject matters.The 1992 Maastricht Treaty amended Article 130r(2) of the EC Treaty so that EC action on the environment 'shall be based on the precautionary principle', and the 1997 Amsterdam Treaty further amended the EC Treaty to apply the principle to Community policy on the environment (Article 174(2)). The European Commission has published a Communication on the precautionary principle which outlines the Commission's approach to the use of the principle, establishes guidelines for applying it, and aims to develop understanding on the assessment, appraisal and management of risk in the face of scientific uncertainty. The Communication considers that the principle has been 'progressively consolidated in international environmental law, and so it has since become a full-fledged and general principle of international law'. The principle has been applied by the ECJ and by the EEA Court, which has ruled that, in cases relating to the effects on human health of certain products, and where there may be a great measure of scientific and practical uncertainty linked to the issue under consideration, the application of the precautionary principle is justified and 'presupposes, firstly, an identification of potentially negative health consequences arising, in the present case, from a proposed fortification, and, secondly, a comprehensive evaluation of the risk to health based on the most recent scientific information'. The Court went on:

> When the insufficiency, or the inconclusiveness, or the imprecise nature of the conclusions to be drawn from those considerations make it impossible to determine with certainty the risk or hazard, but the likelihood of considerable harm still persists were the negative eventuality to occur, the precautionary principle would justify the taking of restrictive measures.

The precautionary principle or approach has now received widespread support by the international community in relation to a broad range of subject areas. What does the principle mean, and what status does it have in international law? There is no clear and uniform understanding of the meaning of the precautionary principle among states and other members of the international community. At the most general level, it means that states agree to act carefully and with foresight when taking decisions which concern activities that may have an adverse impact on the environment. A more focused interpretation provides that the principle requires activities and substances which may be harmful to the environment to be regulated, and possibly prohibited, even if no conclusive or overwhelming evidence is available as to the harm or likely harm they may cause to the environment. As the Bergen Ministerial Declaration put it, 'lack of full scientific certainty should not be used as a reason for postponing measures to prevent environmental degradation'. Under the Rio Declaration, the requirement is stated to be mandatory: lack of full scientific certainty 'shall not be used' to prevent action. What remains open is the level at which scientific evidence is sufficient to override arguments for postponing measures, or at which measures might even be required as a matter of international law.

A more fundamental change would be adopted by an interpretation of the precautionary principle, one increasingly widely held, which would shift the burden of proof. According to traditional approaches, the burden of proof currently lies with the person opposing an activity to prove that it does or is likely to cause environmental damage. A new approach, supported by the precautionary principle, would tend to shift the burden of proof and require the person who wishes to carry out an activity to prove that it will not cause harm to the environment. This interpretation would require polluters, and polluting states, to establish that their activities and the discharge of certain substances would not adversely or significantly affect the environment before they were granted the right to release the potentially polluting substances or carry out the proposed activity. This interpretation may also require national or international regulatory action where the scientific evidence suggests that lack of action may result in serious or irreversible harm to the environment, or where there are divergent views on the risks of action.

There is growing evidence to suggest that this interpretation is beginning to be supported by state practice, even if it still falls short of having sufficient support to allow it to be considered a rule of general application. Examples include the EC's 1991 Urban Waste Water Directive, which allows certain urban waste water discharges to be subjected to less stringent treatment than that generally required by the Directive providing that 'comprehensive studies indicate that such discharges will not adversely affect the environment'. Under the 1992 OSPAR Convention, parties (France and the United Kingdom) which originally wanted to retain the option of dumping low- and intermediate-level radioactive wastes at sea were required to report to the OSPAR Commission on 'the results of scientific studies which show that any potential dumping operations would not result in hazards to human health, harm to living resources or marine ecosystems, damage to amenities or interference with other legitimate uses of the sea'.

The practice of international courts and tribunals, and of states appearing before them, sheds some light on the meaning and effect of the precautionary principle. Before the ICJ the principle appears to have first been raised in New Zealand's 1995 request concerning French nuclear testing. New Zealand relied extensively on the principle, which it described as 'a very widely accepted and operative principle of international law' and which shifted the burden onto France to prove that the proposed tests would not give rise to environmental damage.

Five 'intervening' states (Australia, Micronesia, the Marshall Islands, Samoa and the Solomon Islands) also invoked the principle. France responded that the status of the principle in international law was 'tout a` fait incertain', but that in any event it had been complied with, and that evidentiary burdens were no different in the environmental field than any other area of international law. The ICJ's order did not refer to these arguments, although Judge Weeramantry's dissent noted that the principle had 'evolved to meet [the] evidentiary difficulty caused by the fact [that] information required to prove a proposition' may be 'in the hands of the party causing or threatening the damage', and that it was 'gaining increasing support as part of the international law of the environment'. In the *Gabcikovo-Nagymaros* case, Hungary and Slovakia also invoked the precautionary principle.

Again, the ICJ did not feel the need to address the principle, limiting itself to a passing reference to Hungary's claim that the principle justified the termination of the 1977 treaty and its recognition of the parties' agreement on the need to take environmental concerns seriously and to take the required precautionary measures. Of particular note was the failure of the ICJ to refer to or apply the principle in its consideration of the conditions under which Hungary could invoke the concept of ecological necessity to preclude the wrongfulness of its suspension of works on the two barrages in 1989. Having acknowledged without difficulty 'that the concerns expressed by Hungary for its natural environment in the region affected by the Gabc'ýkovo-Nagymaros Project related to an "essential interest" of that State', the ICJ nevertheless found that Hungary had not proved that 'a real, "grave" and "imminent" "peril" existed in 1989 and that the measures taken by Hungary were the only possible response to it.' The ICJ found that there were serious uncertainties concerning future harm to freshwater supplies and biodiversity, but that these: could not, alone, establish the objective existence of a 'peril' in the sense of a component element of a state of necessity. The word 'peril' certainly evokes the idea of 'risk'; that is precisely what distinguishes 'peril' from material damage. But a state of necessity could not exist without a 'peril' duly established at the relevant point in time; the mere apprehension of a possible 'peril' could not suffice in that respect. It could moreover hardly be otherwise, when the 'peril' constituting the state of necessity has at the same time to be 'grave' and 'imminent'. 'Imminence' is synonymous with 'immediacy' or 'proximity' and goes far beyond the concept of 'possibility' . . . That does not exclude, in the view of the Court, that a 'peril' appearing in the long term might be held to be 'imminent' as soon as it is established, at the relevant point in time, that the realization of that peril, however far off it might be, is not thereby any less certain and inevitable.

This is not precautionary language, premised as it is on the need to establish the certainty and inevitability of serious harm. However, it must be recognised that the ICJ was concerned here with the application of the law as it stood in 1989, when Hungary had wrongfully (in the view of the ICJ) suspended work on the project. At that time, the precautionary principle had not yet emerged and could not realistically be applied as general international law. It may be that the ICJ also had this in mind when it indicated later in the judgment that '[w]hat might have been a correct application of the law in 1989 or 1992, if the case had been before the Court then, could be a miscarriage of justice if prescribed in 1997'.

The International Tribunal for the Law of the Sea has also been presented with arguments invoking precaution, and has shown itself to be notably more open to the application of the principle, albeit without express reliance. In 1999, in the *Southern Bluefin Tuna* cases, Australia and New Zealand requested the Tribunal to order 'that the parties act consistently with the precautionary principle in fishing for Southern Bluefin Tuna pending a final settlement of the dispute'. Japan, the respondent state, did not address the question of the status or effect of the principle. In its Order the Tribunal expressed the view that the parties should 'act with prudence and caution to ensure that effective conservation measures are taken to prevent serious harm to the stock of southern bluefin tuna' (para. 77), that there was 'scientific uncertainty regarding measures to be taken to conserve the stock of southern bluefin tuna' (para. 79), and that, although it could not conclusively assess the scientific evidence presented by the parties, measures should be taken as a matter of urgency to preserve the rights of the parties and to avert further deterioration of the southern bluefin tuna stock (para. 80). In ordering the parties to refrain from conducting experimental fishing programmes, the Tribunal was plainly taking a precautionary approach, as Judge Treves recognised in his Separate Opinion.

In 2001, in the *MOX* case, Ireland claimed that the United Kingdom had failed to apply a precautionary approach to the protection of the Irish Sea in the exercise of its decision-making authority in relation to the direct and indirect consequences of the operation of the MOX plant and international movements of radioactive materials associated with the operation of the MOX plant. The principle was invoked by Ireland at the provisional measures phase to support its claim that the United Kingdom had the burden of demonstrating that no harm would arise from discharges and other consequences of the operation of the MOX plant, and to inform the assessment by the Tribunal of the urgency of the measures it is required to take in respect of the operation of the MOX plant. For its part, and while accepting that in assessing the level of risk in any given case considerations of prudence and caution may be relevant, the United Kingdom argued that in the absence of evidence showing a real risk of harm precaution could not warrant a restraint of the rights of the United Kingdom to operate the plant. The Tribunal did not order the suspension of the operation of the plant, as Ireland had requested, but instead ordered the parties to co-operate and enter into consultations to exchange further information on possible consequences for the Irish Sea arising out of the commissioning of the MOX plant and to devise, as appropriate, measures to prevent pollution of the marine environment which might result from the operation of the MOX plant. That Order, which has a certain precautionary character, was premised on considerations of 'prudence and caution'.

The principle has also been addressed by the WTO Appellate Body. In 1998, in the *Beef Hormones* case, the European Community invoked the principle to justify its claim that it was entitled to prohibit imports of beef produced in the United States and Canada with artificial hormones, where the impacts on human health were uncertain. The Community argued that the principle was already 'a general customary rule of international law or at least a general principle of law', that it applied to both the assessment and management of a risk, and that it informed the meaning and effect of Articles 5.1 and 5.2 of the WTO's Agreement on Sanitary and Phytosanitary Measures (the 'SPS Agreement').

The United States denied that the principle represented a principle of customary international law, and preferred to characterise it as an 'approach' the content of which may vary from context to context. Canada referred to a precautionary approach as 'an emerging principle of international law, which may in the future crystallize into one of the "general principles of law recognized by civilized nations", within the meaning of Article 38(1)(c) of the ICJ Statute'.

The WTO Appellate Body agreed with the United States and Canada that the precautionary principle did not override Articles 5.1 and 5.2 of the SPS Agreement, although it considered that it was reflected in the preamble to and Articles 3.3 and 5.7 of the SPS Agreement, which did not exhaust the relevance of the principle. Recognising that the status of the principle in international law was the subject of continued debate, and that it was regarded to granting the provisional measure requested by Ireland regarding the suspension of the commissioning of the plant.').

Some as having crystallised into a general principle of customary international environmental law, the Appellate Body said:

> Whether it has been widely accepted by Members as a principle of general or customary international law appears less than clear. We consider, however, that it is unnecessary, and probably imprudent, for the Appellate Body in this appeal to take a position on this important, but abstract, question. We note that the Panel itself did not make any definitive finding with regard to the status of the precautionary principle in international law and that the precautionary principle, at least outside the field of international environmental law, still awaits authoritative formulation.

The principle has also been raised before other courts, such as the European Court of Human Rights. In *Balmer-Schafroth* v. *Switzerland*, the applicants claimed that the failure of Switzerland to provide for administrative review of a decision extending the operation of a nuclear facility violated Article 6 of the European Convention on Human Rights. The claim was rejected by the majority, because the connection between the government's decision and the applicants' right was too remote and tenuous. The Court ruled that they had failed to establish a direct link between the operating conditions of the power station . . . and their right to protection of their physical integrity, as they failed to show that the operation of Mühleberg power station exposed them personally to a danger that was not only serious but also specific and, above all, imminent. In the absence of such a finding, the effects on the population of the measures which the Federal Council could have ordered to be taken in the instant case therefore remained hypothetical. Consequently, neither the dangers nor the remedies were established with a degree of probability that made the outcome of the proceedings directly decisive.

A dissenting opinion by seven judges, however, criticised this finding, on the grounds that it 'ignored the whole trend of international institutions and public international law towards protecting persons and heritage, as evident [*inter alia*] in . . . the development of the precautionary principle'. At the national level, there have also been several decisions addressing the status of the precautionary principleininternationallaw. In *Vellore,* for example,the IndianSupremeCourt ruled that the precautionary principle was an essential feature of 'sustainable development' and as such part of customary international law. By contrast, a United States federal court appears more restrained in its approach, holding that the principle was not yet established in customary international law so as to give rise to a cause of action under the Alien Tort Claims Statute.

The legal status of the precautionary principle is evolving. There is certainly sufficient evidence of state practice to support the conclusion that the principle, as elaborated in Principle 15 of the Rio Declaration and various international conventions, has now received sufficiently broad support to allow a strong argument to be made that it reflects a principle of customary law, and that within the context of the European Union it has now achieved customary status, without prejudice to the precise consequences of its application in any given case. Nevertheless, it must be recognised that international courts and tribunals have been reluctant to accept explicitly that the principle has a customary international lawstatus, notwithstanding the preponderance of support in favour of that view, and diminishing opposition to it. The reluctance may be understandable, in view of its inherently commonsensical approach, even if the practical consequences of its application fall to be determined on a case-by-case basis.

POLLUTER-PAYS PRINCIPLE

The polluter-pays principle establishes the requirement that the costs of pollution should be borne by the person responsible for causing the pollution. The meaning of the principle, and its application to particular cases and situations, remains open to interpretation, particularly in relation to the nature and extent of the costs included and the circumstances in which the principle will, perhaps exceptionally, not apply. The principle has nevertheless attracted broad support, and is closely related to the rules governing civil and state liability for environmental damage (as described in chapter 18 below), the permissibility of certain forms of state subsidies, and the recent acknowledgment in various instruments by developed countries of the 'responsibility that they bear in the international pursuit of sustainable development in view of the pressures their societies place on the global environment', as well as the financial and other consequences that flow from this acknowledgment. The practical implications of the polluter-pays principle are in its allocation of economic obligations in relation to environmentally damaging activities, particularly in relation to lia-bility, the use of economic instruments, and the application of rules relating to competition and subsidy.

The polluter-pays principle has not received the same degree of support or attention accorded over the years to the principle of preventive action, or the attention more recently accorded to the precautionary principle, although its use is now being taken up in other regional agreements. It is doubtful whether it has achieved the status of a generally applicable rule of customary international law, except perhaps in relation to states in the EC, the UNECE and the OECD. The strong objections of some countries to the further development of the polluter-pays principle, particularly for international relations, is evident from the compromise language adopted by Principle 16 of the Rio Declaration, which provides that:

> National authorities should endeavour to promote the internalisation of environmental costs and the use of economic instruments, taking into account the approach that the polluter should, in principle, bear the costs of pollution, with due regard to the public interests and, without distorting international trade and investment.

This text, which falls short of the more specific language of EC, OECD and UNECE instruments, includes language which limits the extent of any obligation which might apply to states. This derives, at least in part, from the view held by a number of states, both developed and developing, that the polluter-pays principle is applicable at the domestic level but does not govern relations or responsibilities between states at the international level.

The polluter-pays principle in treaty law can be traced back to some of the first instruments establishing minimum rules on civil liability for damage resulting from hazardous activities. The conventions on civil liability for nuclear damage, the 1960 Paris Convention and the 1963 IAEA Liability Convention,were influenced by the desire to channel compensation from those responsible for theactivitycausingdamage tothevictims.Underthe 1969CLC,however,the shipowner is precluded from relying on the limitation of liability if the incident occurred as a result of his actual fault or privity. Similarly, the Preamble to the 1971 Oil Fund Convention reflects the consideration that the economic consequences of oil pollution damage should be borne by the shipping industry and oil cargo interests.

OECD

The first international instrument to refer expressly to the polluter-pays principle was the 1972 OECD Council Recommendation on Guiding Principles Concerning the International Economic Aspects of Environmental Policies, which endorsed the polluter-pays principle to allocate costs of pollution prevention and control measures to encourage rational use of environmental resources and avoid distortions in international trade and investment. The Recommendation defined the principle in a limited sense to mean that the polluter should bear the expenses of carrying out the measures deemed necessary by public authorities to protect the environment:

In other words, the cost of these measures should be reflected in the cost of goods and services which cause pollution in production and/or consumption. Such measures should not be accompanied by subsidies that would create significant distortions in international trade and investment.

The 1972 Recommendation does not, on the face of it, apply to the costs of environmental damage. In 1974, the OECD Council adopted a further Recommendation on the Implementation of the Polluter-Pays Principle which reaffirmed that the principle constituted a 'fundamental principle' for member countries, that aid given for new pollution control technologies and the development of new pollution abatement equipment was not necessarily incompatible with the principle, and that member countries should strive for uniform observance of the principle. The 1989 OECD Council Recommendation on the Application of the Polluter-Pays Principle to Accidental Pollution extends the principle to imply that the operator of a hazardous installation should bear the cost of reasonable measures to prevent and control accidental pollution from that installation which are introduced by public authorities in conformity with domestic law prior to the occurrence of an accident. According to the Recommendation, however, this does not necessarily require that 'the costs of reasonable measures to control accidental pollution after an accident should be collected as expeditiously as possible from the legal or natural person who is at the origin of the accident'. Such a domestic legal requirement is merely 'consistent with', rather than implied by, the principle. Examples of specific applications of the polluter-pays principle cited by the 1989 Recommendation include adjusting fees or taxes payable by hazardous installations to cover more fully the cost of certain exceptional measures taken by public authorities to prevent and control accidental pollution, and charging to the polluter the cost of reasonable pollution control measures decided on by public authorities following an accident to avoid the spread of environmental damage and limit the release of hazardous substances (by ceasing emissions at the plant), the pollution as such (by cleaning or decontamination), or its ecological effects (by rehabilitating the polluted environment). The Recommendation also provides guidance on 'reasonable' measures: they depend on 'the circumstances under which they are implemented, the nature and extent of the measures, the threats and hazard existing when the decision is taken, the laws and regulations in force, and the interests which must be protected'. The Recommendation cites certain exceptions to the principle, including the need for rapid implementation of stringent measures for accident prevention (provided this does not lead to significant distortions in international trade and investment), or if strict and prompt implementation of the principle would lead to severe socio-economic consequences. The application of the principle does not affect the possibility under domestic law of requiring the operator to pay other costs connectedwiththe puolic authorities' responseto an accident, or compensation for future costs of the accident. *European Community*

The polluter-pays principle is also established under EC law. The EC adopted the principle in its first programme of action on the environment in 1973.Two years later, the EC Council adopted a Recommendation regarding cost allocation and action by public authorities on environmental matters which recommended that the EC at Community level and the member states in their national environmental legislation must apply the polluter-pays principle, according to which natural or legal persons governed by public or private law who are responsible for pollution must pay the costs of such measures as are necessary to eliminate that pollution or to reduce it so as to comply with the standards or equivalent measures laid down by the public authorities.

This formulation is broader than early OECD recommendations in respect of the costs which might be covered by the principle. The EC Council Recommendation, which is not legally binding, identifies standards and charges as the major instruments of action available to public authorities for the avoidance of pollution, allows certain exceptions to the principle, and says which acts will not be considered to be contrary to the principle. In 1986, the EEC Treaty was amended to provide that EC action relating to the environment shall be based on the principle that 'the polluter should pay'. In 1992, the EC member states and EFTA member countries agreed that action by the parties was to be based on the principle that 'the polluter should pay'. A number of acts of EC secondary legislation also refer to, or incorporate, the principle, and the ECJ has occasionally considered its practical implications. The principle has also been applied by the European Commission in relation to state aid.

CONCLUSIONS

The international organisations and other members of the international community has given rise to a body of discrete principles and rules which may be of general application. Their legal status, their meaning and the consequences of their application to the facts of a particular case or activity remain open. There are several reasons for this. First, they have emerged over a relatively short period of time, some only within the past fifteen years. Secondly, each has emerged in the context of sharp differences of view as to what they mean in practice, and what they should mean. And, thirdly, the extent to which state practice interprets and applies these principles and rules is still evolving, and requires further consideration by reference to what states do both at the national level and in their international affairs. Nevertheless, rational arguments can be made in favour of each having significant legal consequences, and states and international courts and tribunals have increasingly been prepared to rely upon some of these principles and rules to justify their actions and to enable them to reach conclusions in their application of substantive legal obligations to particular sets of facts. In some cases, such application has had far-reaching consequences, for example in the *Southern Bluefin Tuna* cases at the provisional measures phase.

Bibliography

Harris, Stephen L. : Fire and Ice: The Cascade Volcanoes, Seattle, The Mountaineers, 1980.

Jane A. Bullock : Introduction to Emergency Management, Amsterdam, Butterworth-Heinemann, 2003.

Jones S. : Building an Emergency Plan: A Guide for Museums and other Cultural Institutions, Getty Conservation Institute, Los Angeles, 1999

Keyes K.E. : Emergency Management for Records and Information Programs, ARMA International, Kansas, 1997.

Ling, Ted. : Solid, Safe, Secure: Building Archives Repositories in Australia, National Archives of Australia, Canberra, 1998.

Norris, Debra Hess : Disaster Recovery: Salvaging Photograph Collections, Philadelphia, PA, 1998.

Robert A. : Insurance for Libraries: Part I and Insurance for Libraries: Part II, Conservation Administration News, 1994.

Stommel, Elizabeth : Volcano Weather: The Story of 1816, The Year Without a Summer, Newport, Seven Seas Press, 1983.

Walker, Bridget : Women and Emergencies, Oxford, Oxfam, 1994.

Waters, Peter : Procedures for Salvage of Water-Damaged Library Materials, Washington, DC, Library of Congress, 1979.

Watson, Lyall : Earthwork: Essays on the Edge of Natural History, London, Hodder and Stoughton, 1956.

Worster, Donald : Dust Bowl: The Southern Plains in the 1930s, New York, Oxford University Press, 1979.

Index

□□□